Suspect Citizens

Suspect Citizens offers the most comprehensive look to date at the most common form of police–citizen interactions, the routine traffic stop. Throughout the war on crime, police agencies have used traffic stops to search drivers suspected of carrying contraband. From the beginning, police agencies made it clear that very large numbers of police stops would have to occur before an officer might interdict a significant drug shipment. Unstated in that calculation was that many Americans would be subjected to police investigations so that a small number of high-level offenders might be found. The key element in this strategy, which kept it hidden from widespread public scrutiny, was that middle-class white Americans were largely exempt from its consequences. Tracking these police practices down to the officer level, *Suspect Citizens* documents the extreme rarity of drug busts and reveals sustained and troubling disparities in how racial groups are treated.

Frank R. Baumgartner holds the Richard J. Richardson Distinguished Professorship at University of North Carolina at Chapel Hill. He is a leading scholar of public policy and has written extensively on agenda-setting, policy-making, and lobbying. His work on criminal justice includes two previous books on the death penalty.

Derek A. Epp is Assistant Professor of Government at the University of Texas at Austin. In *The Structure of Policy Change*, he explains how the capacity of governmental institutions to process information affects public policy. He also studies economic inequality with a particular focus on understanding how rising inequality affects government agendas.

Kelsey Shoub is a graduate student in the Department of Government at the University of North Carolina at Chapel Hill. Her research focuses on using publicly available big data to answer questions about what influences policy change, policy outputs, and the context within which they take place.

Suspect Citizens

What 20 Million Traffic Stops Tell Us about Policing and Race

FRANK R. BAUMGARTNER
University of North Carolina, Chapel Hill

DEREK A. EPP
University of Texas, Austin

KELSEY SHOUB
University of North Carolina, Chapel Hill

CAMBRIDGE
UNIVERSITY PRESS

CAMBRIDGE
UNIVERSITY PRESS

University Printing House, Cambridge CB2 8BS, United Kingdom

One Liberty Plaza, 20th Floor, New York, NY 10006, USA

477 Williamstown Road, Port Melbourne, VIC 3207, Australia

314–321, 3rd Floor, Plot 3, Splendor Forum, Jasola District Centre, New Delhi – 110025, India

79 Anson Road, #06-04/06, Singapore 079906

Cambridge University Press is part of the University of Cambridge.

It furthers the University's mission by disseminating knowledge in the pursuit of education, learning, and research at the highest international levels of excellence.

www.cambridge.org
Information on this title: www.cambridge.org/9781108429313
DOI: 10.1017/9781108553599

First published 2018

Printed in the United States of America by Sheridan Books, Inc.

A catalogue record for this publication is available from the British Library.

Library of Congress Cataloging-in-Publication Data
Names: Baumgartner, Frank R., 1958– author. | Epp, Derek A., author. | Shoub, Kelsey, author.
Title: Suspect citizens : what 20 million traffic stops tell us about policing and race / Frank R. Baumgartner, University of North Carolina, Chapel Hill, Derek A. Epp, University of Texas at Austin, Kelsey Shoub, University of North Carolina, Chapel Hill.
Description: New York: Cambridge University Press, 2018.
Identifiers: LCCN 2018003783 | ISBN 9781108429313 (hardback) | ISBN 9781108454049 (paperback)
Subjects: LCSH: Racial profiling in law enforcement – United States. | Discrimination in law enforcement – United States.
Classification: LCC HV7936.R3B38 2018 | DDC 363.23089/00973–dc23
LC record available at https://lccn.loc.gov/2018003783

ISBN 978-1-108-42931-3 Hardback
ISBN 978-1-108-45404-9 Paperback

Contents

Contents

Figures

Tables

Acknowledgments

This project began in 2011 with a phone call from local attorney Chris Mumma, asking if Baumgartner could volunteer to do some data analysis for a commission looking into racial disparities in criminal justice. The state had collected data on traffic stops but had never analyzed them. Baumgartner quickly recruited graduate student Derek Epp into the project, though Derek was working on a dissertation on a different topic. We both worked on this project "in parallel" with our other priorities for a time. Later, we recruited Kelsey Shoub and eventually an entire team of undergraduate students, then two more graduate students, to join us. Now, seven years later, Epp is an assistant professor of government at the University of Texas at Austin, Shoub is on the verge of receiving her PhD, and we have completed a book, several articles, and have begun (with new collaborators) to expand our studies of traffic stops nation-wide. This book, and the research that it reports, was the object of considerable institutional support which we are happy to acknowledge. We also want to thank many individuals for various other kinds of help and feedback.

First, the Department of Political Science at UNC-Chapel Hill has been a wonderful place to do the research. The highly trained and motivated graduate students, bright and hard-working undergraduates, and institutional resources made it a fantastic environment for Baumgartner to build a team. This was further facilitated by the funds from the Richardson Professorship, for which he is grateful.

Thanks to Karla Slocum and the staff of the UNC Institute for African American Research for a faculty fellowship allowing Baumgartner to devote more time to this project in fall 2015. The IAAR also hosted

Baumgartner for a talk where we were able to get excellent feedback on the work.

We also want to thank our UNC colleagues Chris Clark, Andrea Benjamin, Isaac Unah, Candis Watts Smith, Debbie Stroman, Pat Parker, Whitney Robinson, Mosi Ifatunji, Navin Bapat, and numerous faculty and students who participated in seminars and shared stories of their own encounters with the police. We appreciate all the support and encouragement.

Sociology student Carmen Huerta-Bapat completed a dissertation in 2016 using the underlying data from this book; she focused on Hispanic–White disparities, and we learned a lot from her study. Baumgartner was privileged to serve as the co-chair of her committee.

Epp would like to recognize the support of all the faculty and staff at the Rockefeller Center at Dartmouth College. In particular, thank you to Ron Shaiko for believing in the project from the start and providing much needed institutional support.

Shoub in turn would like to recognize the support of the University of North Carolina Political Science Department for graduate assistant funding as well as the Graduate School for research fellowships in summer 2017 and academic year 2017–18 allowing her to focus solely on her dissertation and this book.

We also acknowledge the assistance of the NC Department of Justice and State Bureau of Investigation for making available the official statistics on which this analysis relies, and for answering technical questions about the organization of this complex database.

We want to thank the following students from UNC-Chapel Hill who have worked on the project that led to this book, and in some cases continue to work on analyses of traffic stops nation-wide, helping us gather and analyze mountains of data. These include graduate students Leah Christiani and Kevin Roach, who have coauthored some papers with us looking beyond North Carolina, and the following undergraduates: Katherine B. Elliott, Amirah Jiwa, Morgan Herman, Reena Gupta, Dana Corbett, Colin Wilson, Julio Zaconet, Justin Cole, Brenden Darouge, Eliza Duckworth, Audrey Sapirstein, Enrique Lambrano, Alex Bennett, Sarah McAdon, Isabelle Zawistowska, Amanda Witwer, Libby Doyle, Patrick Archer, and Arvind Krishnamurthy.

This project would not have gotten off the ground, or even have been conceived, if not for the long-lasting efforts of James E. Williams, who retired during the time our book was in preparation from a long career as the public defender for Orange and Chatham Counties, NC and a leader in the study of racial inequalities in the courts. James convened and chaired the task force on racial inequities in the criminal justice system for the North Carolina Advocates for Justice, and later was instrumental in creating the North Carolina Commission on Racial and Ethnic Disparities in the Criminal Justice System (NC-CRED). Our original contact about this project came from Attorney Chris Mumma, who was involved with the task force James Williams set up, and who initially asked Baumgartner if he could undertake some analysis of a state database. It was a fortuitous stroke of good fortune, generating an entire stream of research activities and insights into our criminal justice system. Rich Rosen and Raul Pinto also deserve thanks for their feedback in those early years of the project.

Chief Chris Blue of the Chapel Hill Police Department, along with several of his top staff members met with us several times in an effort to understand local police traffic statistics and consistently showed great openness to the challenges of transparency; these meetings were very helpful. Orange County Sheriff Charles S. Blackwood and his staff similarly were helpful in meetings several times. In all, we met with police chiefs, other police leaders, and municipal leaders in Chapel Hill, Carrboro, Charlotte, Roanoke Rapids, Durham, and Fayetteville, and we appreciate all of their time and feedback.

Mike Fliss has been involved in some elements of the project, but he has taken the work much further than we have as he completes his PhD in Epidemiology at UNC with a combination of the data we are also using as well as supplements from many other data sources. We look forward to seeing the final results of his impressive work. Bayard Love worked on the initial stages of the project, independently from us and later as a collaborator on an article (see Baumgartner, Epp et al. 2017); we thank him for his insights, ideas, and commitment.

Ian Mance of the Southern Coalition for Social Justice has been involved in projects related to this for at least as long as we have. His entrepreneurial efforts led to the creation of a website that makes available all the data we use here in a user-friendly and simplified format. Then he did it for Maryland. Then Illinois. His Open Data Policing site (https://opendatapolicing.com/) makes possible many of the things that we believe our book demonstrates to be so important. At the same time as Ian has accomplished all this he has also defended clients and advocated for important reforms in criminal justice. It has been a pleasure to collaborate with him on occasion over the past few years.

We would further like to thank the many judges, public defenders, and district attorneys who have participated in various legal trainings we have presented, in some cases jointly with Attorney Ian Mance and Fayetteville Police Chief Harold Medlock, over several years; these have been sponsored by the UNC School of Government and by Wake Forest University School of Law. We learned so much from our discussions with Chief Medlock, in particular. As readers of this book will learn, he came into a difficult situation and made his city a better place.

We appreciate the work and feedback of UNC School of Government professors Emily Coward and Alyson Grine (now at NC Central University School of Law), whose manual, *Raising Issues of Race in North Carolina Criminal Cases*, explains in detail how attorneys can use the data on which this book is based in their cases (see Grine and Coward 2014). We thank them for their important and careful work.

We have received useful feedback from talks and presentations at the annual meetings of the American and Midwest Political Science Associations, and at the Universities of Antwerp (Belgium), Aarhus (Denmark), Leiden (Netherlands), Arizona, Harvard, Michigan, Edinburgh (Scotland), CIDE (Mexico City, Mexico), Glasgow (Scotland), Duke, Oklahoma, the State Politics Working Group at UNC-Chapel Hill, community forums in the Chapel Hill area including the Fearington Democratic Club, the Ethnical Humanist Society of the Triangle, and a community meeting at the United Church of Chapel Hill organized by UNC professor Debbie Stroman.

A number of local and other journalists have taken an interest in this work and have produced excellent studies of their own; we appreciate their work. This includes Sharon LaFraniere and Richard Oppel, Jr. of the *New York Times*, Virginia Bridges and Jim Wise of the *Raleigh News and Observer*, Sean Collins Walsh, Jeremy Schwartz, Eric Dexheimer, and Christian McDonald of the *Austin American-Statesman*, Brian Collister of KXAN-TV in Austin, Texas, Frank Stasio and Leoneda Inge of WUNC-FM in Chapel Hill, Andrew Barksdale of the *Fayetteville Observer*, Joe Killian of the *Greensboro News and Record*, and Michael Gordon and Eric Frazier of the *Charlotte Observer*.

Texas State Representative Garett Coleman (D-Houston), Chair of the Committee on County Affairs, and Rep. Ramon Romero (D-Fort Worth) have been active in addressing similar issues to those discussed in this book through their legislative work in Austin, Texas, and we thank them for their devotion to the issue. It will be apparent to readers in Chapter 2 of this book that none of this would have been possible without the active legislative leadership of a number of members of the North Carolina General Assembly. While we were not here at the time, we thank them for their work as well. We hope that this book stands as a clear documentation that their concerns were well-founded and deserving of more investigation.

Over the years during which this project has been developing, we have posted a wealth of information to the following website: www.unc.edu/~fbaum/traffic.htm. This includes reports on each of the largest police agencies in North Carolina as well as spreadsheets with officer-level metrics of traffic stops and searches by race. The site also includes links to various media stories and other related items.

We have created this page for materials associated with this book: www.unc.edu/~fbaum/books/SuspectCitizens/. The site includes all the data and replication do-files associated with the analysis reported here, appendices to certain chapters in the book providing technical and statistical details as well as robustness tests for certain analyses, links to relevant sites such as the NC Department of Justice traffic stops office, Ian Mance's Open Data Policing initiative, and other resources. The site will also be updated regularly with links to media coverage, reviews, and other materials associated with the book after its publication.

I

Suspect Citizens

Fighting the War on Crime with Traffic Stops

On a cold December morning in 2012, Durham Police Officer Kelly Stewart, working undercover from an unmarked car, observed Carlos Riley drive off from a "known drug area" (actually, not far from the Duke University campus) in his red two-door car after conversing with an individual through the open passenger window. Officer Stewart pulled the car over, identified himself as a detective, asked the driver to get out of the vehicle, frisked him and checked his identification. After submitting to the frisk, Mr. Riley got back into his car, with the engine still running, and attempted to drive away. Officer Stewart, standing right at the open door to the car, lunged inside and was able to put on the emergency brake, bringing the car to an abrupt stop. Then, while engaged in a close physical struggle, he tried to put handcuffs on the driver, but Riley fought off that attempt. The officer pulled his service revolver from his holster, pointed it at the driver, and the struggle continued. With the officer holding his gun with both hands and Mr. Riley attempting to deflect it from being aimed directly at him, a shot was fired. The officer was hit in the leg; accounts differ as to who was holding the gun. With the officer shot and in pain, Mr. Riley pushed him from the car and drove off. The officer's badge and handcuffs had fallen into the car, and Riley had possession of the gun.

In a Durham courtroom three years later, Carlos Riley was acquitted on all charges associated with the shooting of Officer Stewart. Evidence presented showed that Officer Stewart had engaged in a pattern of racially profiling drivers, with Attorney Alex Charns noting that more than 76 percent of the traffic stops he made had been of African-American males. The particular stop that led to the confrontation was not recorded at all in the police database. Community organizers and minority residents in Durham argued that the case reflected broad patterns of "racial profiling, police abuse, and illegal searches" (Bridges 2015a). Riley faced charges of reckless driving, robbery with a dangerous weapon, assault on a law enforcement officer inflicting serious injury, assault on a law enforcement officer with a vehicle, and assault on a law enforcement officer with a gun. In the 2015 Durham trial, the jury likely concluded that Officer Stewart had conducted a legally suspect search following a racial profiling incident, that he had shot himself during a struggle, and that Mr. Riley was guilty only of robbery (driving away in possession of the officer's gun, handcuffs, and badge). In any event, none of the charges of assault on the officer were sustained, nor was the reckless driving charge which was the initial justification for the stop (see Bridges 2015b). We can never know, of course, exactly what the jury was thinking or collectively concluded, but with their verdict they made clear that the official version of events, presented by the officer and his legal team, did not sway them.

This is highly unusual. How was it that a jury acquitted a person accused of shooting an officer, particularly a young African-American male with a felony record? (Carlos Riley had previously pled guilty to federal gun possession charges.) What drove a jury of twelve North Carolinians to such a verdict? In most American communities, citizens trust the police. Police testimony in court is typically treated with considerable deference, especially in comparison with young men accused of serious crimes and with previous felony convictions. Moreover, the facts of the case, in particular the shooting of an officer in an altercation with a civilian, were not seriously disputed. Rather, who shot whom, and under what circumstances, was in doubt. There was no doubt that an officer ended up with a bullet in his leg. Obviously, from the outcome of the Carlos Riley trial, trust in the police was lacking in that particular courtroom on that particular day in Durham in 2015.

This book is about how community trust in the police can be enhanced or eroded. We conduct the most comprehensive analysis to date of traffic stops in a single state, North Carolina, in order to explore the complex relations between police and the communities they serve. By looking in detail at over 20 million traffic stops over more than a decade, we explore the patterns apparent in the data. These make clear that powerful disparities exist in how the police interact with drivers depending on their outward identities: race, gender, and age in particular. These disparities could be justified by differences in the likelihood of criminal behavior, they could be based on stereotypes, or a mixture of both factors might explain what we document here. Regardless, as we explore the patterns of racial, gender, and age-based difference in how police interact with members of the public, several things become clear. First, there are stark differences. Second, young men of color are clearly targeted for more aggressive treatment. Third, these differences are not fully justified by differences in criminality. Fourth, the aggressive use of traffic stops as a tool to investigate possible criminal behavior, though justified as part of the war on crime, is surprisingly inefficient, rarely leading to arrests for contraband. When we contrast the costs of targeted and aggressive policing with the benefits of it, we find that the social and community costs are high (in terms of reduced trust in and cooperation with the police) but that the number of crimes solved by traffic stop-related investigations is minimal. Finally, we show that there are feasible solutions to these issues, and that they can actually enhance community safety while simultaneously restoring trust. In fact, they enhance safety precisely because they restore trust. When large pockets of the population lose their trust and confidence in the local police, no one wins.

Two reasons explain the disjuncture between the low benefits but high costs of aggressive traffic policing of those who fit police profiles. First, the very targeting which characterizes a "criminal patrol" ensures that most middle-class white Americans are unaware of it. That is, police behavior seems normal, respectful, and appropriate to most of us. To individuals who fit into certain demographic profiles, however, it is anything but. Since most Americans, particularly voters, are not subjected to these behaviors, however, it has remained off the radar, far from mainstream political discussion, and supporting the police has remained the accepted norm. The second reason why we have not compared the costs to the benefits of these new police practices has been that we have assumed the costs to be zero. If the costs of the policy are zero, and there are any benefits at all, then by definition the benefits outweigh the costs. As we will see in detail below, traffic stops, and the detentions and searches that sometimes result from them, have traditionally been considered only as momentary, trivial inconveniences, meriting no special concern. We argue that this perspective is misguided. If police searches within a neighborhood or of a certain class of citizens are repeated, intrusive, and upsetting, these can place a significant burden on that group of individuals, a high cost indeed. Only if we assign a value to those detentions and searches can we reasonably assess whether that cost is greater or lesser than the corresponding benefit.

As America continues to struggle to understand how to balance public safety needs with respect and equity for all its citizens, in particular its most socially vulnerable, we hope that this analysis can inform reasoned debate. Such debate must be based on the best available evidence, and our goal is to provide that here. While we have no simple solutions, we can document very clearly the extent and nature of those racial disparities that do exist. These are substantial, growing, and unjustified by the crime-fighting value of the policies that lead to them.

Traffic Stops and Public Perceptions of Them

No one likes being pulled over by the police. But we can all recognize when we have been caught after perhaps inadvertently applying a little too much gas. We know when we deserve a speeding ticket (though we hope to avoid it), and we know when failing to signal a lane change merits and does not merit police attention; typically it does not. A long line of legal research has established that while no one likes to come into contact with the law, even those who receive a judicial sanction can accept it if they feel the process has been fair. John Thibaut and Laurens Walker (1975) found that individuals' assessment of court proceedings is affected not only by the outcome, but by their sense of whether the procedures were fair. Tom Tyler and Robert Folger (1980) expanded on this idea outside of the courtroom setting, looking at citizen interactions with police. They found that here too when citizens call the police, or are stopped by them, their perception of how fairly they were treated by the police affects their satisfaction. This was independent of the outcome, such as whether they were issued a citation or whether the officer solved the problem that led to the contact. Tom Tyler and Jonathan Jackson (2014) make the point that people comply with the law because they perceive it to be legitimate.

While white Americans typically have very high ratings for the legitimacy of the police and courts, these numbers are lower for African-Americans. Crucially, this sense of legitimacy is linked to cooperation with the police (e.g., helping to solve a crime) and appears to affect citizens' interactions with government in general, beyond the judicial system. For example, rates of voting move from 36 percent among those with high legitimacy to just 23 percent among those ascribing low levels of legitimacy to the police and the courts (Tyler and Jackson 2014, 89). So feelings of how one is treated by the police, or the courts, affect both future cooperation as well as more general factors of democratic participation such as voting. Recall that legitimacy, throughout Tyler's various works, is unrelated to the favorability of the outcome the individual received in their interaction with the legal system; rather it has to do with the sense of fairness of the procedures.

Since 1999, the US Department of Justice has conducted a Police–Public Contact Survey every three years, drawing from a large sample of Americans aged sixteen and older. Between 17 and 21 percent of the public reported contact with an officer in the previous twelve months in surveys between 2002 and 2008. Consistently, across all the surveys, traffic stops and traffic accidents were the most common reason for the contact: between 53 and 59 percent of all citizen contact with the police related to this (in 2008, 44 percent were drivers in a traffic stop, 3 percent were passengers, and 12 percent were involved in a traffic accident). Other reasons for interactions with the police were (in declining order of frequency): reporting a crime or a problem to the police (21 percent in 2008), receiving assistance or service from the police (6 percent), police investigating a crime (6 percent), and police suspecting the citizen of wrongdoing (3 percent). Altogether, fewer than 10 percent of citizen interactions with the police involve criminal investigations, and almost 60 percent involve traffic stops or accidents, with routine traffic stops by far the most common source of all police contact (see Eith and Durose 2011, 3, Tables 2 and 3).

It is no exaggeration then to say that traffic stops are the epicenter of police–citizen interactions. Perceptions about their fairness will go a long way toward shaping citizens' opinions of the police and even the government more broadly. So it is good news that, among those having contact, the vast majority felt that the interaction was legitimate and that the police acted respectfully. Whereas 74 percent of African-American drivers pulled over in 2008 for a traffic stop perceived that they were stopped for a legitimate reason, this number was much higher (79 percent) when it was a speeding stop than when it was for a vehicle defect (61 percent). Among White drivers, 92 percent of those stopped for speeding, and 87 percent of those stopped for a vehicle defect believed the stop was for a legitimate reason (Eith and Durose 2011, 8, Table 11). These are high numbers in both cases, but clearly white drivers perceive some extra legitimacy for the police, and there may be good reasons for this racial divide. A recent study by a team of Stanford psychologists and computer scientists analyzed audio transcripts taken from police body cameras in Oakland California in April 2014. Looking at the language used in the interactions, and comparing how the officers interacted with black and white drivers, this study of 981 traffic stops and over 36,000 utterances found that officers used more respectful language when interacting with white drivers: they were more likely to refer to them by their last names rather than by their first name or by a nickname, more likely to say "please," less likely to use negative words, and so on (see Voigt et al. 2017). If officers are apologetic, hesitant, grateful, and formal in their addresses to white drivers, but informal, disfluent, negative, and commanding in their interactions with blacks, then there should be no surprise that the two population groups express different levels of satisfaction following such interactions. To be clear, the differences in the Voigt et al. study were subtle rather than stark. But they were consistent and statistically meaningful.

This sense of the appropriateness of police interaction is fundamental to how citizens can be expected to respond to it. Virtually all Americans appreciate the value of the police investigating crimes. Everyone understands the need to patrol the highways for unsafe drivers. But given the enormous range of traffic laws, we all know that we routinely violate some of them. We do not expect to be given a problem by the police for such issues, however, and we have an intuitive sense of whether a police stop was legitimate or may have been based on a technical violation of the law that was then used as a pretext. Legally speaking, we may understand that a technical violation is indeed a violation, but seeing that used as a pretext for a police interaction would be recognized as just that: a pretext for something else based on a suspicion. We may be prepared to "face the music" when caught driving 15 mph over the posted limit, but would understandably be annoyed if pulled over for driving just 2 mph over the limit.

We will come back to the question of how the police interact with the public, and pay particular attention to the question of whether the member of the public is likely to feel that their traffic stop or interaction was legitimate, or may have been motivated by something other than safety on the roads.

A Transformation in Police Crime-Fighting Strategies

Our interest in the subject of police traffic stops and their repercussions draws from a gradual shift in police practice that occurred over several decades. As Tom Tyler, Jonathan Jackson, and Avital Mentovich (2015) describe it, the police moved from working on crimes in progress, or on solving crimes that had previously occurred, to a proactive strategy of preventive measures aimed at deterring future crimes. This more proactive approach to policing has led to more frequent police-initiated nonvoluntary public contacts with the legal system, both through increased stop, question, and frisk activities and via zero-tolerance policies that bring more people within the criminal justice system through arrests, court appearances, and even time in jail. (604)

That is, rather than seeking the cooperation of the public to help solve crimes that have already occurred, the "new" model of policing seeks to stop the crime in the first place. Rather than contacting citizens to help them solve a crime that all may want to see resolved, in the new model of policing, police interactions with members of the public are more aggressive and suggest that individuals are under suspicion. While sometimes that suspicion is well warranted, often it is not. This shift in the style of public contacts "so that they have increasingly communicated police suspicion and mistrust of members of the public with whom the police are dealing" (603) is of particular interest in this book.

Especially problematic is that the "risk-management" model is applied unevenly across racial lines; to a considerable extent white neighborhoods still enjoy the old, community-based style of policing, while minority neighborhoods receive more intense scrutiny. The result of this is a significant decline in citizen perceptions of police legitimacy within minority neighborhoods, which has negative consequences for public–police cooperation in fighting crime. Tyler, Jackson, and Mentovich explain:

Our argument is that it is not contact with the police per se that is problematic. In fact, the results of the study suggest that when the police deal with people in ways that they experience as being fair, contact promotes trust and a variety of types of desirable public behavior. Rather, it is contact that communicates suspicion and mistrust that undermines the relationship between the public and the police. (603)

At the same time as these non-voluntary contacts have increased, their nature has changed. The

police now more frequently approach members of the public with an attitude of suspicion and distrust as they search for signs of criminal character and likely future criminal behavior (e.g., 'a regulatory gaze'). Consequently, an increasing number of people are having involuntary interactions with the police during which they are more likely to be treated as if they are suspected of having deviant tendencies and suspect character. Rather than communicating reassurance, trust, and respect, the police communicate suspicion, mistrust, and fear. (604)

As these strategies were applied to traffic stops, several innovations occurred. One related to the way sheriffs and highway patrol officers patrolled mostly rural areas with interstate highways. They developed "drug courier profiles" and stopped hundreds or thousands of drivers, often fitting a particular demographic profile, in a needle-in-a-haystack strategy of finding a small number with significant contraband.

The US Drug Enforcement Agency (DEA) promoted the use of profiles largely on the basis of the work of Florida state trooper Bob Vogel, later elected Sheriff of Volusia County, Florida. In a laudatory profile in the *Orlando Sentinel*, Charles Fishman (1991) explains Vogel's laser-like focus on drug couriers, in spite of the fact that they typically were only in transit through his rural stretch of I-95 near Daytona Beach. Fishman writes: "The pipeline wasn't causing much of a law enforcement problem for Vogel. (An early element of the courier profile, in fact, was that cars obeying the speed limit were suspect – their desire to avoid being stopped made them stand out.)" In fact, according to Webb (2007), Fishman's early work on drug interdiction was thrown out by various judges who considered his "hunch" that drugs may be in the car an unconstitutional violation of the need to have probable cause before conducting a search. Vogel responded by studying the Florida vehicle code, finding that there were hundreds of reasons why he could legally pull a car over.

He found them by the hundreds in the thick volumes of the Florida vehicle code: rarely enforced laws against driving with burned-out license plate lights, out-of-kilter headlights, obscured tags, and windshield cracks. State codes bulge with such niggling prohibitions, some dating from the days of the horseless carriage.

"'The vehicle code gives me fifteen hundred reasons to pull you over,' one CHP [California Highway Patrol] officer told me." (Webb 2007)

So, while it was those patrolling rural areas of the country, often focused on "oustiders" in transit through their jurisdictions who developed these profiles, Sheriff Vogel's discovery that he could scrutinize the highway code for various technical violations of the law was later adopted more generally. Anyone driving in a car is at risk for a technical violation, especially when such things as "driving in an unsafe manner" are determined by the observations of the officer, not according to objective criteria. This legal innovation, however, represented a powerful transformation of policing practice.

The shifts associated with "old" and "new" style policing were slow in coming and predate Officer Vogel. In fact, the constitutional seeds of this shift go back to the 1960s, when the Supreme Court ruled in *Terry v. Ohio*, 392 U.S. 1 (1968) that police officers may legally "pat down" or frisk an individual based on "reasonable suspicion" rather than "probable cause." These interpretations were solidified and extended a generation later, in *Whren v. United States*, 517 U.S. 806 (1996). This landmark decision validated the police strategy of targeting individuals who fit a "profile" said to be associated with drug activity. Here the Court validated the right of police officers to pull over a car for any traffic violation, but ruled that there was no constitutional requirement of equity in treatment of traffic offenders. By breaking the law, any law, offenders opened themselves up to the possibility of police action. That action need not be equitable, the Court said. The police were not expected to stop all speeders, all those veering slightly out of their lane as they drive, all those driving in the passing lane of a freeway, or all of those with a cracked brake light, a dangling mirror, or an obscured license tag. Officers could pick and choose those offenders who seemed to be of greater interest. And, with hundreds of traffic laws and great discretion in their interpretation, officers could pull over virtually any car. Once pulled over, officers could seek consent or use probable cause to conduct a search of the driver, passengers, or the vehicle. Effectively, the Court permitted the use of routine traffic stops for targeted criminal investigations. The war on crime was the justification for these actions.

Two Fundamental Supreme Court Cases Create a New Regime

To those readers who are not lawyers, the 1968 movement from "probable cause" to "reasonable suspicion" may not appear to be an important distinction, but suspicion is a very low standard as compared to probable cause. It meant that the police could stop and frisk great numbers of people even if they had no reason to believe they were actively engaged in any illegal activity. Today police use the phrase "Terry stop" to describe situations where they detain an individual momentarily in order to investigate them, including conducting a physical search of their body. Note that even in a Terry stop, the police must be able to point to "specific and articulable facts" that generate a reasonable suspicion toward the individual about to be searched or patted down. Many traffic stops fall under the legal umbrella of a Terry stop: a momentary detention based on suspicion rather than a longer detention based on arrest, or a search based on probable cause.

Justice William O. Douglas was highly critical of the "new regime" he said we were entering in 1968 with the *Terry* decision. He wrote in his dissent in *Terry v. Ohio*:

Until the Fourth Amendment ... is rewritten, the person and the effects of the individual are beyond the reach of all government agencies until there are reasonable grounds to believe (probable cause) that a criminal venture has been launched or is about to be launched.

There have been powerful hydraulic pressures throughout our history that bear heavily on the Court to water down constitutional guarantees and give the police the upper hand. That hydraulic pressure has probably never been greater than it is today.

Yet if the individual is no longer to be sovereign, if the police can pick him up whenever they do not like the cut of his jib, if they can "seize" and "search" him in their discretion, we enter a new regime. (Justice Douglas, dissenting, *Terry v. Ohio*, p. 39)

We may well have entered a "new regime" with policing in the USA with the development of the war on crime, beginning in the 1960s and accelerating in the 1980s and 1990s. While *Terry* was an important shift, the Justices confronted something even more generic in *Whren*, and the combined result of both *Terry* and *Whren* was clearly as Justice Douglas indicated, to "give the police the upper hand." Whereas in *Terry* the Court allowed for a pat-down based on mere suspicion rather than probable cause, in *Whren* the Court acquiesced to the idea that the police may stop a car for virtually any reason. Although the Court ruled in *Whren* that race by itself would be unconstitutional as grounds to decide which cars to stop and which to let alone, it also sustained the legitimacy of a search resulting from a selective traffic stop. Since there was no doubt that the traffic stop had been legally justified (as almost any traffic stop would be), the resulting search was not unconstitutional. The opinion contains this passage, recognizing the allegation of the petitioners that virtually any car on the road can be found to be in violation of some law, and that the police should not be able selectively to enforce the law when they please:

Since, they contend, the use of automobiles is so heavily and minutely regulated that total compliance with traffic and safety rules is nearly impossible, a police officer will almost invariably be able to catch any given motorist in a technical violation. This creates the temptation to use traffic stops as a means of investigating other law violations, as to which no probable cause or even articulable suspicion exists. Petitioners, who are both black, further contend that police officers might decide which motorists to stop based on decidedly impermissible factors, such as the race of the car's occupants. (*Whren*, p. 810)

But, in a unanimous decision written by Justice Scalia, the Court held:

Petitioners urge as an extraordinary factor in this case that the "multitude of applicable traffic and equipment regulations" is so large and so difficult to obey perfectly that virtually everyone is guilty of violation, permitting the police to single out almost whomever they wish for a stop. But we are aware of no principle that would allow us to decide at what point a code of law becomes so expansive and so commonly violated that infraction itself can no longer be the ordinary measure of the lawfulness of enforcement. (*Whren*, p. 818)

And, finally: "The temporary detention of a motorist upon probable cause to believe that he has violated the traffic laws does not violate the Fourth Amendment's prohibition against unreasonable seizures, even if a reasonable officer would not have stopped the motorist absent some additional law enforcement objective" (*Whren*, p. 806). That is, if the stop itself was legal since there was reason to believe a traffic infraction (however minor) had occurred, then any fruit of that traffic stop was legal as well. We moved from "probable cause" to "articulable suspicion" in 1968 and in 1996 we moved to a full constitutional protection for selective application of the letter of every traffic law, including as a pretext for "some additional law enforcement objective." The war on crime was in full swing, and the police now had the legal backing to conduct it as broadly as they saw fit.

Throughout the period from the 1960s through the 1990s, Court interpretation of reasonable search and seizure moved in the direction of greater powers for the police to conduct searches. To be clear, *Whren* would indeed authorize an officer to observe a car or driver, develop a suspicion or an inkling that something may be of interest, and then wait for the driver to violate one of hundreds of different traffic laws, including driving too fast (speeding), driving too slow (impeding traffic), touching a lane marker, or any of a number of equipment or regulatory violations. Once pulled over for what the Court then recognizes as a legitimate enforcement purpose, the officer can then follow up on their suspicion by interviewing the driver, peering into the car, and so on. *Whren* was a watershed moment.

While of course we expect legal professionals to be sure to be operating within the scope of what has been determined to be constitutionally acceptable, members of the public have a different conception of what is fair and what is not. For an officer to follow a driver until that driver commits a traffic infraction is legally permissible, but many would question whether it is fair. Of course, many others would encourage and applaud the police for tracking those who look suspicious and thereby keeping the community safer. Because the cost of increased surveillance is borne largely by young men of color, most Americans are immune to it, ignorant of it, and may well be in favor of it. But it certainly can be expected to generate mistrust and that mistrust should be particularly acute within the demographic communities that receive extra police scrutiny. Thus as Tracey Meares, Tom Tyler, and Jacob Gardener (2016)

explain, police officials may justify their actions as being constitutionally permissible, but members of the public might think they are simply
unfair. Legal professionals and ordinary citizens thus speak a different
language. One of our conclusions in this book is that the ordinary citizens' understanding of fairness is important to incorporate. This, not the
legal details, determines how people think about and respond to disproportionate police scrutiny. It may be legal, but it is not fair.

Community Mistrust as a Response to Disparate and Aggressive Policing

One of the fundamental questions of interest in this book is how community mistrust is generated. Since the 1970s, aggressive police targeting
within the minority community has been justified by the war on crime
and then more specifically by the "war on drugs." Even routine traffic
stops were seen as a means by which the police could target drug couriers
and put an end to the epidemic of drug abuse that has long generated
so much concern. Here we seek to document what has not been fully
documented before: this strategy is a poor tool for catching "bad guys"
and instead generates distrust, anger, and alienation among those the
police are sworn to protect. Concerns about government waste are
always politically salient and so we offer the "risk-management" model
of policing as a prime example.

Consistently in implementing the war on drugs, police agencies have
made clear that "you have to kiss a lot of frogs before you find your
prince" – very large numbers of traffic stops would have to occur before
an officer might interdict a significant drug shipment (see Webb 2007).
Unstated in that calculation was that many Americans would be subjected
to police investigations so that a small number could be searched or
arrested in the hope of finding a large cache of drugs. Those who were
momentarily detained were said by the Court to have suffered only a
trivial inconvenience. The key element in this targeting, which kept it
hidden for so long from those who might have objected, was that middle-
class Americans were largely exempt from its consequences. On the other
hand, members of minority groups, especially young men, were subjected
to a lot more than just an occasional trivial inconvenience. Police routinely targeted poor neighborhoods, individuals with certain forms
of dress, males rather than females, younger people rather than older
ones, and minorities rather than whites. Police cruisers allow officers to
look up the license plate numbers of the cars in front of them at a stop
light, identifying those with outstanding court warrants. This may be a

fantastic opportunity to track down wanted criminals. But statistically it is routinely used to identify those with unpaid tickets, court fees, and other small charges which appear small only to those with the means to pay them. The poor are particularly targeted because of the number of vehicle violations associated with broken tail-lights, equipment problems, and expired registration tags, issues that are more likely to occur among the poor than among the middle class. Where these sociodemographic groups overlap is where police attention is most focused. Thus, millions of Americans have been targeted for more intensive police attention outside of the gaze or knowledge of most middle-class whites. And it has not been trivial at all. It has been humiliating, frustrating, and unfair. Beyond all that, it has been ineffective.

While civil rights attorneys and members of minority communities have long complained of these police activities, the targeted nature of them kept them from the consciousness of most middle-class white Americans. Americans all understand that excessive speeding may well lead to flashing lights in the mirror, and no one enjoys a police encounter leading to a ticket. But we also know the difference between a legitimate, if unwelcome, traffic ticket and a pretextual or targeted enforcement. Being stopped and ticketed is one thing, being asked to justify or explain your whereabouts, your destination, or the car you are driving is something else entirely. When Philando Castile was shot and killed in St. Paul, Minnesota in 2016 after a routine traffic stop, he had been pulled over at least forty-six times from the time he learned to drive until his death fourteen years later; he had had various suspensions of his license and fines for such violations as driving without a license or not having valid insurance. Altogether these violations totaled over $6,000, meaning that he had spent virtually his entire young life as a driver fighting various fines, court fees, and license suspensions (see Peralta and Corley 2016). Many low-income drivers, especially in minority communities, do the same. Of course, these troubles are virtually unheard of in middle-class America. In contrast, poverty keeps many from paying the initial fine, leading to accumulating court sanctions, fees, and penalties.

We should not be surprised that these more aggressive tactics, which effectively (though perhaps inadvertently) treat as criminal suspects large numbers of individuals depending on where they live or work, how they dress, and how they look, would have generated a great deal of mistrust, anger, and alienation. A key but underappreciated element of the new police tactics has been that the cost has been borne almost exclusively by one demographic group: young men of color. Their alienation, frustration, and anger with government is understandable when we consider the disproportionate targeting that they have suffered through these policies and their ratification through the courts.

Increased Attention to an Old Problem

Since the shooting of Trayvon Martin in 2012 and the organization of the Black Lives Matter movement in 2013, police–community relations have been in the news. Of course, friction between police departments and the communities they serve is a perennial issue in urban America. The 1992 Los Angeles riots were in response to the acquittal of police officers for the beating of Rodney King, an unarmed black man pulled over on the freeway for speeding (and who attempted to evade the police, leading them on a high-speed chase). The 1967 Detroit rebellion was sparked by a police raid of a black nightclub. Many of the riots of the 1960s erupted in communities where black neighborhoods were policed by largely white police forces and where trust had eroded beyond the breaking point. There is nothing new, in other words, about problems of trust between the black community and the men and women in blue. However, the last several years have seen unprecedented and consistently high levels of concern, media discussion, and community engagement that have forced or allowed many difficult conversations about race, policing, and citizenship. What is different between the current and previous situations? One key point is shifting social understandings based on changing media coverage.

A turning point in a previous generation of the civil rights movement was when peaceful demonstrators marched from Selma to Montgomery, Alabama in 1965. These marchers were fully aware that Bull Connor's police dogs would attack them, officers would beat them with clubs, drench them with fire hoses, and that some might die. But the iconic photos and national news coverage of these events changed the views of many white Americans living far from the areas where the civil rights demonstrations were taking place. This larger public was appalled, and suddenly more aware, of what had long been happening in communities throughout the South (see McAdam 1988).

Cell phone videos of police shootings may be playing a similar role today. For example, officer Michael T. Slager pled guilty in a Charleston, SC court to firing eight rounds toward the back of fleeing unarmed motorist Walter Scott (see Blinder 2017). Without the cell phone coverage of the shooting, it is unlikely that such a case would have even gone to trial. Dramatic cell phone coverage of many publicized incidents have changed the conversation, giving much greater credence to long-standing but previously discounted complaints in the minority community about differential standards for police encounters with majority and minority populations. The power of the videos, constantly replayed in social media and in the mainstream press, to show the brutality of shooting to kill when a police life is not in danger has galvanized many inside and outside of the minority community. A key element in this conversation is that the videos have created attention, and generated concern, in communities that are not directly affected by such actions.

Until individuals such as Mr. Castile were cast into the national spotlight when videos of their violent deaths were played on national television and reporters delved into their backgrounds, few were asking about the collateral consequences of these large-scale police dragnets. But dry data analytics have backed up these vivid illustrations. New data analytic tools made possible by the routine collection of traffic stop and other types of data on police encounters with citizens have allowed us to document surprisingly large but previously undocumented disparities in the treatment of different racial groups. We will be focusing on the NC case, the longest running statewide data collection of traffic stops data, throughout the chapters to come. While these data do not explain the causes of any disparities, they certainly make clear that they are large. Studies in various states have found the same. The US Department of Justice investigation of the Ferguson (Missouri) Police Department used similar data to show that citizen complaints were indeed based on real, tangible, measurable disparities in treatment of citizens of different race. A particularly egregious finding of the Ferguson report was the degree to which the city had come to use court fees as a source of municipal revenue. The city relied on its poorest residents for traffic fines, court fees, and arrests because all of these were income-generating activities for the city. In effect, the city was financed through selective and targeted enforcement of various laws that did little to make people safer, but which imposed a severe burden on those least able to bear it (see US DOJ 2015).

As mentioned above with respect to Mr. Philando Castile, many individuals living in poverty accumulate traffic and court fees and when they are unable to pay them may be subject to a warrant for arrest. Items which to a middle-class American might be a mere inconvenience or embarrassment can cause others to lose their jobs or go to jail if they cannot pay bail. Walter Scott, shot in North Charleston, SC after a traffic stop for a brake light failure, was behind on child support payments and may have been concerned about the consequences of the traffic stop, as he had an outstanding warrant. Previously, he had gone to jail for this, leading him to lose a job (see Robles and Dewan 2015). Rodney King, whose beating sparked the 1992 Los Angeles riots, attempted to flee from the police in his car, leading to a high-speed chase; he was concerned that the traffic stop would lead to his parole being revoked (see Frontline n.d.). With millions of Americans under some kind of judicial control or supervision, and with many outstanding warrants for such things as unpaid court debts, a "routine" traffic encounter can have very powerful consequences; people can lose their jobs, their homes, or go to jail (see for example Goffman 2014). In other words, whereas the typical middle-class American might be slightly bothered by a traffic stop, they would likely recognize it as a momentary inconvenience with very little chance of long-lasting consequence. For others, those more commonly targeted with more aggressive policing, the calculus is entirely different.

A consequence of the war on drugs and the *Whren* decision is to allow police great leeway in using the traffic laws as they please to target certain individuals. If drug couriers all shared some obvious indicator making them easily identifiable on the roadways, then these police powers would find an appropriate outlet. But, the data reveals that traffic stops only rarely lead to significant contraband hits. Whereas 3 percent of traffic stops lead to a search, only about one-third of those searches lead to contraband. Further, only about half of those contraband hits lead to arrest, which is not surprising because when we look at the amounts of contraband found, it is typically that associated with a user, not a distributor, of the item in question. In the rare instances when large amounts have been found, bona fide drug dealers or couriers may hire qualified attorneys to search deeply into the arresting officer's background and patterns of traffic stops. If they find that the officer has indeed "kissed a lot of frogs" before "finding his prince" – that is, subjected hundreds or thousands of law-abiding minority citizens to traffic stops or searches while letting white motorists go on their way – the charges may be dropped or reduced. Wearing a certain type of cap or driving a car registered in another state do not constitute probable cause. So, throughout the book we will want to compare the costs associated with racially disparate policing with the benefits of the policy. If the benefits are high, perhaps they could be argued to out-weigh the costs. But if the benefits are very low, this becomes more unlikely, and we have to look at other reasons to understand why such disparities exist.

Causes of Racial Differences

Throughout this book we will be looking at patterns of police interactions with motorists and looking at how they differ by race, age, gender, and other factors. We want to be clear that the mere existence of a disparity in any given outcome does not mean that the disparity is unjustified. For example, young people commit more violent crime than older people, and males more than females. If the police arrest people in the exact proportion that they commit crimes, then arrests and police contacts will also show these disparities. In plain English, some disparities are caused by differences in the likelihood of breaking the law, not by any bias or differential treatment by race. There is no doubt that blacks and other minorities are vastly over-represented in the criminal justice system, and in this book we will show that North Carolina traffic stops show similar patterns.

Racial Profiling versus Racial Difference

Racial disparities are ubiquitous in criminal justice, housing, education, health care, and in other areas of American life. The presence of a difference does not by itself mean that it was the result of profiling. Jack Glaser defines racial profiling as "the use of race or ethnicity, or proxies thereof, by law enforcement officials as a basis for judgment of criminal suspicion" (Glaser 2015, 3). He does not say that race must be "the" basis for judgment, just "a" basis. Glaser notes that others disagree, and some even find racial profiling to be a positive. Lorie Fridell, a respected voice in the debate, prefers simply to avoid the term:

We believe "racial profiling" has frequently been defined so restrictively that it does not fully capture the concerns of both police practitioners and citizens. For instance, racial profiling is frequently defined as law enforcement activities (e.g., detentions, arrests, searches) that are initiated solely on the basis of race. Central to the debate on the most frequently used definitions is the word "solely." In the realm of potential discriminatory actions, this definition likely references only a very small portion. (Fridell et al. 2001, 3; quoted in Glaser 2015, 15)

Fridell and her team prefer the phrase "racially biased policing" (see Glaser 2015, 15; Fridell et al. 2001, 3–4). One reason she gives for this is apparent in the two definitions just given. Glaser's definition (race as any part of a judgment) is close to what many civil rights advocates use; Fridell's definition (race as the sole basis of a decision) is close to what police officers themselves might recognize as profiling. Indeed Fridell's team avoided the term partly because they found that stakeholders used the term to mean very different things.

Our sense is close to Glaser's in that the US Constitution guarantees equal protection of the law without regard to race, ethnicity, and other demographic features. Racial differences are clear in many areas of life, but race itself should not be the basis (or even a basis) of decisions by the police which generate those differences: behavior should. The police perspective that profiling only occurs if race is the "sole" determinant of a decision is so restrictive that it would virtually never come into play. When we look for evidence of profiling, as opposed to mere disparities, we will be looking for instances where racial differences remain even after we remove other possible reasons for an observed disparity. For example, if blacks and whites are equally likely to break the law but blacks are arrested more often, this would be a sign indicating that profiling may be occurring. But if blacks commit more crimes than whites, and are arrested in proportion to that, then this is a disparity with no sign of having been caused by police profiling; it would be a difference or a disparity, but would not indicate biased policing.

No matter what we call it, racial differences in criminal justice are real, and they may stem from a great number of possible causes. To the degree that differences are caused by differences in actual criminal behavior, we certainly cannot suggest that profiling has occurred or that police practices should be called into question. If poverty, housing, job, educational and health-care opportunities are systematically different across groups, then we certainly cannot expect the police to solve those problems, and it may be those larger problems which are generating differences in the propensity to be involved in crime. The police simply come to reflect these social pathologies. So we certainly want to be careful to attribute criminal behavior an important place in our analyses, controlling for it whenever we can before we assess the residual impact of race, over and above differences in behavior.

On the other hand, there can be additional factors which generate differential policing, and those will be of interest to us throughout the book. In the chapters to come, we will be interested in controlling for behavior and then assessing if there is a residual effect of race, gender, age, and other legally irrelevant factors on the likelihood that individuals face different experiences in their interactions with the police following a traffic stop.

Four Causes of Racial Disparities

Racial differences in traffic stop outcomes could logically come from four distinct sources. First, as Michael Tonry (1995) makes clear, there is no reason to expect that white and black motorists break the law at the same rate. If black motorists are more likely to speed egregiously, or carry illegal contraband in their cars, then we would expect that the police would be relatively more likely to stop and search black drivers. Differential criminality is the first possible cause of differential contact with the police. Second, there could be some number of "bad apple" police officers who simply do not live up to the standard of fair and impartial policing. Whether because of "old fashioned" racism, implicit bias, or a lack of proper training, racial disparities might be traceable to a small fraction of the police force who treat black drivers much differently than white drivers. Third, there could be widely shared, but relatively subtle, differences in how white and minority drivers are treated following a traffic stop. These differences might be statistically only moderate but widely spread across the vast majority of officers in a given department. Perhaps, due to implicit bias shared by most Americans, a large share of officers tends to treat black drivers just slightly more aggressively than white drivers. Consider the recent study in Oakland, California finding subtle differences in how officers spoke to white and black citizens they encountered (Voigt et al. 2017). These subtle but system-wide differences could be due to inaccurate statistical assumptions or over-wrought stereotypes. Fourth and finally, there could be institutional practices which lead to racial differences in outcomes. For example, a given department might emphasize regulatory traffic stops, stops for equipment failures, or it might have more aggressive search policies in certain neighborhoods or precincts which themselves might differ by race. If there are more police assigned to a given area, and that area is a predominately black neighborhood, then blacks will have a higher chance of coming into the criminal justice system, even with an equal likelihood of engaging in criminal behavior.

Given our extensive statistical evidence, we will differentiate among these different possible causes of the racial differences we observe. Note that institutional practices such as differential policing in different neighborhoods could have a significant racial impact, but might be an inadvertent, unintentional corollary or consequence of policing decisions that were made for other reasons. From the data, we cannot always judge whether those reasons might justify the racially disparate outcomes, but by pointing out the racial disparities that may stem from them, we can allow a conversation that has not previously been made explicit.

Differential Criminality

Tonry (1995) notes that the first explanation of dramatic racial differences in blacks compared to whites in prison, jail, or under some kind of judicial

oversight has to be different rates of criminal behavior. He cites obser-
vers from W. E. B. DuBois (writing in 1899) to Thorsten Sellin (in 1928),
Guy Johnson (1941), and Gunnar Myrdal (1944) all making essentially
the same argument: given 400 years of American history, systematic and
institutionalized lack of access to education and jobs, and differences in
poverty, health care, housing, wealth, and income, it would be astounding
if the racial groups did not differ in levels of criminality. And indeed they
do. Tonry writes:

> For as long as the FBI has collected and reported national arrest data in its
> *Uniform Crime Reports*, blacks have experienced substantially higher arrest rates
> than whites relative to their respective shares of the population. This should sur-
> prise no one. Criminality and other serious antisocial conduct flow from social
> disorganization and social and economic disadvantage. (1995, 52)

The key point, according to Tonry, then, is to attempt to estimate what
share of the difference in differential outcomes from the criminal justice
system can be attributed to different levels of criminal behavior versus
differential treatment once the justice system comes into contact with
individuals of different racial groups. His evidence clearly points in two
directions: racial differences in criminality are real and should not be
ignored, but also the war on drugs had a dramatic and unjustified effect
magnifying the criminality of the black population disproportionately
compared to whites.[1] Something changed in policing during the 1980s in
particular, leading to dramatic increases in black arrest, over and above
what could be explained by differences in rates of involvement with
crime. That something was the rise of a new style of policing, focused on
drugs (see Tonry 1995, chapter 4). So while some elements of the story
are long-lasting, some are new. The new part relates to an aggressive
style of policing focused on drugs and minor crimes (for more detail,
see Withrow 2004, 2006; and various works by David A. Harris: 1997,
1999a, 1999b, 2002a, 2002b).

"Old Fashioned" Racism versus Implicit Bias

Whereas Bull Connor and other enforcers of the legal separation of blacks
and whites during the Jim Crow period explicitly laid out their beliefs in
the superiority of whites, we rarely see such "old fashioned" or explicit
statements of racial hierarchy, at least in official documents. At the same
time, the American experience, reinforced in everyday life, movies, television, and popular culture, makes race a prominent signal or marker,
and most Americans harbor implicit, subconscious biases even if they

are careful to be racially neutral in their conscious decision-making and would hate to think of themselves as having any racial prejudices. Kristin Anderson (2010) starts her book, *Benign Bigotry*, by pointing out that racial stereotyping has "gone underground" and is much more difficult to see today than when it was written into law as it was during the Jim Crow period. Whereas once one could look for explicit and unabashed outward signs of racism, today's racism must be found in different forms. She explains:

> Explicit prejudice is a set of feelings about others that are consciously access-ible, seemingly controllable, and self-reported. Racism based on explicit preju-dice is referred to as *old-fashioned* or *overt* racism. Implicit prejudice may or may not be consciously accessible, and may be difficult or impossible to control. Implicit prejudice is believed to be a consequence of years of exposure to associ-ations in the environment, it tends to be impervious to conscious control, and it is relatively stable. Racism based on implicit prejudice has various names: *subtle, covert, modern, ambivalent,* or *aversive.* (Anderson 2010, 4)

Particularly important is one group's set of stereotypical assumptions about another group. As Anderson writes, this might be about men or women, about gay, married or single people, people of a given nationality, or by racial group. People from another group are wrongly assumed to be "all the same," that is, out-group homogeneity is a common assumption (see Anderson 2010, 22–81).

The sources of covert racial bias are found all around us and are parts of US history. They are not particular to the criminal justice system, but given the powerful effects of race on criminal justice matters, and the over-representation of minorities in the criminal justice system, there should be no surprise that many associate crime with minorities, particu-larly young males. Crucially, according to the accumulated social psycho-logical literature, no one growing up in mainstream US culture would be immune to these pressures (see for example Gillian and Iyengar 2000). Furthermore, within the police profession, there is ample reason to expect that such biases may be especially strong. In particular, as relates to the decision to shoot or not to shoot a hypothetical suspect in an ambiguous experimental setting, the black suspects are typically shot in a higher per-centage of the cases than an identically situated white suspect (see for example Correll et al. 2002; Correll et al. 2007; Correll 2009).

Clearly, a police officer stopping a moving vehicle, or approaching a driver after a traffic stop is called upon to make quick decisions. Just as clearly, officers go through training and are required to treat all citizens in the same manner. In later chapters we will be looking for indications of differential treatment of white and minority drivers after traffic stops are initiated. Implicit biases are not the only possible reason for racial disparities in traffic stops outcomes, but they are a strong contender. Social psychologists have found covert or subtle bias throughout various experimental settings and there is no reason not to expect it in the context of a traffic stop. In fact, there are reasons to believe that the circumstances governing traffic stops, particularly, the high-volume nature of modern police patrolling tactics, encourage officers to act upon subtle biases.

Inaccurate Profiling and Stereotyping

Jack Glaser has written extensively about the causes and consequences of racial profiling, which he defines as "the use of race or ethnicity, or proxies thereof, by law enforcement officials as a basis for judgment of criminal suspicion" (2015, 3). He also notes: "Reasonable people can and do disagree over whether racial profiling is legal, fair, ethical, and effective" (3). He cites US government (Bureau of Justice Statistics) data projecting that as of 2003, 5.9 percent of white boys born will serve time in prison as compared to 17.2 for Latinos and 32.2 percent for blacks (6). So, he notes, there can be no question about differential likelihood of imprisonment. Much of this, he notes, is related to differential offending rates, but a large percentage of the difference relates to drug offenses, where there are few racial differences in use by race (with the notable exception of powder versus crack cocaine use). He cites a Centers for Disease Control (CDC) study noting the rates at which young men reported having carried a gun in the past thirty days: 17.2 for blacks, 18.2 for whites, and 18.5 for Hispanics. But blacks were three times as likely to be arrested on weapons charges as compared to whites (Glaser 2015, 7). These and other unexplained disparities led Glaser into an investigation of whether the profiles used by police might be inaccurate.

Police agencies and the FBI have long used criminal profiles; attempts to understand the common patterns of how individuals engage in certain types of crimes. Airplane hijackers, for example, were the subject of extensive psychological efforts to generate a profile, even before 9/11, and similar efforts are made for school shooters, serial killers, and Islamic terrorists. By building a profile, police officials hope to be able to focus on those most likely to commit a crime. Some of the first drug courier profiles were constructed by airport security personnel attempting to understand which of tens of thousands of airplane passengers might be transporting drugs. These profiles often targeted individuals who: travelled alone, stayed in their destination city for a very short time, had little baggage, and who were travelling between two cities with significant traffic in drugs (see for example Glaser 2015, 43ff., Harris 2002a).

More generally, police have extensive information about criminals based on those they apprehend. They know where they commit crimes, their age, race, gender, mode of dress, type of car, where they live and work, and many other characteristics. There should be no surprise, and there is no problem, when this information is put to work in order to fight crime. Glaser refers to this as an "actuarial" police profile; constructing these can be a sign of good policing. The problem comes in when particular elements of the "actuarial" profile are over-emphasized, particularly the demographic elements. As discussed in previous sections in this chapter, stereotyping is a common, if not ubiquitous human tendency; members of an "out-group" are wrongly assumed to share traits more than they really do. Therefore it is only a small step from creating a profile to over-emphasizing it.

Glaser (2006 and 2015) provides an example and a statistical illustration. Imagine two groups with the same level of criminality. If one is policed more heavily than the other, it is obvious that one will have more members in prison. But assume perhaps more realistically that one group has higher criminality than the other. What will profiling do in that case? His various simulations, using a wide variety of different parameters, show that the effect of profiling is to exaggerate whatever criminality differences might be in the population. That is, if one group commits twice as much crime (per capita) than the other, but is policed more closely, the ratio of arrests will be significantly higher than two-to-one. The targeted group is over-arrested with respect to their criminality, and the other group is under-policed, leading to fewer arrests in that group than their underlying criminality would warrant. Of course these are hypothetical examples, but the logic is powerful and the mathematics are very consistent.

One key element in Glaser's simulation should be particularly disturbing: if the targeting is inaccurate with respect to the underlying criminality, then a lower percentage of the total number of criminals will be arrested. As the targeting gets further away from that which is statistically justified by behaviors, so the overall proportion of criminals who are arrested declines. Increased percentages of criminals within the targeted group are arrested, but decreasing percentages in the (larger) non-targeted group are found. Therefore, his simulations show not only much sharper disparities in who is arrested than could be explained only by differences in criminality, but they reach a point where they produce fewer arrests altogether. Profiling, combined with stereotyping, can be counter-productive.

Glaser's (2006 and 2015) simulations do not explore changes in the behaviors of possible criminals in response to the inaccurate targeting by the police. As he notes, some suggest that racial targeting can be justified because it may deter crime in communities where crime rates are highest (see for example Schuck 2006). But, Glaser notes, if the deterrence argument is to be introduced, it has to work both ways: while one group recognizes it is under increased surveillance, another group sees the police moving away – "reverse deterrence." If the police are looking disproportionately for criminals in one neighborhood, or among one demographic group, then individuals with criminal tendencies who are immune to that targeting may decide to commit more crime. Consider an experiment. Amy Hackney and Jack Glaser (2013) put subjects in a situation where cheating was possible. In one treatment group, black subjects were clearly and loudly singled out for cheating and in the other monitoring for cheating was racially neutral. In the case where blacks where targeted, white subjects cheated more, presumably because they felt they were unlikely to be caught: the monitors were so focused on the black subjects the whites knew they could get away with it. "The effect of the profiling of blacks was consequently a net increase in cheating" (Hackney and Glaser 2013, 348). Glaser's point in assessing the likely impact of over-targeting is that if the police devote their limited resources inefficiently, over-policing one group, then by definition they will be under-policing another. That other group will certainly notice and adjust its behavior accordingly. When the cat is away (or distracted by other prey), the mice will play.

There are many potential problems with inaccurate profiling. As Glaser has persuasively argued, it can be inefficient. But we should also recall that differential policing calls into question the constitutional guarantee of equal protection of the law. By putting particular individuals into the position of "suspect" merely because of where they live or work or their membership in a certain demographic group (rather than on the basis of their observed criminal behavior), we collectively send a powerful message that they are not full members of the community, that they are not to expect equal treatment, and that the most visible government agents they are likely to encounter view them as dangerous threats. No wonder people subjected to this respond with anger and withdrawal, a point to which we will return in later chapters.

Differential Policing by Place

Policing in the USA is a highly local affair, with almost 18,000 state and local police departments in operation in 2008, including over 12,500 local police agencies, more than 3,000 county sheriff's offices, fifty state agencies, and over 2,000 special jurisdiction and constable / marshal's offices (see Reaves 2011). With such an emphasis on local control, there should be no surprise that different local agencies might have different characteristics. So, for example, if a given agency has, say, a 6 percent search rate, and officers in another agency search only 2 percent of the drivers, then there could be racial disparities in search rates driven entirely by institutional practice combined with different racial make-ups of the populations served by various police agencies. In a review of 649 publicly available annual traffic stops reports from 132 different agencies, Baumgartner, Christiani, and colleagues (2017, Table 3) found that highway patrol departments had search rates of 2.12 percent on average, whereas police departments had much higher rates (6.33 percent on average). Further, black, white, Hispanic, and overall search rates typically varied greatly from agency to agency. Clearly, to understand policing as it is experienced by citizens we must take into account the dramatic differences that stem from the localized nature of policing in the USA.

Just as we must be attuned to agency-effects in policing, within larger agencies there may also be substantial "precinct" effects or neighbor-hood differences in how the police interact with citizens, including during traffic stops. Because of racial differences in residential patterns, these neighborhood, or place-based differences in policing, may have substantial racial implications and can help explain differential outcomes in policing by race.

Indeed, the very localized and place-based patterns of policing are strong possible explanations of racial difference. With housing substantially segregated by race (see Sharkey 2013), a simple cause of racial difference in contact with the police could simply be that the police patrol more intensively on one side of town than the other. Naturally, the police go where the crime is, whether by design or by responding to calls for service. And this may bring them into contact with minorities with greater frequency than whites. But, crucially, while sending more patrol units to crime-ridden neighborhoods is a perfectly reasonable approach to fighting crime, developing different thresholds for searching (higher in some neighborhoods, lower in others) is more problematic. In a country governed by laws, probable cause should mean the same thing regardless of the zip code. Still, we want to be careful throughout our analyses to look within police departments since many racial differences might be due to institutional or agency-level differences across them. Simply put, we will want to ensure that our analyses do not mistakenly attribute to race something that might only be associated with place.

When Community Trust Evaporates

A number of scholars have addressed the high cost of intensive policing of particular social groups. Todd Clear and Natasha Frost (2014) assess what they call "the punishment imperative" in describing the confluence of trends that led to increasingly punitive crime policies from the 1960s to the 1990s. Most notably, they note that the number of individuals imprisoned per 100,000 population was steady for many decades at about 100, but began a dramatic rise in the 1970s until it reached over 500 in the 2000s. Remarkably, this dramatic rise has not been correlated with a rise in either property or violent crime (p. 35). Because imprisonment is a function of how many individuals commit crimes, the proportion of those sentenced to prison, and the length of those prison sentences, it is clear that one could expand net imprisonment by increasing sentencing rates or sentence lengths even in the absence of rises in crime. And this is exactly what occurred in the late 1990s.

Further, the rise in imprisonment was highly concentrated geographically: specific neighborhoods were particularly affected. Clear and Frost cite the influential work of Tucker and Cadora, who wrote: "There is no logic to spending a million dollars a year to incarcerate people from one block in Brooklyn – over half for non-violent drug offenses – and return them, on average, in less than three years stigmatized, unskilled, and untrained to the same unchanged block" (2003, 2). Tucker and Cadora suggest that a better use of incarceration funds would be to invest in jobs, economic vitality, health care, and social services in those neighborhoods hardest hit by crime. The highly localized nature of crime, and the police response to it, is an important element of the patterns we will explore throughout this book.

A number of authors have explored the dynamics of life in these places of crime and marginality. Alice Goffman (2014) writes of a strongly disordered neighborhood in Philadelphia, based on intensive fieldwork there over six years during which she observed hundreds of police actions and was able to come to know many of those living "on the run." In a neighborhood where police surveillance is a daily occurrence, where large percentages of the young male population are under judicial super-vision – on parole or subject to an outstanding warrant (often for an unpaid court fee) – many social pathologies develop. Injured individuals avoid the hospital, fathers avoid their children's schools, people cannot keep regular hours and so cannot work even if they find a job, as all these things create opportunities to be found by the police. Not only do "dirty" individuals (those on the run) suffer from such a life but their "clean" neighbors, friends, and relatives do as well (that is, those with no legal entanglements). As she describes, there is no doubt that the "6th Street" neighborhood that she studied was crime-ridden. But, she writes, "under these conditions the role of law enforcement changes from keeping com-munities safe from a few offenders to bringing an entire neighborhood under suspicion and surveillance" (2014, 201). She continues:

Under these conditions, the highly punitive approach to crime control winds up being counterproductive, creating entirely new domains of criminality. The level of social control that tough-on-crime policy envisions ... is so extreme and difficult to implement that it has led to a flourishing black market to ease the pains of supervision. A new realm of criminal activity is produced as young people supply the goods and services that legally compromised people seek to evade the authorities or live with more freedom and com-fort than their legal restrictions permit. This black market runs second to the fugitive status as a kind of corollary illegality. Moreover, mothers and girlfriends find themselves committing a seemingly endless series of crimes as they attempt to hide, protect, and provide for their legally entangled sons and partners. Thus, the great paradox of a highly punitive approach to crime control is that it winds up criminalizing so much of daily life as to foster widespread illegality as people work to circumvent it. Intensive policing and the crime it intends to control become mutually reinforcing. The extent to which crime elicits harsh policing, or policing itself contributes to a climate of violence and illegality, becomes impossible to sort out. (Goffman, 2014, 201–202)

Naturally, she writes, this generates frustration and anger:

From the perspective of 6th Street residents, distrust and anger at the police are understandable. The police (along with the courts, the jails, and the prisons) are not solving the significant problems of crime and violence but instead are piling on additional problems to the ones residents already face. (2014, 202)

The police, of course, are not solely to blame: they are called upon to solve social problems but are equipped only with "handcuffs and jail time" (203). Goffman is not the only one to review these processes; important work has also been done by such authors as Elija Anderson (1978, 1990, 1999), Bruce Western (2006), Sudhir Venkatesh (2006),

Devah Pager (2007), and Loic Wacquant (2009). These authors collectively paint a picture of poverty being addressed with punitiveness, and the
consequences of that. Of course, crime is more complicated than poverty,
but the point here is simply that where punitiveness is a logical response
to criminality, it has become a response to poverty, and by subjecting
entire communities to harsh policing practices it has eroded trust sometimes to a breaking point.

Traci Burch (2013) addresses a different point: many of the most
disordered and heavily policed areas of American life have been socially
and politically destroyed as well. Fear and mistrust of the authorities extends to voting, making use of government services, and even
engaging in political action. Far from mobilizing the poor to demand
change, aggressive policing and incarceration policies alienate and
demobilize them.

Our analysis in the chapters to come focuses on traffic stops, not
policing in general, and not incarceration at all. So what is the connection
between our analyses and these studies? There are two important
linkages. First, these studies document and explain a puzzle: how can
community trust be eroded so greatly that juries fail to convict an individual when a police officer is shot with his own service revolver during a
scuffle following a traffic stop? This was one of the central questions for
Epp et al. (2014), whose analysis of citizen experiences with traffic stops
poignantly included a discussion of drive-by shootings where dozens of
witnesses proceeded to avoid the police despite clearly seeing more than
fifty shots fired on a crowded street (152). Understanding how community trust can be so severely eroded is an important goal.

Second, the tight geographic focus of the aggressive policing tactics
documented in the studies cited above, and the consequences of these,
explain a paradox: most middle-class white Americans can be completely
unaware of the different experiences of others. This creates what we can
refer to as an "empathy gap." By that we mean a lack of understanding
at the most basic level. For example, most middle-class white Americans,
including the authors of this book, have never been treated with disrespect during a traffic stop. Many members of the white middle class
responded with disbelief or surprise when they saw video of the shooting
of Walter Scott in April 2015 in North Charleston. Mr. Scott had been
stopped for an equipment violation and attempted to flee; he was shot
in the back while running away. Similarly, Sandra Bland, who was found
dead in a jail cell in Waller County, Texas in July 2015, had been stopped
by a trooper for a traffic violation, but the traffic stop quickly escalated

into a heated argument leading to a charge against Bland for assaulting an officer. The ideas of running to escape, or getting into a verbal or physical altercation with an officer following a routine traffic stop, seem alien to most middle-class Americans. Given our experiences with the police, this behavior just does not make sense; we cannot empathize.

We want to close this empathy gap. By documenting and exploring stark differences in how individuals are treated by the police following a traffic stop, we want to give credence to those members of minority communities who say to middle-class Americans: you just don't get it. We hope that our data and explorations here will move us some way to better mutual understandings.

Using Traffic Stops Data to Explore Racial Disparities in Policing

Chapter 2 explains in detail the database on which our analysis is based, a record of every traffic stop in the state of NC from 2002 through 2016. Traffic stops, of course, are but one way in which the police interact with the community. They are certainly not the reason for the massive increase in incarceration of the 1980s and beyond that we referred to earlier in this chapter. But, as we also noted, they are by far the most common avenue by which citizens encounter law enforcement. Wesley Skogan (2008) studied citizen interpretations of their encounters with the police, emphasizing the long-lasting negative consequences of interactions judged to be painful, unhelpful, or disrespectful on the part of the police toward the citizen. In Skogan's view, positive, respectful interactions have little impact but negative ones can have a strongly detrimental impact on citizen views of the police. Tom Tyler, Jeffrey Fagan, and Amanda Geller (2014) review young adults' experiences with "stop and frisk" policing behaviors in New York. They note, logically enough, that adolescents and young men often have many encounters with the police, and that each one of these is a "teachable moment" in the lives of that young man. They find that about 20 percent of all these pedestrian encounters "appear to fall short of constitutional grounds of legal sufficiency" and that "almost none turn up guns (0.11 percent of all stops) or other contraband (1.5 percent). The high rate of error in these stops, both constitutionally and in effectiveness, is a potential sore spot that could poison citizen support for and cooperation with the police" (Tyler, Fagan, and Geller 2014, 752).

When the police interact with citizens rarely, respectfully, and lightly, we can expect little effect on citizen feelings of belonging. But when the interactions are common, aggressive, and seemingly unjustified, then the citizen so treated may well develop an angry response. Given that traffic stops are the most common type of encounter that Americans have with the police, we believe it is an important place to start. What lessons are different demographic groups being taught?

Why Bother?

One might think that it is unnecessary to document in a book-length study that there are strong racial disparities in traffic stops. Others have already shown strong differences in how blacks and whites are treated throughout the criminal justice system, so why should there be any surprise if we find differences here as well? We believe it is important for a number of reasons. First, we fill a gap that was intended in the original NC law when it was discussed, debated, and passed; indeed the 1999 law mandated periodic reports to ascertain whether there might be important and statistically significant disparities in traffic stops, but no official state analysis was ever done, and the most extensive study done so far focused only on the State Highway Patrol for calendar year 2000 (see Smith et al. 2004). Second, more generally, even if we may not be surprised that disparities exist, we need to put numbers to it: a 10 percent difference is not the same as a 300 percent difference, and we do not know until we do the study how strong any disparity may be. Third, we want to know if the disparities are widening or lessening, and again the only way to know is to look. Fourth, we want to know the various avenues that these disparities may take: are they similar between black and Hispanic drivers compared to whites; how do they differ by age and gender, for urban and rural areas, across police departments, sheriffs, and the highway patrol; whether they are caused by just a few officers or are more widespread; and so on. By understanding the shapes and contours of the disparities, we can understand better what may be causing them. Finally, we want to know what explains them, what correlates with high and low scores on our measures of disparity, and what policies therefore might be effective in curtailing them. The North Carolina dataset (as we will explain in the next chapter) is uniquely suited to answering these questions as it is by far the most comprehensive record of police traffic stops currently available. Not to spoil the punchline, we will indeed document racial disparities. But our point in writing the book goes much deeper than that simple question. We aim to understand the scope and nature of them so that we can know what to do about it.

The Plan of the Book

North Carolina was the first state in the nation to mandate the collection of demographic data following any traffic stop, passing the law in 1999. Beginning on January 1, 2000 for the State Highway Patrol, and in 2002 for all but the smallest police agencies, officers have recorded the age, race, and gender of every driver pulled over, why they were stopped, and the outcome of that stop. Based on the analysis of over 20 million of these records, we focus on racial differences in the likelihood of various outcomes, with a particular focus on whether the officer searches the driver of the car. Very few traffic stops lead to a search; just about 3 percent. But searches are highly targeted at young men of color; over 20 percent of those stopped are searched in some jurisdictions. The majority of these searches yield no contraband, and when there is a contraband "hit" the amounts involved are rarely those associated with a dealer or a courier. In fact, courier-level contraband hits are vanishingly rare.

If searches associated with traffic stops were justified as a means to catch drug "kingpins" or couriers, they have been extremely ineffective. In North Carolina alone, millions have been pulled over for minor violations – equipment problems, expired registration tags, and for other reasons that could well be pretexts (fully allowed by the Court in *Whren*) rather than because of excessive speeding, drunk driving, or other serious safety concerns. Disproportionately, these traffic stops, and hundreds of thousands of fruitless searches that followed from them, have been targeted at those fitting a "drug courier profile": young men of color. The disproportionate weight of the war on drugs in these communities is an important component of a larger discussion about mass incarceration, citizenship, and belonging.

We focus on traffic stops and document sustained and troubling disparities in how racial groups are treated in routine traffic stops. These disparities are robust to controls for the purpose of the stop and whether the stop occurred on a weekend evening, late at night, or during the morning rush hour. They are both institutional and officer-based. That is, we can identify individual "bad apple" officers who have particularly wide disparities in their treatment of drivers by race. But the causes of the disparities are much broader than only a few bad apple officers.

Across the state, various police and sheriff's departments have higher and lower levels of disparity in their treatment of drivers of different racial, ethnic, age, and gender groups. Further, the disparities vary over time. Looking both over time and across different agencies, we explore the causes and consequences of racially targeted search and arrest patterns. Individual police officers, sheriff's deputies, and state troopers are identified by a unique ID number. While the identity of the officer is unknown, and therefore we cannot analyze whether officer demographics influence their traffic stops, we can identify individual officers who have high and low rates of search, high and low rates of racial disparity in their stops and searches, and from that identify "bad apple" officers: those with the most marked disparities in the rates at which they search drivers by race. With that information, we can then test whether these officer-level differences explain the patterns of racial disparities seen across the database. While they contribute to them (by definition they must), they by no means explain the bulk of the variance in racial disparity that we observe.

When we compare every community in the state both across space and time, we find that those with the highest levels of racial disparity are systematically related to: higher poverty, smaller size, and lower political power for blacks. That is, controlling for the poverty rate and the size of the city, greater political empowerment of the black community generates lower rates of racial disparity in the police department. We measure black political empowerment as a combination of three factors: the black shares of the population, the voting population, and the elected officials. These three factors are of course highly interconnected, so we treat them as one. The bottom line in our research predicting where disparities are high and low, however, comes down to this: where blacks are politically weak, disparities are strong; where blacks are fully mobilized politically and share in the governance of their local community for example by having seats on the city council, the local police have lower rates of disparity. Lerman and Weaver (2014) documented that disparate treatment by police can stimulate reduced voting turnout and involvement in politics by those affected by their interactions with police. We provide further evidence of the importance of this finding: where disparities are high, the voting share of the black population is lower.

Racial disparities in the outcomes of traffic stops naturally generate alienation among those who sense they have been targeted for unequal treatment. Largely unremarked in this debate is that those not targeted may not even be aware that the targeting is occurring, unless a family member or close friend is routinely targeted. This lack of awareness, we believe, has contributed to a large-scale lack of empathy and understanding. Since the rise of the Black Lives Matter movement beginning in 2012, however, cell-phone videos documenting harsh, sometimes fatal, police interactions with young men of color have awakened all Americans to these realities. The massive scale of what we observe convinces us that the diversion of routine traffic patrols into a targeted practice of aggressive search for those who fit a "profile" in the name of the war on drugs has been extremely costly, much more so than has previously been identified. Further, while members of our nation's minority communities have long been aware of these disparities, middle-class whites are only slowly being made aware of them. Of course, understanding can only start with knowledge and acknowledgment. And repair and reform can only come from understanding.

In this book, based on a comprehensive analysis of one state's experience with traffic stops, we add to our collective understanding of the high cost and the low benefit of diverting routine traffic patrols into the wars on crime and drugs. This decision, dating back a generation, has paid little benefit in terms of fighting crime, but has secretly tarnished our democracy. The tarnish has been real, as very few young men of color have escaped the knowledge that they could be pulled over for a pretext, potentially subjected to search, and possibly arrested while their white equivalent on the other side of town would not have to fear these events. The tarnish has been secret as well, since those not targeted by the practice may be completely unaware of it. Of course, police are not allowed to pull over drivers unless they break the law. But many of our traffic and vehicle laws allow for considerable officer discretion, and others put all of us routinely on the wrong side of the law. While the Court has not so ruled, the disproportionate application of the law in some groups but not in other groups has generated resentment, alienation, and a sense of degraded citizenship. Many Americans are only now becoming aware that this is even happening, though it has been going on for decades.

Our chapters proceed as follows. Chapter 2 reviews the passage of the law in 1999 mandating collection of demographic data following every traffic stop in North Carolina and outlines the contours of the data that have been collected. Chapter 3 focuses on who gets pulled over compared to baseline population and driving data. Chapter 4 deals with the outcomes of stops: who gets a warning, a citation, arrest, or is subjected to a search. Chapter 5 focuses on contraband: how much is found, of what type, how good officers are at predicting which drivers should be searched, and what is the outcome of a contraband hit. Perhaps surprisingly, most of those found with contraband are not arrested. Chapter 6 compares search and arrest patterns officer-by-officer and agency-by-agency, noting huge variation, as we see throughout the book. Chapter 7 ends our analysis of disparities by focusing on Hispanic drivers. Most of our analysis focuses on the differences between white and black drivers, but here we note some particular differences in what officers appear to be looking for when encountering a Hispanic driver as compared to a black one. In Chapter 8, we shift focus away from exploring the degree or the nature of disparity and we seek to explain when is it high and when is it low. We document that disparities detrimental to black drivers are highest when the black community has little political power, and that in those communities where blacks are visible and have strong political representation in the government, disparities are markedly lower. Voting matters. Representation matters. In Chapter 9, we explore what can be done about disparate policing, highlighting two simple police reforms: focusing on traffic safety rather than investigations, and using written forms before conducting consent searches. Through detailed comparisons of reforms put in place in Fayetteville, Durham, and Chapel Hill, we document the value of these reforms, but also the need for police agency buy-in for the reforms to be effective. Finally, we show that citizen cooperation with the police can be significantly enhanced, leading to improved public safety, with an in-depth analysis of citizen calls for service in Fayetteville before and after trust-enhancing reforms were put in place by Chief Harold Medlock in 2013. Chapter 10 concludes. Our appendices provide additional documentation for the analysis presented here.

A Legislative Mandate to Address Concerns about Racial Profiling

North Carolina was one of the first states in the nation to mandate the collection of data on every traffic stop, passing legislation in 1999. The goal of the legislation was clear: to answer the question, once and for all, of whether state troopers and other law enforcement personnel were treating minority and white motorists differently. The data collected would involve each traffic stop, even if no arrest or citation occurred, and would include demographic information about the driver. The resulting data would, according to some, put to rest baseless accusations that white and minority drivers systematically faced different experiences on the highway, or it would point to a problem that various police agencies would take immediate steps to remedy.

In this chapter, we explain the impetus for this legislative reform and describe the purposes to which the North Carolina legislature expected the data to be put. As these data provide the backbone for all of the analysis to follow, we explore in detail the data collection mandated by the statute. Later chapters analyze the trends and patterns apparent in the data, but here our focus is on the database itself as well as the original legislative intent. We start with the background, reviewing the context of the legislative debate and the arguments for and against the bill, and then turn to the substance of what the law requires.

We should note at the outset that while North Carolina was at the forefront of passage of such a law and is a national leader in making the resulting database publicly available with minimal administrative hurdles, it has never provided any official analysis of the traffic statistics collected under the law. This book constitutes the largest such analysis ever conducted. Thus, one essential part of the original intent of the law, to answer the question of whether profiling occurs on the roadways, has never been answered by any official agency. We can clearly answer the question here, however: disparities are significant. Black, Hispanic, white, male, female, young, and older drivers face dramatically different odds of search and arrest following routine traffic stops. Black and Hispanic males are roughly twice as likely to be searched as white males. In this sense, North Carolina may be no different than other states. But to the extent that the General Assembly sought answers to the question of whether there might be any profiling on the highways, the answer is clear: yes, there certainly could be, as the numbers show large disparities. But officially, the Attorney General has never said so, and the state has never recognized it.

Driving while Black Comes to the Attention of America

Driving while black has never been a crime. Racial profiling has of course been widely known in minority communities in the USA through long periods of history, but this particular aspect of it surged to the general public consciousness in the late-1990s. Because government officials are sensitive to such shifts, legislation followed. North Carolina has a significant black population (almost 22 percent in the 2000 census) with significant voting power and representation in the Democratic Caucus of the General Assembly. As Cheryl Miller (1990) describes for the modern period (i.e., since reconstruction), the first black member of the North Carolina General Assembly was elected in 1969. Membership in the legislative black caucus increased to sixteen by 1987, all Democrats, comprising 9 percent of the overall Assembly membership. By 1998, the black caucus was up to 14.1 percent of the seats, double that of the nationwide average, and seventh largest in the nation (Clark 2017a; see also Clark 2017b). As we see later in this chapter, several members of the black caucus were important figures in pushing for passage of this law, one of their most important legislative accomplishments in decades. (See Miller 1990 for a comparison with previous accomplishments; Sullivan 2000 for more historical background on the NC legislative black caucus.)

We conducted a series of keyword searches of major national newspapers for different combinations of terms reflecting racial profiling and found an unmistakable pattern each time. The topic was virtually absent in the media during the period before the mid-1990s but by 1999 was generating large amounts of coverage. This surge in attention lasted just three years, through 2001. The events of 9/11 in that year drove attention to this issue off the media agenda. (Indeed, those events may have pushed law enforcement and members of the public in a different direction, as the perceived terrorist threat brought forward a different form of racial profiling, one beyond the scope of this book, directed at people of Middle Eastern descent.) In the short period of intense media attention to racial profiling before 9/11, however, a number of states enacted reforms. By 2004, twenty-two state agencies mandated the collection of race and ethnicity data for all traffic stops, and seven more required such data collection for certain types of stops only (see Hickman 2005). The list of states mandating data collection, and of agencies doing so voluntarily or through local agreements, continues to grow (see Baumgartner, Christiani et al. 2017).

At least fifteen states considered legislation during 1999 mandating the collection of traffic-stop information, and North Carolina was the first in the nation to pass such a law (GAO 2000, 15). Figure 2.1 shows the timing of the North Carolina legislation in the context of increased media attention. Each line in the figure indicates the number of stories published using three different sets of key words to identify newspaper stories.

Increased media coverage of the issue of possible disparities in the experiences of black and white drivers on the nation's highways set the tone for legislative concern on the issue. This is particularly notable because in the period since 2012 there has been another increase in such attention, this one focusing on the deaths of such individuals as Trayvon Martin, Eric Gardner, and Philando Castile. (This surge is not shown in the figure, as it concerns violence, not "driving while black.") As discussed in Chapter 1, unease in police–minority relations has been a perennial issue in many localities across the country. While the underlying tensions may have been with us for a long time, media attention, public concern, and legislative action appear to be much more sporadic. All this suggests that social movements, focusing events, and other elements that drive media attention can have a big impact, as they provide the impetus for legislative action. Legislators feel the need, or the opportunity, to "do something" in the face of such media coverage and related public concern. Even for such a long-standing problem as police–minority relations, bringing increased attention to the problem can have legislative results (for studies looking at these linkages, see Lipsky 1968; Burstein 1979; Baumgartner and Jones 1993; McAdam 2002; Burstein and Linton 2002; King, Bentele, and Soule 2007; Warren and Tomaskovic-Devey 2009).

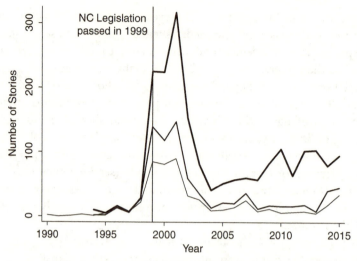

FIGURE 2.1. Media Attention and Legislative Action on "Driving while Black"
Note: The three data series correspond to related searches using different
keywords and newspapers. The thickest black line tracks hits from the following
keywords: SUBJECT("racial profiling" AND ((police) OR ("traffic stop")));
Newspapers used: *Baltimore Sun, Los Angeles Times, Washington Post, New York
Times, USA Today*; 75 percent true hits. The middle line corresponds to the
following keywords: ((racial w/5 disparit!) OR (racial w/5 profil!)) AND ((traffic
w/5 police) OR (traffic w/5 stop) OR ("driving while black") OR ("driving while
brown") OR (minority driv!)); Newspapers used: *Washington Post, New York
Times, Los Angeles Times, Baltimore Sun,* and *USA Today*; 92 percent true hits.
Finally, the thinnest bottom line uses: (SUBJECT("racial profiling" AND (police
OR "law enforcement")) AND BODY((police AND "traffic stop") OR "driving
while black" OR "driving while brown")) OR (SUBJECT("race and racism")
AND BODY((police w/5 "traffic stop") OR "driving while black" OR "driving
while brown")); Newspapers used: *Washington Post, New York Times, Los
Angeles Times,* and *USA Today*; 92 percent true hits.

This is exactly what happened in North Carolina. The relatively large
black caucus naturally provided a number of highly motivated legislative entrepreneurs with direct personal experience in what appeared to
them to be pretextual traffic stops. And the national attention provided a
window of opportunity for reform.

The Legislative Response: NC Senate Bill 76 of 1999

The North Carolina legislature confronted the issue of racial profiling on
the highways in the winter and spring of 1999. Senate Bill 76, "An Act

to Require the Division of Criminal Statistics to Collect and Maintain Statistics on Traffic Law Enforcement" was introduced on February 15, 1999 and referred to committee; it was signed into law by Governor James B. Hunt, Jr. on April 22, 1999.

Before going into detail on the content of the bill and the data collected following its passage, it is worth reviewing what was said at the time in media coverage of its debate and passage. This can give an idea of the "legislative intent" – clearly, legislators expected that the law would either absolve the State Highway Patrol (SHP) and other agencies from accusations of profiling, or provide clear evidence that it was happening. Here we summarize the background leading to the bill's passage and concerns apparent from news coverage of the 1999 debates.

Entrepreneurship by Individual Legislators and the Black Caucus

The primary Senate sponsor of SB 76 was Sen. Frank Ballance, a black Senator who had served as a State Representative from eastern North Carolina from 1983 until 1986, then in the Senate from 1988 through 2002, when he was elected to the US House of Representatives. Republican Sen. and Minority Leader Patrick J. Ballantine co-sponsored. Ballantine, a conservative, was motivated to co-sponsor when contacted by the national coordinator for the American Civil Liberties Union (ACLU), who happened to be a high-school friend. Reggie Shuford had attended the Cape Fear Academy in the early 1980s, one year behind the future Sen. Ballantine. According to a local newspaper profile, the two were an odd couple, but established a bond of mutual respect: " 'We were like night and day in backgrounds,' Mr. Shuford said. 'Even then, it was obvious to me that he [Sen. Ballantine] had sensitivities to racial prejudice.' " " 'He [Shuford] was sandwiched by ridicule,' Sen. Ballantine said. 'He was the only black in a white community, and his own black community accused him of trying to act white. He had it tough, but he made it.' " Both Shuford and Ballantine later attended UNC-Chapel Hill, and Shuford later became a lead attorney for the ACLU, working out of the New York Office. " 'He's a hero of mine, a true American success story,' Sen. Ballantine said" (Ramsey 1999).

With bipartisan support, a national surge in attention to "driving while black," and several legislators willing and able to tell personal stories about their own experiences, the bill quickly made its way through the legislature. These passages from newspaper coverage of the debate illustrate the key roles that personal stories from black legislators played in convincing their colleagues of the need to get to the bottom of accusations of racial bias:

- Rep. Pete Cunningham keeps a "Retired Navy" sticker on the back of his car, not because he's proud of his former career, though he is, but because he's hoping police will spot it before they notice the color of his skin. "Too many times I've been stopped for no good reason," Cunningham, D-Mecklenburg, told the N.C. House on Thursday. "Probable cause? The probable cause is I'm driving a new Mercedes, and I'm black." After an hour of tense debate between black Democrats and white Republicans, House members voted 85–20 to tentatively approve a law requiring the Highway Patrol and other state police agencies to keep detailed statistics on the age, gender and race of every motorist stopped in North Carolina. The goal of the bill: To assure black motorists, especially young black men, that they aren't being stopped more frequently than other drivers. "This happens," Cunningham said. "But even if it doesn't, even if people think there's a problem, we need to deal with that" (Griffin 1999).
- "If you think we don't get harassed simply because of the pigmentation of our skin, I wish you could be black for a week." Cunningham, who keeps a "Retired Navy" decal on his car, said: "I don't do that trying to recruit for the Navy. Too many times I have been stopped in my car. The probable cause was I'm driving a new Mercedes and I'm black ... All is not right in America, folks. Let's not kid ourselves" (Bonner 1999b).
- "I guess if you don't have a point of reference about something, maybe you can't appreciate what's going on. I guess you have to be black to understand this," said Rep. Alma Adams, a black Democrat from Greensboro. "People do things to you, whether it's right or wrong, because of the color of your skin. "If you come from where I come from, if you live where I've lived, it's a daily occurrence" (Griffin 1999).
- In response to Ballance's bill, the Highway Patrol has already begun studying stops in an effort to prove troopers don't stop a disproportionate number of blacks. Republicans say the study, which will include figures from a sampling of counties, should be enough. But black Democrats say the problem, whether real or perceived, needs close study over a number of years and across the state. "If you think we don't get harassed in America because of the pigment of our skin, I wish you could be black for a week," Cunningham said. "You'd

understand some of the things we go through … and you'd understand why we need this" (Griffin 1999).

- For black members of the Senate, there was little doubt it [racial profiling] is happening. "I have three brothers and a husband who have been stopped on several occasions unnecessarily," said Sen. Jeanne Lucas, D-Durham, who also listed other friends who have been stopped. "These people are innocent." She thanked Ballance for "putting the spotlight on something that is occurring in our state. And if it is not occurring, we simply need to say to our law officers we are glad it is not of the magnitude that we think" (Patterson 1999b).

A first key element in understanding why North Carolina passed this progressive bill is therefore the powerful lobbying of minority representatives including those listed above as well as Rep. Ronnie Sutton, the primary House sponsor of the bill and the only Native American member of the General Assembly at the time. Minority elected officials have acted powerfully to bring these issues to the fore in the US Congress (where Rep. John Conyers (D-MI) has long led efforts to combat racial profiling) and elsewhere. Recently Texas Rep. Garnet Coleman introduced comprehensive legislation to ban racial profiling in Texas; while the Sandra Bland Act was significantly reduced in scope by the time it was passed (see Silver 2017), its motivation was clearly associated with Coleman's own experiences. During a legislative hearing in which Baumgartner participated, Chairman Coleman (a black Rep. from Houston) and Rep. Ramon Romero (Hispanic from Fort Worth) both commented on their own repeated personal experiences with what they considered to be racially motivated and unfair treatment as younger men during traffic stops (for coverage of this hearing see Schwartz and Dexheimer 2017).[1]

A Few Bad Apples or a Systemic Problem?

An early theme in the discussion of the traffic stop data-collection initiative was the exact nature of the problem, if one existed at all. Specifically, a number of stories focused on the question of whether any disparities could be attributed to "a few bad apples" or reflected a broader institutional problem. Deborah Ross, executive director of the ACLU of North Carolina (and later the Democratic nominee for the US Senate in 2016) said: "'I think it will be an excellent method of showing whether or not this is a systemic problem or whether there are only one or two troopers who have this problem'" (see Bonner 1999a). The following newspaper selections highlight the question of differentiating a few bad apples from a broader pattern or practice of disparate treatment, and the value of the data in doing so:

- Supporters said the information would reveal the facts behind the widely held perception that troopers target African-Americans and Native Americans for traffic stops. "There is a perception in certain parts of the state, if not all over the state, that police stop minorities more than they do Caucasians," said Rep. Ronnie Sutton, a Democrat from Pembroke and the legislature's only Native American. Collecting the information also would help the Highway Patrol identify troopers who target drivers by their skin color, Sutton said (Bonner 1999b).
- North Carolinians have enough to worry about as their fellow drivers whiz around them in traffic. They need not be concerned that some rogue officer plans to pull them over solely because they are not the right color, creed or gender. North Carolina's highway patrolmen, to their credit, are not opposing the bill. Speaking through the leadership of their troopers' association, they have said that they are ready and willing to participate in the study, and anxious to learn if there are any bad apples in their barrel (see Editorial Board 1999c).

To the extent that the data are used to measure disparities in outcomes following a traffic stop, we will see in the chapters to follow that it is indeed easy to test the "bad apple" hypothesis, since the law mandates a unique number to be assigned to each officer in the state. Chapter 7 reviews these data, showing that there are indeed some bad apples, but that disparate treatment of minority and white drivers goes far beyond only this factor.

Two-to-One Ratio in Drug Interdiction Team Unacceptable

Another question that arose during debate of the issue was what exactly should count as a disparity. After all, it is unlikely that officers stop, search, and arrest black and white motorists at exactly equal rates, but some low level of disparity might not be particularly problematic. At least one story noted that a two-to-one ratio of the percent of minority and white drivers who were searched should be alarming. Notably, this search-rate-ratio statistic was associated with the State Highway Patrol's "I-Team", a drug interdiction unit operating mostly on the state's busy interstate highways, I-85 and I-95, which are the main corridors from Atlanta or Miami, respectively, to Washington DC and further north. According to an editorial in the *Raleigh News and Observer*:

Sen. Frank Ballance, a Warrenton Democrat, has introduced a bill that, if enacted, would provide pertinent facts. And those facts are needed. The bill also would provide the patrol leadership with an excellent management tool to help judge how wisely its resources are being used. Under Ballance's bill, troopers would be required to note the race, age and sex of every driver they stop, regardless of whether they were arrested, cited, warned or sent on their way. Such data is collected now only when the driver is ticketed or stopped by the patrol's special drug interdiction team. The attorney general's office would issue a report to the General Assembly every two years based on that information. As recently as 1996, The *N&O* found that black male drivers on I-95 and I-85 were being charged by the patrol's so-called "I-Team" at nearly twice the rate they were charged by other troopers patrolling those same roads. In most cases, no drugs were found and drivers were cited for minor traffic violations. Patrol statistics show that last year, blacks and other minorities were twice as likely as white drivers to have their cars searched by the drug squad. Officials with the Department of Crime Control and Public Safety say they are concerned that black drivers are searched more often than white ones, but deny that troopers single out blacks for stops. The numbers, which the patrol says would be relatively easy but expensive to collect, should settle this issue of equitable treatment once and for all. It is an investment of time and money that is well worth making. If the patrol is, as many blacks believe, unfairly targeting them, it must be stopped immediately. If not, the patrol deserves to be exonerated. Ballance's bill would go a long way toward showing who is right. (Editorial Board 1999a)

This editorial is worth noting for two specific statistical points of reference as well as its hopeful conclusion. First is the idea that the State Highway Patrol special drug interdiction team (the "I-Team") was of particular concern, with a much higher rate of stopping black drivers as compared to other police agencies. Second is that existing statistics of racial disparity in search rates indicated that officers were "twice as likely" to search black drivers compared to whites. These two elements combined suggest that the overall, statewide search rate disparity was expected to be relatively low, since the unit generating the greatest deal of concern was thought to maybe have a two-to-one ratio. Finally, the Editorial Board asserts that the data collection will "settle this issue of equitable treatment once and for all." Either the SHP must be exonerated, or the unfair targeting must be stopped immediately, according to the Raleigh paper board.

In the chapters to come, we will see clearly that a two-to-one search rate ratio is close to the state average, with many agencies, and hundreds of individual officers, having much higher rates. The SHP actually has a relatively low search rate and a lower racial disparity in search rates compared to other police agencies. But, as the data will show, not only has the SHP not been exonerated, but neither have various state agencies been mandated to "stop immediately." One reason for this may be that the Attorney General's office has never issued a single report analyzing the data so painstakingly collected over all these years.

Low Contraband Hit Rates Prove Many Searches are Wasteful

One lawmaker was quoted during the debate making a particularly prescient point about low contraband hit rates.

The state Highway Patrol is conducting too many roadside searches if it is finding illegal drugs in only 20 percent of those stops, a state lawmaker said Thursday. "This business of stopping a car and bringing in drug dogs, that's serious business," said Rep. Martin Nesbitt, D-Buncombe. Nesbitt's comments came as the House Judiciary Committee took up a plan to try to determine if the Highway Patrol and other statewide law enforcement agencies are stopping a disproportionate number of black drivers. (Mooneyham 1999)

As we will see in later chapters, Rep. Nesbitt was certainly onto something. While the war on drugs has been an important justification for discretionary traffic stops and searches, large amounts of drugs are rarely found following a routine traffic stop; very rarely in fact, as we show in Chapter 5.

Republican Party Outreach to the Minority Community

According to one newspaper account, frustrations in the black community with a lack of responsiveness in the Democratic Party led to a sense of opportunity among Republicans in the legislature that they could reach out to members of the minority party. Writing of efforts to mobilize a potential black Republican voting group, the *Greensboro News and Record* explains:

The group Republicans likely will reach out to first is the Minority Strategic Planning Coalition. The coalition first met two weeks ago to devise a political strategy for winning legislative battles for minorities. By then, many black leaders already had met privately with [Sen. Patrick] Ballantine and Rep. Leo Daughtry. Those early talks already are breeding results. Ballantine is co-sponsoring a bill with veteran black leader Sen. Frank Ballance designed to stop "harassment" of black drivers by patrol officers who some people think often stop black drivers without cause. "There's been a chasm between Republicans and blacks for decades," Ballantine said. "But things are changing. The blacks are in a very powerful position now." (Nash 1999)

Sen. Ballantine was joined by Sen. Virginia Foxx, currently a member of the US House of Representatives, as the two Republican co-sponsors of the legislation. While support was dominated by Democrats, and members of the black caucus in particular, the Republican Party was not uniformly opposed to the legislation, and votes for its passage were lopsided.

Counter-Arguments and Concerns

A number of counter-arguments were brought up against the idea of collecting traffic stop statistics, but the national mood was so strong in favor of it that even the State Highway Patrol initiated its own study, convinced that it would show no bias, but committed to correcting any if it were found. Among the most prominent arguments against the law were mentioned in an article from the *Greensboro News and Record*:

- "The N.C. Troopers Association opposes the bill. A lawyer for the group, David Horne, said oral warnings – meant to quickly admonish drivers and then allow them to carry on without legal consequences – would decline if the legislation is passed. Instead, the troopers would simply write more tickets" (Kirkpatrick 1999).
- Insurance agencies may raise rates on black and Hispanic drivers. The argument here was that official records would now document the rates at which drivers were pulled over, and that inevitably this would find its way into insurance underwriting calculations, even though individual driver information would not be kept (see Kirkpatrick 1999).
- The data will be inconclusive, since we don't know which drivers are breaking the law (Kirkpatrick 1999).

While the *Greensboro News and Record* may have been prescient on continued controversy and the "benchmark problem" (see Chapter 3), they were quite optimistic about the next technological innovation:

- One possible solution is the tamper-proof video cameras some police departments are installing in their cars. An unbroken video record of every stop would show not only demographics, but the all-important circumstances. Researchers could draw real meaning from that data (Editorial Board 1999b).
- Profiling promotes good law enforcement: "Some House Republicans worry that requiring detailed record-keeping will discourage troopers from pulling over drivers who have committed a crime. Several argued Thursday that investigators need to be able to stop drivers who fit the profile of suspected criminals. 'Good management in the patrol ought to be able to tell who's racist,' said Rep. Chuck Neely, R-Wake. 'This

bill is not needed, but worse than that I think it could have a real adverse effect on law enforcement'" (Griffin 1999).

Thus, while a few concerns were raised, the bill went through the legislature with few hurdles, perhaps as a result of large Democratic majorities. Still, those majorities had been in place for decades previously before the opportunity arose to pass such a sweeping bill. The most important response to the bill, of course, came from the Highway Patrol itself, the principal target. (The bill was initially targeted only at the NC State Highway Patrol, but widened to apply to all but the smallest police agencies statewide shortly after passage.)

Accusations of Bias are Unfounded

Leaders of the NC State Highway Patrol (SHP) were adamant that they had policies in place to eliminate racial profiling by their officers, but also clear that they were committed to doing something about it if any studies revealed that it was occurring. Two newspaper reports from the time focus on statements by the SHP leadership:

The N.C. Highway Patrol said Thursday it'll do its own study to prove troopers don't pull over motorists for "driving while black." State Crime Control Secretary Richard Moore said patrol leaders and rank-and-file troopers alike want to knock down any perceptions among blacks and Native Americans that they're targeted on N.C. roads. Patrol policy prohibits any unfair or discriminatory enforcement, he said. "If it, in fact, does exist, we have to do something. We can't tolerate it." He conceded the study is being launched in response to a proposal introduced last week in the General Assembly that would require the attorney general to track the race, age and gender of every driver stopped by the patrol and other state law agencies. "They certainly deserve credit for getting us to look at this," Moore said of the bill's main sponsors, Sen. Frank Ballance, D-Warren, and Rep. Ronnie Sutton, D-Robeson. Ballance welcomed the study but said it doesn't replace the bill. "Citizens do not want stops based on race," he said. "The police say they're not doing them. The facts will speak for themselves." "There could be a big gap, but it could be explained by things other than race," said study coordinator Matthew Zingraff, an associate dean for research at N.C. State University. "If you can't explain it with issues other than race, then you're in serious trouble." (Rhee 1999)

In a similar article (Patterson 1999a), Moore acknowledged that almost 25 percent of tickets went to black drivers, though they account for only 17 percent of licensed drivers in the state.

"There is no doubt that there is a perception in minority communities across North Carolina, particularly in the African-American and Native American communities, that some law enforcement officers target the drivers that they stop based on race," Moore said Thursday. The study results likely will prove troopers are abiding by a strict Highway Patrol policy against racial profiling, Moore believes. He said troopers with laptop computers in their cruisers will start noting the race and sex of each driver they stop. Matthew Zingraff, an associate dean at N.C. State University, said he hopes to have a preliminary report ready before the legislative session ends. He said a final version should be completed in the fall. "Because we understand that the perception exists, we want to make sure, as an organization, that we establish a factual basis for our claim that it doesn't exist," he said. "And if it does in fact exist, we must do something about it." (Patterson 1999a)

So with the NC SHP committed to studying the issue, and the legislature rapidly moving to enact a landmark law to require new statistics to be collected from every traffic stop, the law was passed in April 1999. Beginning in January 2000 for the SHP, and two years later for all but the smallest police agencies throughout the state, every traffic stop would be recorded and reported to the State Attorney General.

Passage of the Law, Subsequent Amendments, and State of the Law in 2017

The text of the 1999 law as passed is reproduced verbatim in Appendix A. The law clearly mandated the State Highway Patrol to make a record of every traffic stop, with one exception: roadside checkpoints would lead to a record only when an adverse action was taken against the driver, such as a search, ticket, or arrest. (Those who passed through the checkpoint with no action would not be recorded, in other words.) Demographic data on the driver would be systematically collected, as well as information about the purpose of the stop, any search that might have been conducted associated with the stop, the discovery of contraband, violence directed toward the stopping officer, use of force by the officer, and the outcome of the stop. (Information concerning passengers would be collected only if adverse action ensued, such as search or arrest. We generally exclude checkpoints and passengers from our analyses, unless otherwise noted.) Further, the law mandated that the data be reported to a new office set up by the Attorney General, which was mandated to "make scientific study" of the collected data and to make periodic reports to the Governor and the General Assembly.

In the 2001–02 session, Senate Bill 147 (sponsored again by Sen. Ballance, the original 1999 sponsor), expanded the scope to apply to almost all law enforcement agencies. This major expansion of the law was eventually adopted as part of a technical revisions bill passed into

law as part of Session Law 2002–159 and an appropriations bill, Session
Law 2001–424. There was little fanfare associated with this expansion,
but it was a major change. Starting in January 2002, the law applied
to all police agencies in the state except for the very smallest ones (see
Appendix B for the exact wording of the current law). Not only did the
expansion double the scope of the law, by expanding from an exclusive
focus on the SHP (responsible for approximately half of all traffic stops
in the state) to county sheriffs, municipal police departments, and other
police agencies, but it also added a significant inter-governmental aspect
to the law. After all, the SHP is a state agency, so legislative mandates can
be seen as part of the legislature's executive oversight function within
state government. But county sheriff's departments and local police
agencies are not part of the state government. In spite of the importance of the scope of the 2001 expansion of the law, our search of the
NewsBank archive of North Carolina newspapers found no significant
coverage of the bill (just a few short mentions in coverage of legislative
actions generally), but one revealing column in the *Chapel Hill News*:

Two years ago, Sen. Frank Ballance and other black legislators pushed a bill
through the General Assembly that requires the Highway Patrol to report the race
of every driver it stopped.
   While the bill passed by a comfortable margin, it became law only after lengthy
committee meetings, considerable public discussion, and a wealth of compromise.
   Thursday, the Senate enormously expanded the scope of the bill without any
committee or floor debate, without public comment, and apparently, without
compromise. Ballance, D-Warren, did so by putting the expansion into the 285-
page budget that passed along party lines.
   The initiative was designed to either prove, or disprove, the notion that police
stop African-American drivers more often than white drivers. Early indications,
based on data collected under the law, are that there is no such discrimination
with the Highway Patrol.
   When Ballance originally proposed the law, he wanted all law enforcement
covered. But he couldn't get political support for a measure that broad. He got
the bill through the Assembly by compromising, saying it would cover only the
patrol. Now there's a good chance that he'll get all he originally wanted.
   Ballance's tactic is fairly common in the legislature. Powerful lawmakers like
Ballance – he's the Senate's deputy president pro tem – get substantive legislation
placed into the monstrous budget bill. (O'Connor 2001)

   O'Connor goes on to explain how this is a good thing, that the legislative process sometimes must involve giving lawmakers some political cover for decisions that might not stand well on their own, and the
budget process allows that. But it is more interesting for the purpose of
this book to note that it took two years, substantial compromise with

the first passage of a law, and the determination of an African-American legislator in a position of institutional power to bring this legislation into place. If O'Connor's interpretation and facts are correct, it suggests substantial influence within the Democratic Party caucus of a committed group of African-American lawmakers and allies. Our search for news coverage of the 2001–02 expansion of the law – which came up empty – suggests that O'Connor at least got that part right; there was indeed little acknowledgment of the expansion in the press. Lawmakers used a window of opportunity in 1999 to pass landmark legislation to great fanfare and with considerable media discussion, then expanded the law quietly two years later to almost no media coverage or legislative debate.

Since 2002, few revisions have been made. Amendments were quietly passed through Senate Bill 464 in 2009 to clarify the care to be taken if a driver had in their custody a young child and to make other minor wording changes to the law; these amendments did not substantially alter the legislation in other ways. There was one potentially important revision added in the 2009 bill, however: the law specified for the first time that the data must be submitted in a timely fashion (no later than sixty days after the close of a month) and that failure to submit the required data would cause the agency to be ineligible for any state grants. From 2002 through 2009, in other words, there were no penalties for failure to comply with the law; these were added only in 2009. Following the first reports by Baumgartner and Epp on the results of their initial analysis of the dataset in 2012, which showed significant racial disparities in the likelihood of search after a traffic stop, Sen. Thom Goolsby introduced legislation to cease all data collection. This bill was referred to committee but no further action was taken (see Appendix B).

Appendix B provides the full text of the currently applicable law in North Carolina, as of July 2017. Appendix C reproduces the SBI-122 form, which is the paper version of the form officers fill out. The State maintains a website allowing any user to create simple reports on stops and searches for any reporting agency: http://trafficstops.ncsbi.gov/. The site has other information about the law as well. The data and reports available on the site are limited to simple tables. We contacted the administrators of the database and they graciously provided the entire database on several occasions. Our most recent version was received in spring 2017, covering all stops from the beginning of reporting through December 31, 2016. The State SBI office in charge takes its mandate of public dissemination very seriously and has been very cooperative. Because of the large amount of data the office provides, they have established an FTP (file transfer protocol) server allowing members of the public to log in directly to their servers to retrieve the data. The office is a model of transparency and open data.

Previous Analyses and Reports

There can be no doubt that the legislative intent of the original drafters of SB 76 in 1999 included not only the collection of data, but its analysis and interpretation. News reports at the time were full of discussions about how the data would either exonerate the Highway Patrol, or indicate that there was a problem in need of immediate correction. The law amended section 114-10 of the North Carolina code, which mandates the Attorney General to have a Division of Criminal Statistics whose duties include "To make scientific study, analysis and comparison from the information so collected and correlated with similar information gathered by federal agencies, and to provide the Governor and the General Assembly with the information so collected biennially, or more often if required by the Governor" (see the text of the law in Appendix A, Section 1, part 3). (Note that this section of the law requiring the division to compile statistics and report on their analysis dates at least to 1939.)

It is perhaps surprising, then, that no reports have ever been issued (see Mance 2012, fn. 3). The state has never publicly taken a position on whether these mountains of data include any indications that might cause concern. Neither has the state publicly concluded that police agencies refrain from racial profiling. State officials simply have not addressed the question.

As discussed above, the SHP cooperated with a team of researchers from North Carolina State University (NCSU) and North Carolina Central University (NCCU) in research that was on-going by the time the law was passed in 1999. Eventually this research team received additional funds from the US Department of Justice and compiled a comprehensive report (Smith et al. 2004). This team was particularly focused on providing the proper baseline ("denominator") measures of the driving population. Following from the intent of the legislators, and concern within the leadership of the SHP, they wanted to know if those stopped by the troopers reflected those speeding or otherwise breaking the law. Their attention also focused on the different units of the SHP, particularly the "Criminal Interdiction Team" (CIT), a unit with a particular focus on drugs, guns, and other forms of contraband. The research team spent time driving in vans at exactly the speed limit, observing the race of drivers passing them and thereby getting an estimate of how often drivers of each race were speeding, using this as the benchmark to compare with who was pulled over. They also conducted a survey of black and white drivers who had been given tickets, asking about driving behavior, contact with the police, and other factors. They verified that the CIT officers were more likely to search blacks than whites (Smith et al. 2004, 11) and suggested that several cognitive biases (e.g. stereotyping) and processes (e.g., interviewing drivers and looking for signs of nervousness) may have been in play, generating these higher search rates for black drivers (12). In one table they summarize significant differences between black and white drivers, based on their survey. Black drivers were significantly more likely: to have been stopped by the police in the past year; to be stopped by the local police; to have a higher number of prior lifetime stops per year of driving; and to travel rarely on the interstate highways. White drivers were more likely to: drive more miles per year; use the interstate; fail to wear a seatbelt; fail to signal when changing lanes; roll through stop signs; run yellow lights; and use more methods to avoid speeding tickets. No significant differences were found for: being stopped by the highway patrol; driving more than 10 mph over the speed limit; speeding; changing lanes frequently in order to drive faster; frequently passing slower drivers (see Warren et al. 2006, table 3).

One of the main concerns of the Smith et al. team was whether the SHP was, on average, guilty as charged of racial profiling. Their data suggested they were not, though there were some troubling "hot spots" such as the CIT drug team. We will show in later chapters that the SHP, with its focus on speeding tickets, actually has a very low rate of search compared to other police agencies throughout the state and is indeed relatively low in its disparity of search between black and white drivers. The agencies with greatest concern are mostly elsewhere, in particular in urban police departments which sometimes have average search rates ten times higher than the SHP average rate. If Sen. Ballance focused the law initially on the SHP as a compromise, he was certainly right to seek to expand it to other agencies. The SHP itself proves to have relatively low racial disparities compared to other agencies. This is reassuring as it accounts for approximately half of all traffic stops in the state.

Academic studies by the NCSU / NCCU team were published in later years based on their analysis of 2,000 traffic stops by the highway patrol. Little fanfare accompanied most of the studies; the initial Smith et al. 2004 article was a final report to the US DOJ; other publications included Tomaskovic-Devey et al. 2004, 2006; Warren et al. 2006;

Tomaskovic-Devey and Warren 2009; Warren and Tomaskovic-Devey 2009; Warren 2010, 2011. While these studies were valuable contributions, particularly to the question of the "baseline" of measuring the driving population, they were focused largely on the SHP and used one year of driving data. These were supplemented with many other forms of data collection, however, and the body of work was very insightful. These did not constitute, however, official findings of the SHP, of any individual police department, and certainly not of the Attorney General. Nor did they generate a lot of media coverage throughout the state.

In 2011, Baumgartner and Epp served as unpaid consultants to a task force for the North Carolina Advocates for Justice and analyzed the statewide data, later issuing a confidential report (see Baumgartner and Epp 2012). In June of that year, the report was distributed to the press and local attorney Ian Mance published an article on our research (Mance 2012), as did a number of local and national reporters. A sampling of these reports includes Barksdale 2012b; Wise 2013; Oppel 2014; LaFraniere and Lehren 2015; Killian 2015; and Maxwell 2016. A sharp rejoinder to the Baumgartner–Epp study was commissioned by the North Carolina Association of Chiefs of Police and the NC Sheriff's Association (see Weisel n.d.). This report contended that our analysis was "deeply flawed" and pointed out some errors but did not contest the fundamental issue of significant disparities. In fact, the report contends that while "racial bias in law enforcement ... cannot be completely eliminated," evidence of disparities should not be considered to be "proof of widespread law enforcement bias" (Weisel n.d., 1).

So, while the data have been collected and made available, no official findings have been reached. Furthermore, it is clear that many conflate issues of bias and disparity. From a law enforcement perspective, discussions of disparity can move quickly into accusations of explicit racial animus. As discussed in Chapter 1, disparities may result from multiple causes, and explicit racial bias may be among the least likely. Our view is that the data collected under the law can provide excellent points of reference and demonstrate conclusively whether or not significant disparities in outcomes occur. The causes of these disparities may range from differences in criminal behavior, differences in institutional practice in police agencies (such as deploying more police in some areas and fewer police in others), "a few bad apples," explicit bias, or implicit bias and inaccurate (or exaggerated) stereotyping. Based on the data, we cannot say what is the cause. But we can look for the disparities in great detail, and we can see if they are systematically related to such factors as officer discretion, the use of investigatory stops, and other factors. We are careful throughout the book to make clear that we are not studying bias; we are studying racial difference. In any case, this book constitutes the most complete analysis of the SBI-122 data so far conducted. In contrast to the NCSU–NCCU team, we have done the work without the cooperation of any official partners, and we have limited ourselves mostly to analyze the data collected as part of the form, not adding such things as surveys of drivers. We are financially independent of any stakeholder in this debate.

The SBI-122 Form and Resulting Data

The most straightforward way to explain what is collected is simply to refer to Appendix C, which includes the SBI-122 form filled out by all police officers after a traffic stop. In this section, we go through the form one section at a time and show the aggregate frequencies at which each item has been observed in the period since 2002. We do not report frequencies for dates and times, individual police agencies, counties or cities, or individual officers. In subsequent chapters where those data are relevant for analyses, we use them, and our website includes a list of frequencies for each police agency. The SHP has over 9 million stops, Charlotte-Mecklenburg has well over a million, and many small agencies are included as well; over 300 agencies appear in the database.

Initial Purpose of the Stop

Table 2.1 summarizes stops by purpose. The form specifies ten reasons why a driver may be stopped, ranging from speeding to criminal investigation. We group the stop purposes as shown in the table by "safety" stops, "investigatory" ones, and "other." In the analysis in later chapters we will make the point that safety-related stops differ in character and in officer motivation from those which we call investigatory. Briefly stated, we argue that stops for "investigatory" purposes are more likely to relate to minor offenses that may serve as a pretext for pulling a driver over. We list Checkpoint stops in the table as "other" and exclude them from all analysis in the book. Checkpoint stops are included, according to the law, only when an adverse outcome ensues. Since we do not know how many drivers went through a checkpoint without search, arrest, or a citation, we exclude these from the analysis below. For the same reason, we exclude passengers from our analysis; they are reported only when they are searched.

TABLE 2.1. *Frequency of Stop Purposes by Race*

Purpose	All Drivers		White Drivers		Black Drivers		Hispanic Drivers	
	# of Stops	% of Stops	# of Stops	% of Stops	# of Stops	% of Stops	# of Stops	% of Stops
Safety	**10,903,991**	**52.41**	**6,685,915**	**55.74**	**3,064,907**	**46.98**	**759,064**	**46.33**
Speed Limit	8,575,792	41.22	5,390,457	44.94	2,349,920	36.02	526,139	32.11
Stop Light/Sign	992,374	4.77	551,345	4.60	319,121	4.89	83,104	5.07
Driving Impaired	182,558	0.88	103,066	0.86	41,854	0.64	32,228	1.97
Safe Movement	1,153,267	5.54	641,047	5.34	354,012	5.43	117,593	7.18
Investigatory	**9,628,598**	**46.27**	**5,191,622**	**43.28**	**3,382,077**	**51.85**	**809,282**	**49.39**
Vehicle Equipment	1,833,213	8.81	913,857	7.62	712,959	10.93	159,549	9.74
Vehicle Regulatory	3,556,772	17.09	1,846,275	15.39	1,393,872	21.37	239,985	14.65
Seat Belt	1,812,175	8.71	1,171,986	9.77	486,004	7.45	99,121	6.05
Investigation	1,410,390	6.78	751,879	6.27	443,981	6.81	177,331	10.82
Other Vehicle	1,016,048	4.88	507,625	4.23	345,261	5.29	133,296	8.13
Other	**273,526**	**1.31**	**116,879**	**0.97**	**76,481**	**1.17**	**70,280**	**4.29**
Checkpoint	273,526	1.31	116,879	0.97	76,481	1.17	70,280	4.29
Total Included Stops	20,806,115	100	11,994,416	100	6,523,465	100	1,638,626	100

Note: This table excludes passengers. We recode race and ethnicity as mutually exclusive categories, but the form lists them as separate variables. The "all drivers" columns include Native American, Asian, and drivers of other races.

A note on language: the SBI-122 form includes "Investigation" as a stop purpose, but Epp et al. (2014) and we distinguish between Safety and "Investigatory" traffic stops. When referring to the SBI-122 stop purpose of "Investigation," we use that term, but readers should note that this is a subset of the broader "investigatory" set of stop purposes. Investigation stops refer to situations where officers are looking for a particular individual, whether following an "attempt to locate" notice, a "be on the lookout for" (BOLO) alert, or similar crime investigations (see Weisel n.d., 87). Investigatory stops include all those stops associated with an officer's desire to find out more about a driver rather than to prevent / reduce dangerous driving habits. So, as indicated in Table 2.1, "investigatory" stops include the stop purpose the form defines as "investigation." It is confusing but we will use the terms consistently.

Vehicle Driver Information

Table 2.2 gives the breakdown of demographic information included in the reports. Clearly, stops are most concentrated among young men and become progressively less common for older drivers. Stops are least common for women over the age of fifty. But recall that we do not know the demographics of the driving population of North Carolina, so we are unable to determine how far stop rates deviate from driving rates, or, for that matter, rates of criminal behavior.

The SBI-122 form lists races as White, Black, Asian, Native American, and Other, and it lists Ethnicity as Non-Hispanic or Hispanic, which it defines as "persons of Spanish culture," consistent with the 2010 US Census definition (see Humes, Jones, and Ramirez 2011). In all of our analyses below, we combine race and ethnicity so that we can look at mutually exclusive categories of white (non-Hispanic) drivers, black (non-Hispanic), and Hispanic drivers. Because of the relatively low numbers of Native American, Asian, and drivers of other races, we do not focus on these racial groups in the chapters to come. Table 2.3 shows how the data is collected and Table 2.4 shows the numbers associated with our mutually exclusive white/black/Hispanic/other variable. We use this mutually exclusive variable for all subsequent analysis. Thus, we use the term Hispanic to refer to any person listed as Hispanic, no matter the race, and white, black, and other to refer to non-Hispanic whites, blacks, and persons of other races.

Enforcement Action Taken

Table 2.5 shows the distribution of outcomes following a stop. In our analyses, we cluster the outcomes as light (no action or a warning), expected

TABLE 2.2. *Driver Age and Sex*

		Number	Percent
By Age:	Younger than 20	1,755,572	8.55
	20–29	6,896,951	33.59
	30–39	4,843,759	23.59
	40–49	3,629,522	17.63
	50 and Older	3,415,109	16.63
	Total	20,540,913	*100.00*
By Sex:	Male	13,118,440	63.89
	Female	7,414,149	36.11
	Total	20,532,589	*100.00*

Note: Includes only drivers. Excludes checkpoint stops. Differences in the N reflect observations where age or gender is missing.

TABLE 2.3. *Driver Race and Ethnicity*

Race	Ethnicity					
	Hispanic		Non-Hispanic		Total	
	# of Stops	% of Stops	# of Stops	% of Stops	# of Stops	% of Stops
White	848,257	6.67	11,877,537	93.33	12,725,794	100
Black	20,684	0.32	6,446,984	99.68	6,467,668	100
Asian	4,670	1.92	239,024	98.08	243,694	100
Native American	2,397	1.51	156,474	98.49	158,871	100
Unknown	692,338	73.92	244,224	26.08	936,562	100
Total	1,568,346	7.64	18,964,243	92.36	20,532,589	100

Note: Includes only drivers. Excludes checkpoint stops.

TABLE 2.4. *A Mutually Exclusive Race / Ethnicity Identifier*

Identifier	Number	Percent
White, non-Hispanic	11,877,537	57.85
Black, non-Hispanic	6,446,984	31.40
Other, non-Hispanic	639,722	3.11
Hispanic	1,568,346	7.64
Total	20,532,589	100.00

Note: Includes only drivers. Excludes checkpoint stops.

TABLE 2.5. *Stop Outcomes*

Outcome	All Drivers		White Drivers		Black Drivers		Hispanic Drivers	
	# of Stops	% of Stops	# of Stops	% of Stops	# of Stops	% of Stops	# of Stops	% of Stops
Light	6,789,225	33.06	3,879,569	32.66	2,313,916	35.89	403,591	25.73
No Action	620,644	3.02	352,063	2.96	213,899	3.32	40,137	2.56
Verbal Warning	3,338,660	16.26	1,720,894	14.49	1,292,794	20.05	224,126	14.29
Written Warning	2,829,921	13.78	1,806,612	15.21	807,223	12.52	139,328	8.88
Expected	13,295,910	64.76	7,799,871	65.67	3,951,937	61.30	1,104,712	70.44
Citation Issued	13,295,910	64.76	7,799,871	65.67	3,951,937	61.30	1,104,712	70.44
Severe	447,454	2.18	198,097	1.67	181,131	2.81	60,043	3.83
Arrested	447,454	2.18	198,097	1.67	181,131	2.81	60,043	3.83
Total	20,532,589	100.00	11,877,537	100.00	6,446,984	100.00	1,568,346	100.00

Note: See note for Table 2.1.

(citation), or severe (arrest). By "expected" we mean simply that this is the most likely outcome after being pulled over by the police.

As the table makes clear, about two-thirds of traffic stops lead to a citation. Arrests follow a stop just 2 percent of the time, and warnings (either verbal or written) constitute about 30 percent of the outcomes. No enforcement action, not even delivering a verbal warning, is taken about 3 percent of the time.

Physical Resistance Encountered

Table 2.6 shows how often officers encounter physical resistance from a driver or passenger, engage force against them, and suffer or cause injuries.

Instances of violence following a traffic stop are rare. Officers encountered violence about 24,000 times, or just over once per 1,000 stops. Injuries are recorded in fewer than 10,000 stops total, more often to the driver than to the officer. While 10,000 injuries and 24,000 incidents with violence are certainly too many, given the scope of the data collection, with 20 million stops over fifteen years, it is clear that the vast majority of traffic stops are indeed routine. In fact, we do not make any further analyses of these variables in the chapters to come. The dataset provides no further information about, for example, shootings or deaths that may result from a traffic stop and in any case the events are so rare statistically that we focus our attention on other factors which are more common.

Search

Just over 3 percent of all traffic stops have led to a search, with almost 700,000 drivers searched. When a search occurs, officers fill out the back of the form, or Part II. Table 2.7 displays the frequencies of search by type: consent, search warrant, probable cause, incident to arrest, or protective frisk.

Three of the search types are quite common, and two are rare. Protective frisks are allowed if an officer has reason to suspect that an individual may be armed; these occur in about one traffic stop in 1,000. Rarer still are search warrants carried out during a traffic stop; fewer than 1,600 have been conducted, or less than one in 10,000 stops. The three main types of search are, in order of frequency: consent, incident to arrest, and probable cause. Searches conducted incident to arrest follow, rather than lead to, the decision to arrest the driver. Whenever an arrest occurs, before taking the individual into custody, the officer should search the individual

TABLE 2.6. *Number of Incidents Resulting in Force or Injury*

	All Drivers		White Drivers		Black Drivers		Hispanic Drivers	
	# of Stops	% of Stops	# of Stops	% of Stops	# of Stops	% of Stops	# of Stops	% of Stops
Encounter Violence	24,026	0.12	10,009	0.08	12,006	0.19	1,611	0.10
Engaged Force	13,215	0.06	6,123	0.05	5,716	0.09	1,115	0.07
Officer Injured	3,628	0.02	1,711	0.01	1,577	0.02	246	0.02
Driver Injured	4,709	0.02	2,162	0.02	1,997	0.03	457	0.03
Total Included Stops	20,532,589	–	11,877,537	–	6,446,984	–	1,568,346	–

Note: See note for Table 2.1.

TABLE 2.7. *Searches by Type*

Search Type	All Drivers		White Drivers		Black Drivers		Hispanic Drivers	
	# of Stops	% of Stops	# of Stops	% of Stops	# of Stops	% of Stops	# of Stops	% of Stops
Consent	304,768	1.48	127,954	1.08	141,190	2.19	30,492	1.94
Search Warrant	1,593	0.01	721	0.01	649	0.01	189	0.01
Probable Cause	153,894	0.75	50,393	0.42	91,549	1.42	9,739	0.62
Incident to Arrest	209,148	1.02	91,832	0.77	82,453	1.28	31,423	2.00
Protective Frisk	20,254	0.10	7,891	0.07	9,494	0.15	2,492	0.16
Total Searches	689,657	3.36	278,791	2.35	325,335	5.05	74,335	4.74

Note: See note for Table 2.1.

for weapons or contraband. We are careful in the analyses below to distinguish between these search types, especially since we typically think of a search as something that might lead to an arrest. Sometimes it is the opposite: arrest leads to search, as a routine matter of protocol. Consent searches differ from probable cause searches because an officer has the right to conduct a search where she has probable cause to believe a law has been broken (e.g., if the officer sees or smells drugs, most typically, or pulls over a car for erratic driving and smells alcohol). Where there is no probable cause, and an officer is interested in conducting a search, she must ask permission of the driver: consent. We pay careful attention to consent searches in the chapters below.

Table 2.8 lays out the "basis for search". Either the driver, a passenger, the vehicle, or the personal effects of the driver or passengers may be searched. Table 2.9 shows the frequency of each type of search.

Erratic behavior is the most common basis on which an officer makes the decision to conduct a search, followed by other official information, observation of suspected contraband, and suspicious movement.

Information about passengers is collected only if there is a search or other adverse outcome. Table 2.10 shows the distribution of passengers searched by sex, race, and ethnicity, as indicated on the form.

Because we know nothing of passengers unless there is an adverse outcome, we do not analyze the passenger data in the following chapters of this book. However, it is notable that a majority (52 percent) of all passengers searched are African-American. Recall that Table 2.1 showed that 31 percent of all stops were of African-Americans, so clearly African-American passengers are being searched at a much higher rate than their white counterparts. This would be consistent with officers being much more likely to search all the occupants of a car if they are black males than otherwise. But since the form contains no information about passengers in general, this is as far as we can take this analysis.

Contraband Found

When contraband is found following a search, officers fill out the section of the form summarized in Table 2.11. The table lists how often contraband of each type was found. Occasionally, either because small amounts are rounded down to zero or because of data-entry errors, contraband is listed as having been found, but no corresponding amount is recorded. We group these instances together in the "no amount recorded" row.

Drugs are the most common form of contraband found, followed by alcohol, weapons, other items (e.g., perhaps stolen goods), and money. (Money is not inherently contraband of course, but may be considered

TABLE 2.8. *Searches by Basis of Search*

Search Basis	All Drivers		White Drivers		Black Drivers		Hispanic Drivers	
	# of Stops	% of Stops	# of Stops	% of Stops	# of Stops	% of Stops	# of Stops	% of Stops
Erratic Behavior	250,336	1.22	109,638	0.92	105,768	1.64	30,437	1.94
Observation of Suspected Contraband	146,003	0.71	55,398	0.47	77,040	1.19	11,308	0.72
Other Official Information	164,741	0.80	64,923	0.55	76,715	1.19	20,332	1.30
Suspicious Movement	89,157	0.43	32,928	0.28	46,258	0.72	8,814	0.56
Informant Tip	23,551	0.11	9,547	0.08	12,020	0.19	1,731	0.11
Witness Observation	15,842	0.08	6,344	0.05	7,520	0.12	1,713	0.11
Total Searches	689,630	3.36	278,778	2.35	325,321	5.05	74,335	4.74

Note: See note for Table 2.1.

TABLE 2.9. *Who or What was Searched*

Who or What	All Drivers		White Drivers		Black Drivers		Hispanic Drivers	
	# of Stops	% of Stops	# of Stops	% of Stops	# of Stops	% of Stops	# of Stops	% of Stops
Vehicle	621,175	3.03	250,131	2.11	295,745	4.59	65,398	4.17
Driver	622,168	3.03	249,552	2.10	295,856	4.59	67,023	4.27
Passenger(s)	250,366	33.37	95,390	31.99	128,790	35.78	22,410	28.02
Personal Effects	151,692	0.74	158,485	1.33	34,908	0.54	5,771	0.37

Note: See note for Table 2.1. Multiple types of searches may occur in a given stop. We exclude passenger searches in the analysis throughout the book. Passenger search percentages are listed as a share of all passengers in the dataset. As noted in the text, passengers are not listed in the form unless search, arrest, or citation follows the stop. This explains the high search rates.

TABLE 2.10. *Passenger Demographics by Search Status*

Status		Not Searched		Searched		Total
		Number	Percent	Number	Percent	
By Age:	Younger than 20	44,384	50.17	44,084	49.83	88,468
	20–29	232,250	65.15	124,232	34.85	356,482
	30–39	122,322	72.34	46,761	27.66	169,083
	40–49	67,317	73.61	24,136	26.39	91,453
	50 and older	33,622	75.05	11,175	24.95	44,797
By Sex:	Male	422,199	68.02	198,536	31.98	620,735
	Female	77,784	60.00	51,849	40.00	129,633
By Race:	White	243,928	68.44	112,467	31.56	356,395
	Black	232,125	64.23	129,286	35.77	361,411
	Native American	2,305	61.50	1,443	38.50	3,748
	Asian	3,256	71.31	1,310	28.69	4,566
	Unknown Race	18,298	75.66	5,886	24.34	24,184
By Ethnicity:	Hispanic	57,556	71.98	22,410	28.02	79,966
	Non-Hispanic	442,338	65.99	227,956	34.01	670,294
	Total	499,912	66.63	250,392	33.37	750,304

Note: Totals sum to 100.00 percent across the rows. Passengers are included in the database only with adverse outcomes (e.g., search, arrest, or citation).

TABLE 2.11. *Contraband*

Contraband Type	All Drivers		White Drivers		Black Drivers		Hispanic Drivers	
	# of Stops	% of Stops	# of Stops	% of Stops	# of Stops	% of Stops	# of Stops	% of Stops
Drugs	96,841	0.48	41,222	0.35	49,875	0.79	4,248	0.27
Alcohol	34,663	0.17	16,571	0.14	13,219	0.21	4,315	0.28
Money	27,688	0.14	10,989	0.09	14,577	0.23	1,736	0.11
Weapons	20,731	0.10	7,032	0.06	12,043	0.19	1,279	0.08
No amount recorded	50,718	0.25	21,920	0.19	24,411	0.38	3,749	0.24
Total Contraband	200,446	0.99	85,242	0.73	98,348	1.55	13,943	0.90

Note: See note in Table 2.1. The "total contraband" row corresponds to the number of stops where contraband was discovered. Officers sometimes find more than one type of contraband during a single stop, so summing each row in the table would produce a larger number than what we list in the final row of the table.

TABLE 2.12. *Property Seized*

Search Type	All Drivers		White Drivers		Black Drivers		Hispanic Drivers	
	# of Stops	% of Stops	# of Stops	% of Stops	# of Stops	% of Stops	# of Stops	% of Stops
Motor Vehicle	18,742	0.09	7,205	0.06	9,043	0.14	2,181	0.14
Personal Property	54,922	0.27	22,235	0.19	28,820	0.45	3,092	0.20
Other Property	44,802	0.22	19,966	0.17	21,617	0.34	2,578	0.16

Note: See note in Table 2.1.

so if related to illegal activities.) Some amount of contraband was found in 149,728 traffic stops, or 0.73 percent of all stops. In Chapter 5, we provide complete summaries of the amounts found. Note that the form leaves some elements ambiguous. Drugs, for example, may be listed as ounces, pounds, dosages, grams, or kilos, but the form does not indicate what type of drug was found: heroin, marijuana, meth, prescription painkillers are all lumped together. Similarly, if weapons are found the form clearly specifies that the number be recorded, but not the type: was it brass knuckles or an AK-47?

Property Seized

Finally, Table 2.12 summarizes the last element of the form, property seized.

Over 18,000 vehicles have been seized over fifteen years as well as more than 54,000 items of personal property and almost 45,000 items of other property. Almost half of the seizures have been taken from black drivers.

Conclusion

Through the determined efforts of a group of highly motivated African-American legislators, including one with a position of significant institutional power, lawmakers insisted on the collection and analysis of data in order to find out if rumors and insinuations of racial profiling had a basis in fact. They succeeded in getting the data, but no public and officially sanctioned statewide analysis has ever resulted from this massive effort. In the chapters to come, we attempt to fulfill this mandate.

3

Who Gets Stopped?

Regardless of the time period of any news story, official investigation, and/or internal review, one question is always asked when the topic turns to police race relations: are departments over-policing minority drivers while under-policing whites? The constitution guarantees us "equal protection" of the law, and this can also be understood to mean equal surveillance – none of us should feel targeted for extra police scrutiny merely because of our race. It is unquestionably unacceptable for the police to target individuals *solely* because of their race, but what if race is one of several factors that the police use to determine the level of scrutiny that a given driver or citizen deserves? Or what if the police use something associated with race, such as the neighborhood, to determine how aggressive or proactive to be? Such questions are at the core of the dispute about what is "racial profiling" that we reviewed in Chapter 1. There is no agreement on the degree of statistical disparity that would clearly indicate unacceptable racial profiling. Even powerful statistical evidence of disparity, if explained by a non-racial characteristic such as differential criminality, would just show a difference, not an indication of bias.

Because traffic stops are the most common way that any of us interact with the police, our focus on them provides an important insight into policing practices in general. And, of course, minority drivers have long sensed that they are indeed subjected to greater police scrutiny on the highways, a point which was one of the primary motivations for the passage of the 1999 legislation mandating data collection on this issue. If "driving while black" is indeed a problem, a key element is the concern that minority drivers are more likely to be pulled over than white drivers.

It would seem simple enough to answer the question statistically; simply compare the share of drivers of different races with the share of those stopped. If all drivers face the same scrutiny, then the shares should be the same. But in fact a number of issues plague these comparisons. They can all be summed up by one question: what is the proper baseline for comparison? Everyone does not have a car. Some people drive more than others. Some people drive safely while others speed, change lanes erratically and without signaling, or drive while impaired. In sum, there is little reason to believe that the population of those pulled over by the police should necessarily be exactly the same as the population living in an area. On the other hand, one would expect some correspondence: in an area with a higher percentage of black or Hispanic drivers, one would expect a higher percentage of those pulled over to be of those racial groups. While we acknowledge these concerns and discuss them in greater detail later in this chapter, we do believe that population comparisons can be enlightening and that such comparisons were specifically called for by those who passed the legislation designed to look into this issue.

One reason to proceed with a population comparison is that, on average, whites drive more than blacks and Hispanics. This is because having a driver's license, owning a car, and driving regularly are all more common among white Americans than black Americans or Hispanics (see Tal and Handy 2005; Withrow and Williams 2015). If whites drive more than blacks or Hispanics, and we show with population comparisons that whites are less likely to be pulled over, then it means that whatever disparity we document using population numbers would be an under-, not an overestimate of the true degree of disparity. We will address the question of the proper baseline and show the impact on our analysis when we use different baseline measures later in the chapter.

Regardless of the definition of the baseline population, there are many ways to measure potential disparate attention. Here we focus on two of these measures. We show that regardless of how one calculates it, black drivers in North Carolina are consistently over-policed, compared to whites. Additionally, we show that this does not occur at the same rate or degree across agencies; rather it appears that agencies make decisions that result in these disparities. This means that it can be changed. We conclude by addressing the "benchmark" or "baseline" question and underscore that disparities found in comparisons to the community population are *low* estimates of disparate treatment rather than high ones, since whites can on average be expected to be more likely to own a car and drive more miles compared to blacks and Hispanics. Thus, whatever imperfections

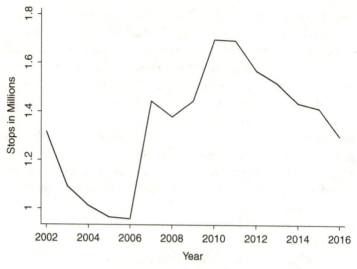

FIGURE 3.1. Traffic Stops by Year

might be associated with our analyses in this chapter, our estimates of disparity are highly likely to understate the severity of the problem.

Traffic Stops over Time

Before making comparisons to local communities, we look at trends in the number of stops and proportion stopped by race over time from the entire state. Figure 3.1 provides the first look at these trends. It simply shows the total number of traffic stops over time for the entire state.

Looking across time, dramatic fluctuations occur in the number of stops across the state. The number of stops decreases from 2002 until 2006, increases from 2006 to 2011, and has fallen since then. The total number of stops from 2002 through 2016 ranges from a low of just under 1 million in 2005 and 2006 to a high of just over 1.7 million in 2010 and 2011. There were 1.3 million stops in 2016. The population of the state, and of course most likely the driving population, has increased slowly and steadily throughout this time. In no way could a slowly expanding driving population explain by itself why the number of traffic stops was 70 percent higher in 2010 than it was in 2006. Nor can it explain why that number has declined by 30 percent since its peak; the population has continued to grow, after all.[1] It is important to recognize the nature of traffic stops: they are not automatic, but depend on the

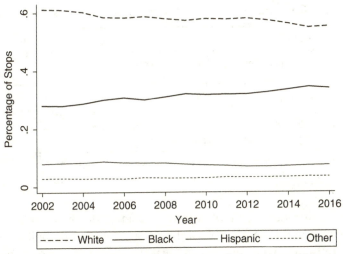

FIGURE 3.2. Racial Composition of Traffic Stops over Time

deployment of police officers and the training and instruction they are given. Their numbers vary dramatically over time, as Figure 3.1 shows, and from agency to agency as well, as we will see below. Of course, they also differ by the race of the driver. Figure 3.2 shows the racial composition of drivers stopped each year. For each stop listed in Figure 3.1, it shows what percentage were from each racial group.

White drivers constituted 61 percent of drivers pulled over in 2002 and steadily declined as a share of the total, reaching 55 percent in 2016. Black drivers were 28 percent in 2002 and rose to 34 percent of the total by 2016. Hispanic drivers constituted a relatively steady share at approximately 8 percent of the total. Other drivers (Asian, Native American, and other race drivers) grow from 2.5 to 3.4 over time. The white share of stops has consistently fallen, while the minority share has increased. The small numbers of Asian, Native American, and drivers of other or unknown races explain why our book focuses on white, black, and (in Chapters 3 and 7) Hispanic drivers.

The Contours of Driving while Black

The first way we estimate the extent to which a "driving while black" phenomenon occurs is by estimating the average percent of the population – overall and by race – stopped over the course of a year. By doing so, we ask and answer: 1) are black and Hispanic drivers pulled

TABLE 3.1. *Comparison of State Population to Traffic Stops, by Race, 2010*

Race	State Population		Traffic Stops		Diff.	Percent Diff.	Stop Rate	Stop Rate Ratio
	Number	Percent	Number	Percent				
White	6,292,572	68.77	843,060	60.12	−8.65	−12.58	13.4	−
Black	2,054,794	22.46	449,012	32.02	9.56	42.59	21.9	1.63
Hispanic	803,288	8.78	110,248	7.86	−0.92	−10.44	13.7	1.02
Total	9,150,654	100.00	1,402,320	100.00	−	−	15.3	

Note: Population data from the US Census. Excludes individuals of other races. Stop Rate Ratios are compared to white drivers.

over at higher rates than white drivers; and 2) do these rates vary by agency? We will show that black drivers are consistently pulled over at higher rates than white drivers, and that these rates vary across agencies. To answer these questions, we first need to establish the baseline number of people who could have been stopped, and then calculate the rate at which traffic stops occur. With those numbers established, the comparison is straightforward. We calculate a Stop Rate, then compare the stop rates for the different groups, ending with a Stop Rate Ratio for blacks compared to whites, and similarly for Hispanic drivers compared to whites. A Stop Rate Ratio of 1.0 would indicate the same odds of search.

Statewide Estimates

The simplest answer to the question of whether drivers of different racial categories are pulled over at the same rates is simply to compare population totals with the numbers of traffic stops. Table 3.1 makes this comparison of the entire state, using 2010 census data and 2010 traffic stops. Figure 3.2 showed that the racial mix of traffic stops varies slowly over time. By looking at a single year, we can gain a rough estimate of the odds of a given driver being pulled over.

Table 3.1 presents several comparisons. First, it shows the population numbers and the breakdown by race, including drivers only of the three racial / ethnic groups shown. (Figure 3.2 and Table 2.3 showed that other racial groups constitute relatively small percentages, so we exclude them here.) Whereas whites constitute 69 percent of the population, they are 60 percent of the traffic stops. That raw difference in percentage, 8.65, represents a 12.58 percentage reduction from the population baseline. For each group, we calculate the stop rate, which is simply the number of stops divided by the population, multiplied by 100 for ease of interpretation. Finally, the Stop Rate Ratio shows that blacks are 63 percent more likely to be pulled over than whites, and Hispanics are 2 percent more likely, or just marginally so.

No matter how we look at these data, Table 3.1 shows that the black population is over-policed, while all other demographic groups are comparatively under-policed. While the broader population is 22.46 percent black, 32.02 percent of those stopped are black. This means that black proportion of those stopped is almost 10 points higher than in the population – a 42.59 percent increased risk. Conversely, the population is 68.77 percent white, while only 60.12 percent of those stopped are white. This is a gap of 8.65 points – a 12.58 percent decreased risk. Similarly, but to a smaller degree, the broader population is 8.78 percent Hispanic, but only 7.86 percent of stops are Hispanic drivers. This is a difference of 0.921 points or a 10.44 percent decrease.

With 843,060 traffic stops in 2010, and 6.3 million whites in the population, the odds of a given white person to be pulled over were 13.4 percent. Blacks, with 449,012 stops and a population of just over 2 million, had much higher odds of being stopped: 21.9 percent. Hispanic drivers had odds similar to those of whites. As the table indicates, the bottom line is that blacks are 63 percent more likely to be pulled over than whites. Driving While Black may be real.

The Stop Rate calculation in the last rows of Table 3.1 is a simplification, and not a perfectly accurate one. Clearly, all those in the population are not at risk for being pulled over: children cannot drive, for example. Some people drive more than others; some take the bus. Because these numbers cannot be expected to be equal across racial groups, the number should be seen only as a rough estimate, a simple guide, to the differential odds of being pulled over. The numbers are quite stark however. We will show later in the chapter that these estimates are likely to be underestimates of the differential odds we are describing.

Agency-level Population–Stops Comparisons

Given the large disparities that characterize the state overall, how do these patterns differ from agency to agency? As reviewed in Chapter 2, various types of police agencies operate simultaneously: state-related agencies such as the Highway Patrol; municipal police departments; county sheriff's agencies; and specialized police agencies such as those associated with universities, hospitals, and parks. Establishing the relevant population for each agency thus has to be done with care. In the previous section we simply compared statewide totals. We can make similar comparisons for any agency where we can compare the relevant local population with those pulled over. Of course, these comparisons are subject to some inaccuracies as the driving population in a given community can be made up of people from neighboring communities or those just driving through. Still, because agencies differ dramatically in their stop and search rates, we can gain significant traction on the question of disparities by looking at the agency level. And if one community has more black drivers "passing through" this should be countered by another agency with more whites driving through, if we look at the entire set of all communities in the entire state.

Given the state database on which we rely, we know the number of traffic stops, so the question is the relevant population statistic with which to compare. For police departments, which patrol a single municipality, the relevant population numbers are those of the municipality. For county sheriff's departments, which have primary responsibilities in those parts of a county not covered by a municipal police department, they are the population numbers of those living in the county minus the population in areas covered by a police department. (Consider Orange County: Chapel Hill, Carrboro, and Hillsborough have separate police departments, so the relevant population for the Orange County Sheriff is the county population minus the populations of those three municipalities.) When looking at individual agencies, rather than statewide totals, we exclude statewide agencies, since their jurisdictions overlap with other agencies and we do not have relevant estimates of the baseline population. We also exclude specialized police departments (e.g. those associated with hospitals, universities, and state parks) since we lack estimates of the local population. We use the 2010 census for these analyses. Let us be clear that it is obvious that individuals drive beyond the boundaries of their own communities, and drivers from out of state come into North Carolina, so these comparisons are imperfect. However, since we are looking at all communities simultaneously, we can look at the overall patterns. Of course, some communities might see large numbers of black or Hispanic drivers crossing into their borders. But logically so then some other communities should see more white commuters, causing the statewide numbers to cancel out, with some showing inaccuracies in one direction and others in the opposite direction. As we will show, this is not what the data reveal.

We calculate the rate of traffic stops per population in a given community. That is, as in Table 3.1, we simply divide the number of traffic stops by the relevant population number for each racial / ethnic group, and overall. This generates a Stop Rate similar to what we presented for the entire state in Table 3.1. Several things are of interest there. First, agencies differ dramatically in their overall stop rates, regardless of race. Some agencies just make more traffic stops than others, controlling for population size. Second, the relative stop rates of white, black, and Hispanic drivers of course are our primary point of interest. But we take seriously the possibility that higher rates of stopping black drivers could be because black drivers happen to live in jurisdictions with higher stop rates. So we want to see if, within a given community, these stop rates differ by race.

We calculate these numbers annually and compare them to the local population, based on the 2010 censuses.[2] Counting up traffic stops by year is trivial, but we make one adjustment because of data reporting problems in the state database. We adjust for missing months. Appendix E (see Table E-3 in the online supplementary materials) shows that many agencies fail to report data for some periods, typically with entire months missing. So we calculate a yearly number of stops for drivers of each race, for each community, based on the number of stops times twelve, divided by the number of months in which the agency reported data to the SBI. For agencies reporting in all twelve months, this has no impact, and for those missing reports in a given month or two, it adjusts their numbers so that it is an estimate of the annual total, if all months had been reported.

Table 3.2 shows, separately for police and sheriff's agencies, the stops compared to the local population. We exclude in the table all those agencies with local populations of less than 25,000. This helps us avoid the problem of analyzing the traffic stop statistics in (say) a small beach town with a large summer influx of tourists, or a small mountain town with many times more visitors than the local population. With that in mind, several points are clear. First, police departments have much higher stop rates than sheriff's departments, on average. Second, blacks have much higher stop rates than whites, across both types of agencies. Third, there is great variability in these statistics from agency to agency – for example, among sheriff's departments, the mean black–white Stop Rate Ratio is 2.95, meaning that blacks are almost three times as likely as whites to be pulled over. However, the standard deviation is 1.93; this means there is tremendous range in outcomes from one agency-year to the next.

Table 3.2 presents a lot of information, but we can illustrate the main point graphically very easily. Figure 3.3 simply compares the percent of the population and the percent of the traffic stops associated with whites,

TABLE 3.2. *Stop Rates by Race by Agency*

Race	Mean Population (2010)	Mean Traffic Stops	Mean Stop Rate	Mean Stop Rate Ratio	St.Dev Stop Rate Ratio	N
Part A. Police Departments						
White	55,119	7,055	13.73%	–		495
Black	32,744	6,452	21.40%	1.60	0.66	495
Hispanic	11,664	1,322	12.75%	0.93	0.37	495
Total	105,944	14,823	14.21%	–		495
Part B. Sheriff's Departments						
White	48,526	923	1.71%	–	–	919
Black	8,197	406	5.03%	2.95	1.93	919
Hispanic	4,444	144	3.06%	1.82	1.56	919
Total	63,880	1,473	2.09%	–	–	919

Note: Stop Rate Ratios are the black or Hispanic search rate divided by the white search rate.

Note: Only agency-years where the local area had at least 25,000 people living in the area are included.

blacks, and Hispanics. Each circle represents an agency-year, with the size of the circle corresponding to the total population of the community; the larger the circle, then the larger the population. (Multiple same-sized circles above or below each other represent multiple yearly observations from the same community; population shares change little over time, but shares of traffic stops change slightly more from year to year. Here we do not impose the 25,000 population threshold to be included, so the smaller circles represent relatively small towns or counties.) The diagonal lines moving from the origin to the upper-right corner in each subfigure indicate equality; data points lying on or near those lines show that a given group makes up the same proportion of the population and of the traffic stops. Observations above the line indicate comparative over-policing of the demographic group compared to its population share, while observations below the line indicate comparative under-policing. This means that if circles are consistently above the line, then that population is consistently over-policed across agencies. Conversely, if circles are consistently below the line, then that population is consistently under-policed across agencies.

In Figure 3.3, we can observe a number of trends consistent with those observed in Table 3.2. First, white populations appear to be consistently under-policed for communities of all sizes; the observations consistently

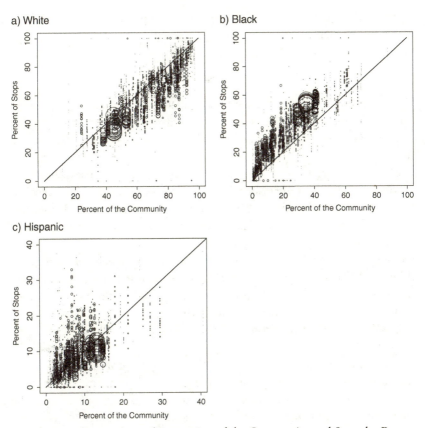

FIGURE 3.3. Comparison of Proportion of the Community and Stops by Race

Note: N's: 3,114 for white, 3,086 for black, and 3,073 for Hispanic. N's refer to agency-years. We exclude 31 outlier observations from Figure 3.3c which make it difficult to see the remaining observations but do not change the interpretation of the plot.

appear below the line in Figure 3.3a. Second, black populations appear to be consistently over-policed regardless of community size; the observations consistently appear above the line in Figure 3.3b. Third, the story appears to be more complex for Hispanic populations. Among the included communities, Hispanic drivers appear to be over-policed in smaller communities, and under-policed in larger communities. Smaller circles – indicating smaller communities – consistently appear above the line of equality in Figure 3.3c, while larger circles – indicating larger communities – consistently appear below the line. The complex relation for Hispanics is reflected in a lower correlation between population share and traffic stop share: 0.59 for Hispanics, compared to 0.84 for whites and 0.88 for blacks.[3]

The "Baseline Problem"

Up to this point, we have used a naïve and simple population baseline to estimate potential disparities and to identify whether communities are over- or under-policed. The residential population of a jurisdiction is a naïve estimate of the baseline population, because it includes non-drivers (e.g., those under sixteen and those without driver's licenses), does not account for differential propensities to drive by race, does not account for those commuting through or visiting the community, and does not account for driving behavior (e.g., whether a particular driver is speeding, and therefore should be stopped). Nor does it distinguish among those communities with higher and lower crime rates, which might explain different levels of police activity. Despite these restrictions, it is a commonly used benchmark, it is intuitive to use the population as a baseline, and such comparisons were clearly in the minds of the legislators who debated and passed SB 76 in 1999 mandating the collection of traffic stops data.

As discussed briefly in Chapter 2, the "baseline problem" is a serious one, and both practitioners and academics have paid attention to this question (for a general overview see Withrow and Williams 2015). The four general types of benchmarks are: adjusting estimates of the residential population (Withrow 2003, Smith and Petrocelli 2001), estimates of the transient population (Lamberth 1994, 1996), vehicle collisions (Alpert, Smith, and Dunham 2004; Withrow and Williams 2015), and internal benchmarks (Walker 2003). Some authors have gone to great lengths to determine such things as the speeding population. For example, as discussed in Chapter 2, Smith et al. (2004) had a team of researchers drive in vans at exactly the speed limit and record the race of those who passed them. However, as noted in Chapter 1, virtually every driver may be found to be in violation of some aspect of the traffic code, if the officer is inclined to find it. Indeed, officers need not look far for reasons to cite a driver, if they choose: speeding is common enough. And in the *Whren* decision the US Supreme Court validated the use of technical violations of the law as pretexts for investigatory stops. Therefore, it is a tricky problem indeed to determine who "deserves" to be stopped. Obviously if one demographic group drives significantly faster than another that would be pertinent information, but this type of data is hard to come by

TABLE 3.3. *Estimated Driving Habits by Race*

	White	Black	Hispanic	BW Ratio	HW Ratio
Own a Car*	83%	53%	49%	.61	.59
Miles Driven per Year*	13,361	11,637	10,303	.87	.77
Driver**	91.1%	79.6%	79.7%	.87	.87
Mean Trips per Day**	2.2	1.8	1.8	.82	.82
Mean Miles Driven per Day**	31.5	25.5	26.1	.81	.83
Miles Driven per Year**	11,515	9,294	9,521	.81	.83

Note: * Results from the US DOT survey from 2009; ** results from AAA Foundation Survey from 2014–15. See Triplett et al. 2016, 7, 11, 12, 14.

on anything approaching a statewide level. Instead, in this section, we focus on how estimates of disparate treatment change as estimates of the residential population are transformed to look increasingly like the driving population.

We showed in Table 3.1 the statewide disparities in stop rates per population. What if we adjust for the differential propensity to drive? This simply requires estimates of the differences in annual driving by race. We can make use of two large surveys in order to do this. The first is the 2009 National Household Travel Survey (NHTS), which is administered by the US Department of Transportation and queries a representative sample of US households on their driving behavior (see US Department of Transportation n.d.). Results from the 2009 survey (the most recent survey data available) revealed that 83 percent of whites owned a motor vehicle, but only 51 percent of blacks and 49 percent of Hispanics. Moreover, white survey respondents drove an annual average of 13,361 miles compared to 11,637 miles for blacks and 10,303 miles for Hispanics (US DOT n.d.). A more recent survey was conducted by the Urban Institute and the AAA Foundation for Traffic Safety (Triplett et al. 2016). They surveyed a total of 7,576 households including 5,774 drivers in 2014 and 2015. This survey found similar results with a slightly different methodology: 91.1 percent of whites were drivers, compared to 79.6 percent of blacks and 79.7 percent of Hispanics. (That is, they regularly drive, whether or not they own a car.) The survey also asked respondents to state how many trips they had made by car the previous day, the length of the trip, and the estimated miles per year they drove. Table 3.3 summarizes the results of these two surveys of driving behavior by race.

Looking at the last two columns, we can see that blacks and Hispanics are considerably less likely to own a car than whites; according to the US Department of Transportation, their rates of ownership are just .61 and .59 those of whites. For all the other indicators, focused on driving rather than owning a car, blacks appear to drive about 80 to 90 percent as much as whites, and the estimates for Hispanics are similar. More precisely, the average of the BW Ratio figures above, not including vehicle ownership, is 0.84. For Hispanics, it is 0.82.

We saw in Table 3.1 that black drivers were 63 percent more likely to be pulled over than whites, based on population statistics. If blacks drive, on average, just 84 miles for every 100 miles that whites drive (e.g., based on the estimates in Table 3.3), then the driving-adjusted Stop Rate Ratio for blacks compared to whites would be: 1.63 / .84, or 1.94. For Hispanics, the 1.02 ratio of stop rates compared to whites, adjusted for driving, is 1.24.

In Table 3.1, we showed powerful disparities, comparing traffic stops to population numbers. Blacks showed a disparity of greater than 40 percent in comparing their share of stops to their share of the population. Here, we see that that is actually a vast underestimate. While we do not want to put too much faith in the exact numbers, since they are based on a national survey in just one year, they clearly suggest the direction of bias: simple population comparisons are inadequate, but they underestimate the racial disparities, not overestimate them. Blacks and Hispanics own vehicles at considerably lower rates than whites, and minorities with access to cars drive significantly less each year than whites. When we adjust for these factors, we see that the ratio of traffic stops to the relevant baseline moves, for blacks, from 1.63 to 1.94. For Hispanics, the estimated difference goes from 1.02 to 1.24. Compared to their share of drivers on the road, blacks and Hispanics are clearly targeted for much greater likelihood of a traffic stop. White drivers are correspondingly exempt from such supervision.

Figure 3.3 presented comparisons of population shares with shares of those pulled over by the police. If we were to adjust each community for the driving population, using the estimates from Table 3.3, the black driving population share would be reduced by approximately 16 percent, and the Hispanic share by 18 percent. The Figure, which already shows significant racial targeting, would be considerably more extreme. Of course, we do not have comparable figures for each community across the state, so we do not push the analysis further than the available data allow. The point is that any estimate presented in this chapter of the differential likelihood of being pulled over is most likely a substantial underestimate, perhaps on the order of 20 percent less than the true value.

Conclusion

Driving while black is not a crime. But most drivers violate the law and police have great discretion in whom to stop and whom to allow to proceed. The rates at which cars are pulled over show tremendous variability over time, from one agency to the next, and within agency by race. White and black drivers are consistently under- and over-policed as compared to their share of the population. Hispanic drivers show a more complicated pattern, perhaps reflecting differences between small towns, where they appear somewhat over-policed.

The baseline problem is a severe one. Small beach towns have more traffic stops in a year than they do population, and it is nearly certain that most of those stopped are not local residents. Clearly, there are inaccuracies when comparing stops to the resident population. Still, when we look across all police agencies in the entire state, and no matter if we base our estimates of the population on census data or more refined estimates of who is driving, we see strong, consistent, and powerful evidence that black and white drivers face dramatically different odds of being pulled over. In the next chapter, we look at what happens after those stops are initiated.

4

What Happens After a Stop?

Once a driver is stopped, what happens? In the last chapter we looked at who gets stopped, and there are problems in establishing the baseline for comparison there. Still, the chapter showed significant (and likely underestimated) differences in the odds of being pulled over, based on race. For those differences to be justified, black drivers would have to break the traffic laws at much higher rates than white drivers. In this chapter, we ask what happens after the stop encounter is initiated. Do drivers of different racial groups see systematically different outcomes once stopped? If so, what are these? How big are the disparities?

In looking at the outcomes of traffic stops, rather than who gets pulled over, we benefit in a number of ways. Crucially, we know both the numerator and the denominator in the equation. That is, we know both the number of drivers with a certain outcome and the number of drivers having been pulled over. The possible outcomes following a traffic stop are several: nothing, a verbal or written warning, citation, or arrest. Any of these outcomes may also be associated with a driver or vehicle search. So, we can pose and answer the questions: who gets searched; who gets arrested; and who gets off light? And we need not worry about the baseline problem, since we have a complete set of all traffic stops. So, our analyses here can be complete.

Previous work points toward a number of expected relationships between outcomes, stop purposes, and driver race. Studies on the implementation of the war on drugs suggest that the police are using traffic stops to search for drug couriers and others who fit the drug profile (Harris 1997; Banks 2003; Hecker 1996; Mucchetti 2005). Following the practice we have established in previous chapters, therefore, we distinguish between safety and investigatory stops in this chapter. In pursuit of their goal of finding contraband, officers may rely on stereotypes, profiles, and hunches associated with drug users and dealers to determine whom to investigate.

Once they determine whom to investigate they may pull cars over that fit their profiles. Officers may use investigatory stops to pursue a "hunch" that an individual is breaking the law or carrying contraband. This is rooted in the logic that an officer can recognize a miscreant from instinct or a set of characteristics; then that officer needs to find a way to justify searching the car to follow up on the hunch. As we will see in later chapters, these investigatory stops have both a much higher likelihood of search (since looking inside the car may have been the reason for the stop in the first place), and the searches that result from investigatory stops have higher degrees of racial disparity associated with them. We therefore pay close attention to this distinction. In a safety stop, officers are maintaining safe driving conditions for all drivers. In investigatory stops, officers are attempting to disrupt suspected criminal activity. One reason for the dramatic differences in search rates over time and by agency is that the relative focus on traffic safety versus criminal interdiction varies. The State Highway Patrol, for example, is clearly active in giving tickets out to speeders and others its troopers find driving in an unsafe manner. Many other departments use traffic stops as a means to investigate suspected criminal behavior. Part of this reflects the nature of the jurisdictions that they police: the level of crime as well as the mission of the agency, traffic safety on the interstate and rural highways versus general police duties in an urban environment.

Informing profiles of whom to investigate, the psychology literature on perceptions of risk tell us that those perceived more threatening trigger greater backlash. Additionally, those perceived as "other" are seen as more threatening than those seen as "like us" (Williams and Eberhardt 2008; Bonilla-Silva, Lewis, and Embrick 2004; Hetey and Eberhardt 2014; Rattan, Levine, Dweck, and Eberhardt 2012; Eberhardt, Davies, Purdie-Vaughns, and Johnson 2006; Eberhardt, Dasgupta, and Banaszynski 2003). Numerous studies have found an implicit bias against blacks in the USA, when individuals are asked to assess risk generated by black individuals and white individuals in various scenarios (Eberhardt, Goff, Purdie, and Davies 2004; Correll, Park, Judd, and Wittenbrink 2002; Sagar and Schofield 1980). Barring specialized training, we are all subject to implicit bias that may lead us to act with suspicion toward certain types of individuals (Plant and Peruche 2005). In the context of policing, all this adds up to the expectation that blacks might be searched and arrested more often than whites. Additionally, blacks may be erroneously searched more often than whites. In more structured environments, we would expect disparities in outcomes to be lower. This is because structure and training may combat biases revealed in situations where decision-makers must react quickly or rely on hunches and their own discretion with few guidelines. In cases where they implement objective rule-based criteria, implicit biases have less room to operate.

Officers may target those they find threatening and those they perceive to be the "other." Officers may target those who dress a certain way, drive certain cars, males rather than females, younger people rather than older people, and minorities rather than whites. In the aggregate this produces discrepant outcomes: minority drivers will be subjected to greater surveillance and harsher treatment than white drivers. Additionally, if training and strict sets of rules counteract the effects of implicit bias and stereotyping, then minority populations will appear over-policed as compared to their white counterparts when comparing outcomes following investigatory stops but not following safety stops. Safety stops typically are justified by bad or dangerous driving, not by a hunch. Speeding stops in particular are more often generated by the objective readings on a radar gun. If an officer starts out with a desire to stop and search a car because of a hunch, they have many ways to pull over that car, as the *Whren* decision made clear and as we discussed in Chapter 1. Safety, or moving violations, are less likely to be used for these purposes, compared to seat belt, equipment, registration tag, or other investigatory purposes. After all, if they so desire, officers can pull cars over for such equipment "failures" as a partially illuminated rear license tag, a crack in a taillight covering, or a tilting rear view mirror; there is often no need to pull out the radar gun.

In this chapter, we evaluate whether young minority males are more likely to be searched and arrested than others and examine whether outcomes following a stop vary based on whether the driver was subject to an investigatory or safety stop. We review the likelihood of these outcomes for each racial and gender group. To do so, we first deconstruct who gets searched and whether this results in racial disparities by search type. Then we conduct a similar descriptive analysis for all the possible outcomes of a stop. We show that minority males are much more likely to be searched or arrested.

The Potential Outcomes of a Traffic Stop

We reviewed in Chapter 2 the possible outcomes of a traffic stop: no action, verbal or written warning, citation, or arrest. Any of these may also involve a search and it is here that we begin our analysis.

Variability in Search Rates

Just as we showed in the previous chapter, outcomes vary substantially by agency. For example, the State Highway Patrol rarely searches drivers, at a rate of 0.6 percent, whereas the search rates in Charlotte and Durham are about 7 to 8 percent, over ten times higher. On average, county sheriff's departments search fewer motorists than municipal police departments, and both of these types of agencies search more than the highway patrol. These trends are similar in other states as well (see Baumgartner, Christiani et al. 2017). There is substantial variability from agency to agency and also from year to year. Figure 4.1 shows variability in search rates over time for the state as a whole as well as for a sampling of some of the largest agencies. Looking at both agency-level and yearly variation makes clear that there is quite a lot of volatility.

Statewide, search rates have varied dramatically over the years, from 4.7 percent in 2002 steadily down to 2.7 percent in 2016. And, as the figure shows, these trends vary dramatically from agency to agency, with the State Highway Patrol only once over 1.0 percent; Winston Salem typically near 2 to 3 percent; but others with higher rates in general. Within any individual agency, we also see large differences over time: the rate in Charlotte was twice as high in 2007 as compared to 2015. Fayetteville, Durham, and Raleigh also show large variability over time.

Looking at the twenty-five largest agencies in the state, a number have had particular years with search rates over 10 percent: Gaston County Police Department (2002, 2003, 2007, 2008, 2009, 2012, 2013), Asheville (2005, 2007, 2008), Charlotte (2005, 2007, 2008), Wake County Sheriff's Office (2004, 2013, 2014), Durham (2007, 2008), Goldsboro (2016, 2013), Guilford County Sheriff's Office (2002, 2005), Burlington (2002), Forsyth County Sheriff's Office (2002), Gastonia (2005), and Fayetteville (2006). The maximum value for any of the twenty-five largest police agencies in any single year was Gaston County Police Department (15.08 percent in 2002, also 14.86 percent in 2008, the second highest value).

While some years and some cities see rates above 10 percent, large numbers of observations also fall in the range of zero to 2 percent search.

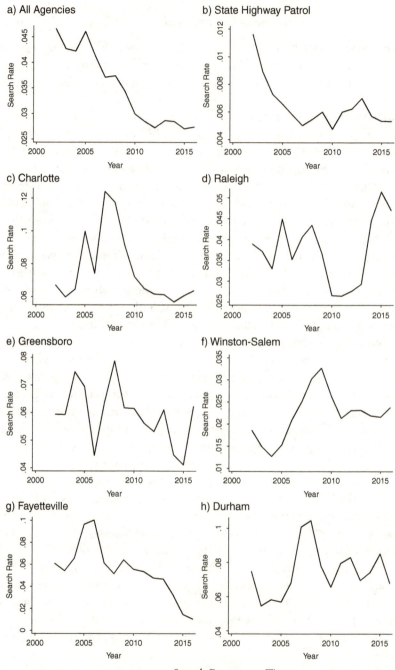

FIGURE 4.1. Search Rates over Time

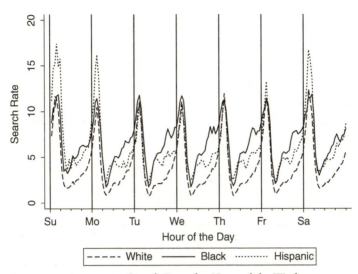

FIGURE 4.2. Search Rates by Hour of the Week

In fact, of 375 agency-year combinations for these large agencies, twenty-seven are below 1 percent, fifty-eight are below 2 percent, and 109 (more than 25 percent of the total) are below 3 percent. In sum, there is wide variability in search rates across time, and across agencies as well. It is not at all clear why such variability exists. Some of the agency-to-agency differences are surely due to regional differences in underlying crime rates. But why the year-to-year differences within a given agency are so pronounced is more mysterious. It is possible that they emerge from changing agency leadership, policing strategies, or political pressures. In any case, Figure 4.1 is a reflection of the intensely localized nature of policing in the United States; clearly there are not statewide standards to which the largest agencies gravitate.

Time of Day and Day of Week

Search rates differ dramatically depending on the time of day, and are marginally higher on weekend nights, as one might expect. Figure 4.2 shows the search rates for white, black, and Hispanic drivers in hourly intervals across a week.[1] Search rates peak each night just after midnight, drop sharply during the morning rush hour, and increase during the afternoon and evening. Rates on the weekends are only marginally different from those during the week, as the figure makes clear. Hispanic drivers have significantly higher search rates on weekend nights, but for black and white drivers, there is little difference.

a) Males

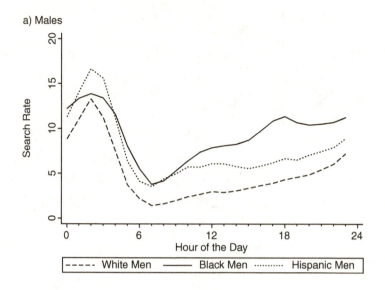

b) Females

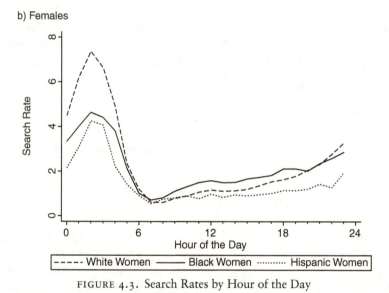

FIGURE 4.3. Search Rates by Hour of the Day

Since the patterns of search are so similar no matter what the day of the week, in Figure 4.3 we combine all the days of the week together to explore in more detail the effect of time of day. We also separate out male and female drivers in two parts of the Figure.

Figure 4.3 clearly documents dramatic differences in search rates by time of day, but also strong race and gender effects. Just like our parents taught us, nothing good happens after midnight. And clearly, the police view individuals they pull over with much greater suspicion during the hours between midnight and 4am. Males of any race have search rates above 10 percent during that time. White females are searched more than 8 percent of the time they are pulled over, if the stop occurs at 3am. Once dawn breaks and the morning rush hour begins, searches decline precipitously for all races. By 8am, fewer than 1 percent of women are searched, and searches of males decline to below 5 percent. Figure 4.3a makes clear, however, that searches of black male drivers begin a steady increase and by noon, they are double the rate of white males. Hispanic males see a particular spike in search rates in the early hours of the morning, over 15 percent at 3am. White males face higher search rates across the day than females of any race, but their rates are always lower than black and Hispanic males, for every hour of the day. Between the hours of noon and 7pm, a large gap is apparent between the search rates of white and black males. Among women, the racial dynamics are quite different: whites are searched much more than others in the early morning hours, but there is little racial difference during the day. If we think of what makes a citizen a suspect, it is being a black male, or being out late at night. Because these hour-of-the-day effects are so strong, we are careful to control for them in the statistical analysis that follows.

Variation in Search Rates by Race

Of the more than 20 million stops that have occurred in North Carolina between 2000 and 2016, almost 700,000 have resulted in a search, as reviewed in Table 2.7. Table 4.1 presents the rates of search already reported in Table 2.7 for white, black, and Hispanic drivers, and the ratios between these rates. The black–white (B-W) Ratio represents the rate for black drivers divided by the rate for white drivers; the Hispanic–white (H-W) Ratio compares Hispanic to white drivers.

Overall, white drivers are searched 2.35 percent of the time, black drivers 5.05 percent, and Hispanic drivers at a rate of 4.74 percent; the B-W and H-W ratios are therefore 2.15 and 2.02: blacks are 2.15 times as likely as whites to be searched, or 115 percent more likely. Hispanics are in a similar situation to black drivers, overall. These ratios differ substantially depending on the type of search. Recall from Table 2.7 that Consent searches are the most common type of search, followed by incident-to-arrest searches, and probable cause, with the other two search types being relatively rare. Probable cause searches have the greatest racial disparity

TABLE 4.1. *Search Rates by Race, by Type of Search*

Search Type	White	Black	Hispanic	B-W Ratio	H-W Ratio
Consent	1.08	2.19	1.94	2.03	1.80
Search Warrant	0.01	0.01	0.01	1.00	1.00
Probable Cause	0.42	1.42	0.62	3.38	1.48
Incident to Arrest	0.77	1.28	2.00	1.66	2.60
Protective Frisk	0.07	0.15	0.16	2.14	2.29
Total Searches	2.35	5.05	4.74	2.15	2.02

Note: data from Table 2.7.

TABLE 4.2. *Search Rates by Race, by Stop Type*

	White	Black	Hispanic	B-W Ratio	H-W Ratio
Safety Stops	1.07	1.59	2.51	1.49	1.20
Investigatory Stops	1.31	3.54	2.30	2.70	2.08
All Stops	2.38	5.13	4.81	2.16	2.02

for blacks compared to whites, with arrest-related searches the highest for Hispanic drivers. Black drivers are more than twice as likely to be subjected to a consent search than white drivers.

The type of search is one way to look at racial disparity, but the stop purpose is another. Table 4.2 distinguishes between searches following a safety stop and those following an investigatory stop. We explained this distinction in Chapter 2.

Following safety stops, black drivers are 49 percent more likely to be searched. But following stops for investigatory purposes, black drivers face a 170 percent increased chance of search, compared to whites. We will follow up on these large disparities in search rates following from investigatory stops in later chapters. A similar pattern can be seen between Hispanic drivers and white drivers: following safety stops, Hispanic drivers are 20 percent more likely to be searched; and following investigatory stops, Hispanic drivers are 108 percent more likely to be searched.

The Final Outcome: Arrests, Tickets, and Warnings

Whether or not a driver is searched, a traffic stop may lead to one of five outcomes: nothing, a verbal warning, a written warning, a ticket (citation), or arrest. We collapse the first three possibilities into one category – a *light outcome*. In this case, either nothing is done to a driver

TABLE 4.3. *Differential Outcomes by Race*

Outcome	White	Black	Hispanic	B-W Ratio	H-W Ratio
Light	32.66	35.89	25.73	1.10	0.79
Expected	65.67	61.30	70.44	0.93	1.07
Severe	1.67	2.81	3.83	1.68	2.29
Total	100.00	100.00	100.00	–	–

Note: Data from Table 2.5.

or the driver receives a warning; the driver does not need to pay a fine or appear in court. A stop resulting in a light action indicates one of two things: the driver is perceived as a negligible threat; or the driver was pulled over because of a suspicion which is immediately relieved once the officer speaks with the driver, perhaps giving an apology for the inconvenience. A warning may also be appropriate for a young driver not fully stopping at a stop sign or in other cases where the officer rightfully uses his or her discretion to avoid the sanction of a ticket and the fees that it entails, but where the driver may have made a minor violation of the law. In any case, a light outcome is one that most drivers appreciate, since there is no ticket. Second, a driver might receive a citation – the most likely outcome once stopped. If a driver receives a ticket or citation, then they must pay a fine, appear in court, or both. Drivers typically prepare themselves for this type of stop: while not pleasant, this is *expected*. Third, a driver might experience the most *severe* outcome; he or she may be arrested.

We saw in Table 2.5 the relative use of each of the outcomes by race. Table 4.3 summarizes these differences for the three types of outcomes we just described.

Black drivers are 10 percent more likely to get a "light outcome," 7 percent less likely to get a ticket, and 68 percent more likely to be arrested, compared to white drivers. Hispanics have lower rates of light outcomes, slightly higher rates of citation, and much higher rates of arrest, even higher than that of black drivers. Of course, the absolute numbers of drivers arrested remains low, lower than 4 percent for Hispanics, 3 percent for blacks, and lower than 2 percent for white drivers. The disparities by race are pronounced, especially for the most severe outcomes, paralleling what we saw for searches in the previous table.

What might the disparities in outcomes indicate? Light action taken against a driver might indicate either that the officer made a mistake in pulling the driver over or that they were barely breaking the law (e.g. going 1 mph over the speed limit). Our data indicates that blacks are disproportionately likely to experience a light outcome. This was a concern motivating the original drafters of the law that mandated collecting data on traffic stops in 1999, as we saw in Chapter 2. Lawmakers were concerned that troopers were pulling over black drivers for no reason. There is some evidence that this occurs; we explore this in greater detail in Chapter 7. Notably, however, blacks are also somewhat less likely to be ticketed than white drivers and Hispanics are only marginally more likely to be ticketed than whites. This suggests that the racial disparities that we do find are perhaps driven less by outright racial animus on the part of police officers (because, in that case, why not ticket blacks at higher rates) than by implicit biases that lead officers to be more suspicious of black drivers. That is, most officers are not necessarily out to punish black drivers but they, perhaps unconsciously, have a lower threshold for stopping and searching African-Americans.

In the broader view, what these rates tell us is that an average interaction between driver and police officer differs based on the race of the driver. Blacks seem to be more likely to experience *negative* interactions with police than whites. They are generally stopped and searched more often. They appear to be stopped and searched more often for relatively trivial offenses, as indicated by their greater likelihood of experiencing "light" outcomes, and (as we will see in Chapter 6), the lower contraband "hit rate" of their searches. Paradoxically, while many might rejoice in getting a warning rather than a ticket, the racial differences consistently apparent in the data suggest another interpretation for black drivers: even the officer recognized that there was no infraction. This of course raises the question of why the driver was pulled over. If the driver had been pulled over for a moving violation such as speeding, no action or a warning is possible, but why would this occur more often for blacks than whites? If the driver is pulled over for an investigatory reason, on the other hand, such as an officer's suspicion that the driver is "out of place" or may have drugs, then a stop may immediately reveal that the suspicion was unwarranted. From a police perspective, such minor inconveniences are inevitable and no harm may be intended. Indeed, this perspective was supported by the US Supreme Court in its *Whren* decision. A key question is whether it is a "minor inconvenience." Most would probably agree that it is if it happens rarely. If it is highly targeted only at a small subset of the population, on the other hand, it may occur repeatedly, reinforcing a notion that the police view those individuals with suspicion. The rest of the population may be "blissfully unaware" that such warrantless stops are occurring, but for the group repeatedly stopped, the unfairness of it all may be truly alienating. Normatively, all of these discrepancies in police treatment following a traffic stop are troubling. They generate anger, disillusionment, a sense of second-class citizenship, and disenfranchisement. They contribute to a decline in trust in government in general and the police in particular. These effects, however, might be apparent only within a small set of the population. For the rest of us, it is hard even to imagine being repeatedly stopped on the roads for no reason, or subjected to search over and over again.

Comparing Outcomes by Age, Race, and Gender

Beyond race, gender and age affect how threatening an individual is perceived to be and are incorporated into stereotypes of drug users, drug traffickers, thieves, and criminals more generally. Before moving to a full multivariate model of the various possible outcomes of a traffic stop, here we make some simple comparisons of the relative frequency of the different outcomes for black and white, male and female, and younger and older drivers. Figure 4.4 shows the results of this analysis. The y-axis in every graph is the occurrence rate. The x-axis indicates which subpopulation is being described. The subfigures are roughly ranked from lightest outcomes to the severest outcomes after being stopped.

Taken as a whole, the six parts of Figure 4.4 show that as the outcome type goes from light to severe, the distribution of who sees what action flips. In parts A, B, and C, which focus on light outcomes, the relative rate for each age group increases as the driver age increases. Race and gender differences are also clear, though with slightly different patterns for each of the three outcomes. The inverse is seen in parts D, E, and F, which present the harsher outcomes: younger drivers are more likely to experience these outcomes relative to older drivers. Citations represent the most common outcome. Black men are less likely to get tickets, and older black particularly so. But when we look at the other figures it is clear that younger black men don't get tickets because they are more likely to be arrested or to get a verbal warning, whereas older black men are much more likely to get a written warning rather than these other outcomes.

Additionally, in part A depicting the rates of the occurrence of no action and in parts E and F depicting the harshest outcomes, two additional patterns can be observed. First, men experience these outcomes at higher rates than women. Second, black men experience these outcomes at higher rates than white men. And whereas no-action stops are more common among older drivers, search and arrest are highly focused on the

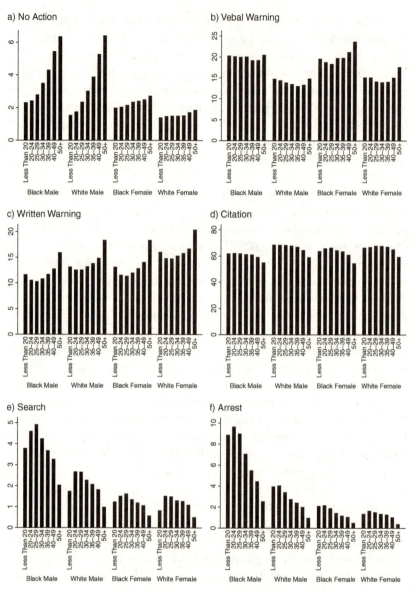

FIGURE 4.4. Outcome Rates by Race, Gender, and Age Group

young. These observations provide further evidence that those fitting the stereotypes vilified by the war on drugs are subjected to greater scrutiny. In some cases, this results in an individual being modestly inconvenienced and in others subjected to a search. In any case, we can see that police actions following a traffic stop are closely connected to who is driving. Males, females, blacks, whites, young and old are treated quite distinctly. No group experiences the harsh treatment that young black men can expect. This may give some insight into why trust in the police, and expectations that the police will treat white and black drivers fairly and equitably, differ so sharply by race. A Pew Research Center poll in 2014 found that 71 percent of whites have a "great deal" or a "fair amount" of confidence that the local police would treat blacks and whites equally, but just 36 percent of blacks agreed. Similar results were found in 2009 and 2007 (see Drake 2015).

Multivariate Analysis

In order to isolate the independent effects of race controlling for other factors, here we estimate logistic regressions predicting the probability of each outcome using our collapsed outcome categories. This is important to make sure that what we have identified as racial disparities really are about race and are not being confounded by other factors that may correlate with race. For example, we know from Figure 4.3 that police officers are more likely to conduct searches at night and if blacks are more likely than whites to drive at night, then they would have a higher risk of being searched, but the difference would be predicated on driving habits and not a race-based judgment on the part of police officers. Each regression uses a mixture of information about the driver and the qualities of the stop.

Table 4.4 presents the results of these estimations. Entries are odds-ratios rather than the raw estimated coefficient to facilitate interpretation of the results. If the odds-ratio is 1 or approximately 1, then the likelihood of a given outcome occurring does not change based on a change in the associated predictor variable. An odds-ratio of 1.25 would indicate that each movement on the independent variable is expected to lead to an increase of 25 percent in the outcome variable; a value of 0.75 would mean that the likelihood is 25 percent less likely. By including demographics and stop characteristics in the same model, we condition the probability of each variable on the overall likelihood of the given outcome occurring. Across all models every variable in the model returns a statistically significant result.

The regressions show that the role of race, gender, and stop purpose vary by outcome and when controlling for other influences. White female drivers have the highest probability of receiving a light outcome. Column 1 in Table 4.4 tells us this by indicating that if a driver is black, Hispanic,

TABLE 4.4. *Predicting Outcomes of a Traffic Stop, 2002–2016*

Variable	Light Outcome	Citation	Arrest	Search
Demographics				
Black	0.98(0.00)	0.99(0.00)	1.43(0.01)	1.94(0.01)
Hispanic	0.56(0.00)	1.68(0.01)	1.52(0.01)	1.02(0.01)
Other Race	1.00(0.01)	1.03(0.01)	0.65(0.01)	0.63(0.01)
Gender (Male)	0.88(0.00)	1.07(0.00)	1.95(0.01)	3.14(0.02)
Age	1.01(0.00)	0.99(0.00)	0.99(0.00)	0.97(0.00)
Search Occur				
Search Occur	0.77(0.00)	1.14(0.01)	1.66(0.02)	–
Contraband				
Contra. Found	0.11(0.00)	0.77(0.01)	19.47 (0.20)	–
Stop Purpose				
Safety				
Speed Limit	–	–	–	–
Stop Light	2.37(0.01)	0.43(0.00)	1.22(0.02)	1.77(0.02)
Impaired	0.91(0.01)	0.06(0.00)	85.75(1.03)	33.33(0.37)
Movement	4.69(0.02)	0.20(0.00)	2.15(0.02)	3.14(0.02)
Investigatory				
Equipment	6.87(0.02)	0.15(0.00)	1.29(0.01)	2.75(0.02)
Regulatory	2.24(0.01)	0.44(0.00)	1.45(0.01)	2.11(0.01)
Seat Belt	1.21(0.01)	0.81(0.00)	1.44(0.02)	2.82(0.03)
Investigation	3.41(0.01)	0.24(0.00)	4.49(0.04)	6.96(0.05)
Other	2.23(0.01)	0.41(0.00)	2.83(0.03)	3.43(0.03)
Time				
Hour of Day	Included	Included	Included	Included
Day of Week	Included	Included	Included	Included
Fixed Effects				
Agency	Included	Included	Included	Included
Constant	0.69(0.01)	1.37(0.03)	0.01(0.00)	0.01(0.00)
N	6,627,813	6,627,813	6,627,813	6,627,813
Psuedo R^2	0.11	0.11	0.28	0.16
Log Likelihood	–4,026,802	–4,062,480	–647,395	–1,159,107

Note: All coefficients are statistically significant at $p<.05$. Entries are odds-ratios, with standard errors in parenthesis. Non-Hispanic whites are the reference category. Speed limit violations are the reference category for stop purposes. Analysis is limited to stops made by the 25 police agencies with the greatest number of observations.

and/or is male the odds of receiving a light outcome decrease. For Hispanic drivers, it is cut nearly in half, quite a substantial effect. Stop characteristics seem to give us the answer here: if no contraband is found and the stop is investigatory in nature then the driver has higher odds of experiencing a light outcome. Thus, the multivariate analysis contradicts the univariate analysis. Black drivers identically situated to white drivers are actually slightly less likely to be sent off with no action or just a warning. The univariate frequencies analyzed in the previous section of this chapter showed them having a higher chance of a light outcome. That suggests that the light outcomes for black drivers stemmed from the fact that they were less likely to have other factors making them suspicious to the officer. When all those are controlled for as in this model, black drivers are found to suffer a (very modest) penalty for their race. Similarly for males: they are 12 percent less likely than females to get a light outcome, other things equal.

A similar pattern emerges when looking at predicting whether an individual gets a ticket. Low values for all the stop purposes mean that speeding is the main driver of getting a ticket. Being black, once all the other factors are taken into account, has only the slightest effect, virtually none for the odds of getting a ticket. Being Hispanic, on the other hand, leads much more often to a ticket. Males are 7 percent more likely to get a ticket than female drivers, other things equal.

The final two columns predict being arrested or searched. Here we see a 43 percent increased chance for arrest and a 94 percent increased likelihood of search for black drivers compared to whites. Males are 95 percent more likely to be arrested, and 214 percent more likely to be searched than females, controlling for the other characteristics of the traffic stop, such as why the stop occurred. The main predictors of being arrested are driving while impaired and having contraband. The main predictors of being searched are being stopped for driving while impaired, for an investigation, and being male. Note that contraband is included in the models for all the outcomes except search, since the contraband is an outcome of the search, and cannot have driven the decision to conduct the search. The powerful findings for contraband and some stop purposes are not surprising and suggest a logical reaction to serious infractions on the road. The key point is the remaining effect of race and gender, on the likelihood of search and arrest, after these legally relevant factors have been taken into account. Black and Hispanic drivers, similarly situated to whites, are 40 to 50 percent more likely to be arrested. Blacks are almost twice as likely to be searched.

Overall, the results in Table 4.4 present a stark picture of the odds of negative outcomes for black drivers. Controlling for other demographic and stop characteristics, black drivers are more likely to be searched or be arrested than white drivers. Of course, the analysis is limited in that we do not know the extent to which motorists were breaking the law when they were pulled over. In part, we account for this possibility by controlling for contraband, but this is incomplete as there are many ways to break the law beyond carrying contraband. Still, these multivariate results corroborate and extend the findings from our earlier presentations of simple ratios and percentages. Minorities are much more likely to be searched and arrested than similarly situated whites, controlling for every variable that the state of North Carolina mandates to be collected when traffic stops are carried out. Even controlling for contraband being found, a powerful race effect remains. If the purpose of the data collection mandated by the state in 1999 was to see if there is prima facie evidence to suggest disparate treatment of drivers of different races, Table 4.4 shows that the lawmakers were certainly onto something. The rates of search and arrest are highly disparate, even controlling for other factors. The effect of being male is very powerful as well. Age appears to have only a moderate effect in the table, with a coefficient of .99 or .97; however, this is an effect per year of age. So, for the arrest model, the annual coefficient of 0.97 suggests a 3 percent decrease in likelihood per year of age: comparing an eighteen year-old to a thirty-eight year-old would imply a difference of 60 percent in the expected odds of being searched. We can clearly see how young men of color are targeted for harsh outcomes, other things equal, even in routine traffic stops.

Conclusion

We find robust patterns that show black drivers and white drivers are searched at differential rates and have different probabilities of being searched. In looking at descriptive statistics, we find patterns by which young, black men are more likely to be searched and arrested than other drivers. In looking at the more rigorous multivariate analysis, black drivers are shown to have increased odds of being searched and arrested following a traffic stop than white drivers. Further, men have increased odds of being searched and arrested over women, and younger people more than older. We found a powerful effect of a legally relevant factor: contraband. We explore this in greater detail in the chapter to come.

5

Finding Contraband

We know why motorists were pulled over by the police and we know the outcomes of those stops. What we do not know is the degree to which motorists were breaking the law. Driving full speed through a red light is a much more serious violation than failing to come to a complete, zero-mph stop at a stop sign; driving 50 mph over the speed limit is more dangerous than going 5 mph over. Pursuant to the *Whren* decision, police have legal justification to stop a motorist who violates the letter of the law in any way. Seeing a driver brush against the double-yellow line is enough to pull someone over for a safe movement violation, for example. Travelling even one mph over the speed limit is technically breaking the law and the police may enforce the law, according to the *Whren* decision, as they see fit. Minor violations of the letter of the law can be used as a pretext for stopping a motorist the officer may want to investigate for other reasons, including general suspicion. And, according to *Whren*, these stops may be racially disparate. That is, if black and white drivers are equally likely to violate a law, officers may legally pull over the blacks at greater rates than the whites, surprising as this may sound. (It may not be the sole reason, of course; that would clearly be unconstitutional racial discrimination. But unless an officer states in court that he pulled all those of one race over but not others, even very skewed statistical patterns have been found to be legally acceptable.) If a thousand individuals break the law, granting mercy to one does not relieve the other from the consequences of breaking the law. Or so the Supreme Court ruled in *Whren*.

We saw in Chapter 2 that black motorists are more likely to experience certain types of stop, particularly those associated with equipment and regulatory violations; in Chapter 3 that minority drivers are much more likely to be stopped than whites, compared to their population shares; and in Chapter 4 that drivers experience dramatically different outcomes following those stops, based on race, gender, and age. It is also possible that minority drivers are more likely to get stopped for comparatively trivial violations, such as driving slightly over the speed limit.[1] On the other hand, we have no guarantees that blacks and whites break the law at the same rate or in the same way. For example, a study by Lange, Johnson, and Voas (2005) of drivers on the New Jersey Turnpike found that speeders were more likely to be black and that patterns of police traffic stops accurately reflected the racial make-up of speeders, rather than the racial composition of the surrounding communities. Other studies have argued the opposite – that blacks are less likely to break the traffic laws (Epp et al. 2014). In any event, if blacks are more likely to break the traffic laws, or more likely to do so egregiously, we would expect them to experience more enforcement actions from the police. The lack of data on driver behavior is a black box at the center of our study, preventing us from linking the gravity of traffic violations to the police responses they provoke.

This is why the data on police searches and contraband finds are so important. When an officer initiates a search, they do so (ostensibly) to find contraband and we know whether or not they were successful. By calculating what percentage of searches lead to contraband – what we call the contraband hit rate – we can determine how effective officers are at finding contraband. So the hit rate can be thought of as the searching success rate and the inverse of the hit rate (the percentage of searches that come up empty) is the rate at which innocent drivers are needlessly inconvenienced, that is, the failure rate.

We believe that the costs associated with failed searches are much higher than has previously been appreciated by law enforcement or the Supreme Court. One failed search may indeed be a minor inconvenience, but after a string of pretextual stops even the most law-abiding young man might start to wonder if the police will always consider him to be a criminal suspect. Failed searches may be inevitable. The police cannot ascertain ahead of time, without looking, who is breaking the law. And such momentary inconveniences have been ruled to be just that by the courts: trivial, momentary, and inconsequential. In this chapter we document just how common they are. When targeted largely at a small segment of the population, we also must consider what would be the cumulative effect of a string of such events. Clearly, it cannot be expected to enhance any sense of citizenship, of belonging, or of trust and respect for the forces of order.

Furthermore, focusing on hit rates allows us to address the question of racial disparities directly because we can compare search rates and contraband hit rates for blacks and whites. In the previous chapter, we showed that blacks are much more likely to be searched by the police. Do these higher search rates find any justification in the contraband hit rates? When evidence shows that contraband hit rates are equal or higher for black drivers, this has generally been considered evidence of effective policing, even if blacks are searched at much higher rates (Knowles, Persico, and Todd 2001). Conversely, when blacks are searched at higher rates but are less likely to be found with contraband, this disparity is taken as evidence for an unjustified targeting of black drivers (Lamberth 1996; Harris 1999a; Meehan and Ponder 2006; Persico and Todd 2008; Bates 2010). As the US Justice Department explains in their report on the Ferguson PD, "the lower rate at which officers find contraband when searching African-Americans indicates either that officers' suspicion of criminal wrongdoing is less likely to be accurate when interacting with African-Americans or that officers are more likely to search African-Americans without any suspicion of criminal wrongdoing. Either explanation suggest bias, whether explicit or implicit" (US DOJ 2015, 65). Recent research by Stanford scientists suggests that this is also a problem in North Carolina (Simoiu, Corbett-Davies, and Goel 2017). The authors, using hierarchical statistical models that leverage geographic variation in stop outcomes, find that officers have a much lower search threshold when interacting with black and Hispanic motorists.

In this chapter, we compare search rates and contraband hit rates. We find that many police agencies are worse at finding contraband on blacks, especially in those searches which are more discretionary. Most alarmingly, these disparities are becoming more pronounced over time, indicating that racial bias on the motorways is a growing problem. Recall from Figure 3.2 that blacks are among an increasing share of those stopped, over time. If at the same time the racial disparities in search rates are also growing, this suggests a ratchet effect: increasing targeting of blacks over time. They are pulled over more than before, and the difference in search rates is also growing. So, we already know there is increasing targeting. We know that the costs of searching can be considerable, both in terms of police resources and community relations. Black Americans are less likely to trust the police. But from a police perspective, perhaps there are crime-fighting benefits to this targeting which outweigh the costs. What are the benefits? To find out, we need to know how often contraband is found and in what quantities. That is our focus here.

How Many Frogs Does It Take?

When asked about the logic behind the Drug Enforcement Agency's (DEA) Operation Pipeline,[2] a California Highway Patrol sergeant famously explained that, "It's sheer numbers. Our guys make a lot of stops. You've got to kiss a lot of frogs before you find a prince" (Webb 2007). The officer's statement reveals what we consider to be the two fundamental limitations of investigatory stops. First, the vast majority of motorists are not involved in any illegal activities (besides trivial traffic code violations). Second, even highly trained police officers have a hard time telling the difference between serious criminals and ordinary drivers. On the motorways, evidence for drug or weapons trafficking is often only circumstantial, so officers are forced to rely on behavioral stereotypes or visible cues that are thought to be indicators of criminality. These are of dubious accuracy and so the strategy quickly devolves into an effort to search as many drivers as possible. Indeed, these limitations have always been a defining feature of the investigatory traffic stops approach. Thus, in the *Tactics for Criminal Patrol*, a popular police training manual, Charles Remsberg (1995) instructs that the exceptional officer "seeks to maximize the number of citizen contacts on vehicle stops during each shift and, through specific investigative techniques, to explore the full arrest potential of each" (9). Rigorous standards for stopping and searching motorists have never been part of the investigatory stop equation, it is purely a numbers game.

Tracey Meares and collaborators (2016) note the different prisms through which ordinary people versus police and legal professionals view the appropriateness of a traffic stop. Police and legal professionals consider their actions through a prism of lawfulness and constitutional rulings: "officers know that the key to avoiding punishment is to follow the letter of the law" (299). Citizens, on the other hand, evaluate their actions based on a looser set of considerations: "people's procedural justice evaluations about the demeanor of the officers during their interactions with them" (300). Tom Tyler, with another set of collaborators (2015), goes further:

> Our argument is that it is not contact with the police per se that is problematic. In fact, the results of the study suggest that when the police deal with people in

ways that they experience as being fair, contact promotes trust and a variety of types of desirable public behavior. Rather, it is contact that communicates suspicion and mistrust that undermines the relationship between the public and the police. (603)

As we reviewed in Chapter 1, these authors suggest that members of the public seek a form of "procedural justice" – to be treated equitably and not singled out as an object of suspicion while simply "driving while black." Our analysis suggests, and a review of policing since efforts to crack down on crime emerged in the 1980s and 1990s reinforces, that police professionals and the courts assign no cost to the officer who comes up short, even many times over.

"Kissing a lot of frogs" may not be the best use of an officer's time. But how do the frogs like it? If indeed a large percentage of the stops and searches are fruitless, and if they are targeted at a small slice of the driving population, then we should pay attention to the potential consequences of these fruitless searches. At a minimum, we should assign some cost to them. The fruitless search rate, as we might call it, has never been part of the equation. And we will see that it is indeed very high. When we think of how targeted it is at young males of color, several things should be apparent: the cost is disproportionately borne by a group with little political power or voice; those with greater power and political voice (e.g., middle-class whites) are virtually immune from its consequences (and ignorant of its occurrence); and finally, we cannot expect these encounters to encourage civic participation or respect for the police.

Of course, not every police search is carried out in a random effort to "crack down on crime." Sometimes officers have good reasons for searching a motorist, such as smelling marijuana after a routine traffic stop or when contraband is in plain sight. Recall from the last chapter that some searches take place pursuant to other actions, such as making an arrest. In these cases, officers carry out a search, not because they necessarily believe that they will find contraband, but because it is mandated by police protocol. Before taking a person into custody, after arrest, officers routinely search for weapons and contraband. Given that these are individuals who have already been arrested, such "incident to arrest" searches often yield contraband. Thus it is important to consider the type of search when considering its effectiveness and we would expect (or at least hope) that searches requiring a judgment call from an officer are more successful than those that are automatically triggered by exogenous circumstances.

Finding Contraband

Data on contraband comes from Part II of the SBI-122 form. Officers are asked to check a box labeled "none" if they conducted a search but did not find any contraband. If an officer did find contraband, then they are asked to indicate the quantity. If it was drugs they can record the quantity as either ounces, pounds, dosages, grams, or kilos; alcohol can be recorded as pints or gallons; money as a dollar amount; weapons as the total number of weapons. Officers can also list contraband as "other." Additionally, the software platform that officers use to enter information from the SBI-122 form rounds down small amounts to zero, so in these cases the data entry shows that contraband was found but without any corresponding information on quantity. We group these contraband hits together into a "no amount recorded" category along with the hits listed as "other." Beyond these general groups, there is no further information about the type of contraband. An officer may report that they found 3 ounces of some drug, but we do not know if the drug was marijuana or heroin. Likewise, a weapon could refer to a pocketknife or an AK-47; we have no way to distinguish from the data. Multiple types of contraband are sometimes listed for the same traffic stop.

Table 5.1 shows the types of contraband found after each type of search. The top row, labeled "Drugs," shows that police have found some type of drug a total of 96,841 times. Reading across this row reveals that 50 percent of contraband found after any type of search is drugs, for consent searches drugs make up 46 percent of all contraband, compared to 56 percent of contraband found with probable cause searches, 39 percent for incident to arrest, 35 percent for protective frisks, and 50 percent of contraband found after executing a warrant. Weapons are typically the rarest type of contraband, followed by money. Note, however, that there is a relationship between the type of contraband the police find and the type of search they are conducting. Weapons make up 35 percent of the contraband found pursuant to a protective frisk, presumably because police are either more likely to conduct this type of search when a weapon is in plain sight, or because the police are more likely to list a weapon as contraband after having frisked a motorist. Similarly, alcohol is relatively common following searches that take place incident to arrest, suggesting that the types of behavior that put motorists behind bars (such as drunk driving) correlate with the presence of alcohol in the car. Often when police find contraband it lands in the "no amount recorded" category, either because it was some type of contraband besides drugs, alcohol, money, or weapons, or because the quantity recorded was so low that the

TABLE 5.1. *Type of Contraband Found, by Type of Search*

	N	All Searches	Consent	Probable Cause	Incident to Arrest	Protective Frisk	Warrant
Drugs	96,841	49.89	46.03	55.59	38.94	34.94	49.52
Alcohol	34,663	17.36	15.58	13.90	27.94	13.37	26.29
Money	27,688	13.86	13.53	14.87	12.61	10.16	16.13
Weapons	20,731	10.38	9.30	9.19	12.63	34.74	12.10
No amount recorded	49,997	25.03	27.75	24.19	22.56	21.71	14.52
Total	229,920	116.52	112.19	117.74	114.68	114.92	118.56

Note: Entries are column percentages. The totals are greater than 100 because searches occasionally uncover multiple types of contraband. The total column simply sums the other rows in the column, and thus some stops are counted twice if multiple types of contraband were discovered.

SBI-122 software rounded it down to zero. These types of finds are especially common for consent searches, making up 28 percent of the total.

Next, we turn to contraband hit rates. How successful are the police at using each type of search to find contraband? Here we must be particularly sensitive to whether or not the search was discretionary. Searches that take place incident to arrest are required by police protocol as are searches that take place when exercising a warrant. In these cases, a low hit rate should not be taken as evidence of any policing inefficiency, but rather a simple reflection of the prevalence of contraband on arrested motorists. On the other hand, the discretionary searches – consent and probable cause – tell us how accurately officers can judge when a motorist has contraband. These are searches that do not need to be carried out, so officers are presumably conducting them only when they feel there is a reasonable chance that contraband will be found. Table 5.2 shows the hit rates associated with each type of search and contraband.

Looking first at the row labeled "Overall," we see that police have found contraband a total of 199,725 times. (The total from Table 5.1 is 229,920, but this corresponds to the total number of times each type of contraband has been found, and sometimes multiple types of contraband are discovered from one search.) Reading across this row reveals that overall officers find contraband after 29 percent of searches. Consent searches result in contraband about 23 percent of the time, but probable cause searches are much more successful, with a hit rate of 55 percent. The other three types of search – incident to arrest, protective frisk, and warrant searches – are procedural, based less on an officer's intuition and

TABLE 5.2. *Contraband Hit Rates, by Search Type*

	N	% All Searches	% Consent	% Probable Cause	% Incident to Arrest	% Protective Frisk	% Warrant
Overall	199,725	28.96	22.98	55.36	19.29	17.35	38.92
Drugs	96,841	14.04	10.58	30.77	7.51	6.06	19.27
Alcohol	34,663	5.03	3.58	7.70	5.39	2.32	10.23
Money	27,688	4.01	3.11	8.23	2.43	1.76	6.28
Weapons	20,731	3.01	2.14	5.08	2.44	3.06	4.71
No amount recorded	49,997	7.25	6.38	13.39	4.35	3.77	5.65

Note: Police officers have conducted 689,657 searches and found contraband 199,725 times for an overall contraband hit rate of 28.96 percent. The number of times each type of contraband has been found exceeds the overall number because officers sometimes find more than one type of contraband from a single search. The dataset records 721 instances when contraband was found but no search was conducted. As our focus in this chapter is on hit rates (i.e. what happens after a search) we exclude these instances from this table, which is why the overall amount of contraband listed is less than what is recorded in Table 2.11.

more on the dictates of protocol. Each of these procedural searches is less effective at finding contraband than probable causes searches, although warrant searches are more successful than consent searches. (Note, that if an officer observes contraband in plain sight and this leads to the arrest of the motorist, this "search" should be recorded under probable cause, so searches incident to arrest are not predicated on the existence of contraband.)

Where we noted above that probable cause searches have the highest "success rate" at 55 percent, we should consider what that number means. Probable cause is a relatively high legal standard, where the officer has the right to conduct a search because of the high probability of success. The fact that this probability is empirically revealed to be 55 percent suggests that the threshold is lower than one might imagine. And, as we will see below, many "successful" contraband hits in fact lead to very small amounts of contraband, including amounts so small that no arrest follows. Table 5.4, later in the chapter, shows that in fact only 23 percent of probable cause searches lead to contraband and arrest. Half of the contraband hits even in the probable cause searches are so small that the officer decides an arrest is not warranted. Looking at consent searches, these numbers are even lower.

Of the two discretionary searches, consent searches are less likely to find contraband than those initiated with probable cause. This makes sense if we consider consent searches essentially to be fishing expeditions. If an officer has good reason to think that a motorist has contraband, then they can search them with probable cause. It is the absence of such "smoking-gun" evidence that necessitates an officer asking for consent in the first place. For each search, when officers do find contraband it is most likely to be drugs. Beyond drugs, the "no amount recorded" category is relatively common, suggesting that when the police do find contraband it is often in very small amounts.

Amounts of Contraband Found

We shift now to looking at the amount of contraband found by officers. Do officers frequently make large drug busts? Or is finding contraband in any substantial quantity a rarity? Remember that the logic of investigatory stops is to crack down on serious criminals: people involved in moving substantial quantities of drugs or weapons across the country. If the police find levels of contraband consistent with drug trafficking only rarely, then this undermines much of the justification of investigatory traffic stops.

Figure 5.1 presents a series of histograms, plotting the frequencies with which officers make contraband seizures of different sizes. The upper-left plot, labeled "Weapons," reveals that when weapons are recovered as contraband, it is almost always only one weapon. Moving to the plot labeled "Pounds," we see the same pattern, usually no more than one pound is recovered. This strong leftward skew is evident in every histogram, indicating that when contraband is found, regardless of the form it takes, it is almost always found in the singular; one pound, one pint, one ounce, one gallon. In fact, for every type of contraband the median size of seizure is one, except dosages where it is two and money where it is twenty. And actually, this leftward skew is underestimated in the figures. Approximately a quarter of all contraband finds are listed under the "no amount recorded" category because the SBI-122 software rounds down very small quantities to zero (although a small percentage of the "no amount recorded" hits are for miscellaneous types of contraband). If these small amounts were included they would all be grouped in the far-left bars of the histograms.

The logic of using investigatory stops to fight crime is to apprehend high-level dealers and their associates who move and sell large quantities of drugs. Like many states, North Carolina has drug trafficking laws that define what quantities of different types of drugs lead one to be considered a trafficker. For example, it takes at least 10 pounds of

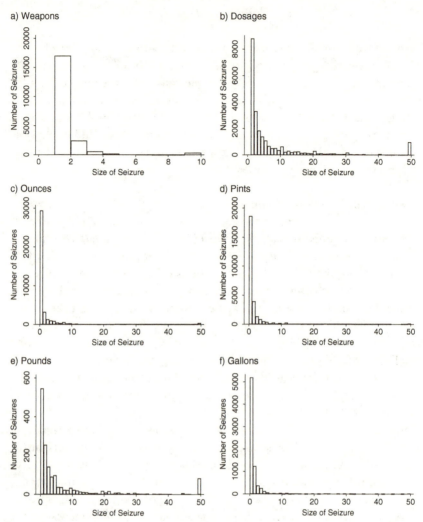

FIGURE 5.1. How Much Contraband is Found?

Note: (a) Weapons were found as contraband in 20,731 stops. The median size of seizure is 1. Large values are clustered at 10. (b) Dosages were found as contraband in 23,630 stops. The median size of seizure is 2. Large values are clustered at 50. (c) Ounces were found as contraband in 39,388 stops. The median size of seizure is 0.98. Large values are clustered at 50. (d) Pints were found as contraband in 27,247 stops. The median size of seizure is 1. Large values are clustered at 50. (e) Pounds were found as contraband in 1,575 stops. The median size of seizure is 2. Large values are clustered at 50. (f) Gallons were found as contraband in 7,489 stops. The median size of seizure is 1. Large values are clustered at 50. (g) Money was found as contraband in 27,688 stops. The median size of seizure is 20. Large values are clustered at 100. (h) Grams were found as contraband in 34,936 stops. The median size of seizure is 2. Large values are clustered at 50. (i) Kilos were found as contraband in 90 stops. The median size of seizure is 2.

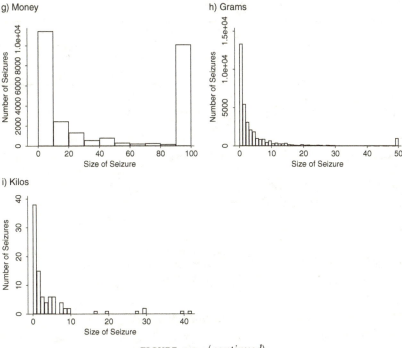

FIGURE 5.1. (*continued*)

marijuana to qualify as a trafficker, and the minimum penalty for being caught with this amount is twenty-five months in prison and a $5,000 fine. For heroin, it takes only 4 grams to qualify as a trafficker and the minimum penalty is seventy months in prison and a $50,000 fine (NC General Assembly 2015).

While we do not know the type of drug associated with the recorded quantities, Figure 5.1 suggests that it is unusual for officers to apprehend drug traffickers on the motorways. Assuming that pounds most often refers to marijuana, officers have stopped someone with enough of the drug to qualify as a trafficker only a handful of times in hundreds of thousands of searches. If we assume that every kilo found is of marijuana, then officers have only caught sixteen marijuana traffickers. To put these numbers in perspective, of the hundreds of thousands of searches in state databases since 2002, only 28 percent of those searches resulted in contraband, and only a small fraction of those contraband finds were for amounts associated with drug trafficking. A major drug bust is a vanishingly rare occurrence on the motorways.

TABLE 5.3. *Police Actions Resulting from the Discovery of Contraband*

Action	Type of Contraband					Total	
	Drugs	Alcohol	Weapons	Money	No amount recorded	N	%
No action	0.84	0.92	1.80	1.50	1.20	1,818	1.14
Verbal warning	4.39	6.39	7.06	6.80	8.97	10,651	6.68
Written warning	4.97	3.97	4.89	6.22	7.14	8,957	5.62
Citation	49.66	58.73	34.54	39.54	52.02	80,105	50.26
Arrest	40.14	29.99	51.71	45.94	30.67	57,839	36.29
Total Percent	100.00	100.00	100.00	100.00	100.00		100.00
N	81,127	23,387	15,633	22,600	40,893	159,370	–

Note: Entries are column percentages, summing to 100 percent for each contraband type. The table excludes 209,148 searches that took place "incident to arrest," as in these cases the arrest precipitated the search, rather than the search determining the outcome.

Most Contraband Hits Do Not Lead to Arrest

We can explore this theme further by looking at what happens after contraband is found. We may not know exactly what type of drug or weapon officers discover, but, presumably, if an officer finds more serious drugs (cocaine or heroin), or more dangerous weapons (automatic rifles or grenades), the consequences for the driver will be more severe. Table 5.3 shows the police actions that took place after various types of contraband were found.

Reading down the column labeled "Drugs" reveals that 50 percent of the time when drugs are found the motorist is issued a citation. In fact, a citation is more likely than an arrest, which occurs in only 40 percent of the stops when drugs are discovered. This strongly indicates the majority of drugs that officers find do not warrant prosecution. In other words, these appear to be relatively minor offenses, perhaps relating to small quantities of marijuana. The story is similar for other types of contraband; in each case, motorists are very likely to receive a ticket. Weapons are the only type of contraband where the likelihood of an arrest is 50 percent or greater, meaning that having been discovered with a weapon, motorists are more likely to be arrested than some other outcome. However, even for weapons, 48 percent of the time motorists are not arrested, suggesting that the weapons in question must not have been contraband at all (e.g., the driver had a legal permit to carry), or that they were such things as

TABLE 5.4. *Arrest-Worthy Contraband Hit Rates, by Search and Contraband Type*

	Arrests	% All Searches	% Consent	% Probable Cause	% Protective Frisk	% Warrant
Overall	57,839	12.04	6.89	22.76	7.09	24.17
Drugs	32,566	6.78	3.89	12.99	2.76	11.11
Alcohol	7,014	1.46	0.80	2.78	0.89	6.53
Money	10,383	2.16	1.13	4.36	4.14	0.85
Weapons	8,084	1.68	0.86	3.20	2.46	3.83
No amount recorded	12,540	2.61	1.46	5.02	1.58	3.64

Note: Entries show the percent of drivers arrested after a given type of search and a given type of contraband found. For example, in the first row, 32,566 individuals were arrested for drugs; these represented 6.78 percent of all searches, 3.86 percent of all consent searches, and so on. The table excludes 209,148 searches that took place "incident to arrest," as in these cases the arrest precipitated the search. More than one type of contraband may be found in a given search.

pocket knives. A search yielding an unauthorized lethal weapon such as a gun would certainly lead to arrest, but only slightly more than half of all weapons found as contraband lead to arrest.[3]

In light of these findings, we update Table 5.2, which looked at contraband hit rates, to consider only "arrest-worthy" hit rates. We want to know how often the police found contraband in amounts consistent with serious criminal activity. The results, shown in Table 5.4, cast further doubt on the efficacy of widespread searching of motorists as an approach to fighting crime. The first row in Table 5.2 showed that police find contraband after 29 percent of searches, but, when we limit our focus to arrest-worthy contraband, the hit rate plummets. Only 12 percent of total searches result in contraband that leads to an arrest.

Hit rates suffer greatly across the board. Whereas 55 percent of probable cause searches result in some type of contraband, only 23 percent of those searches result in contraband serious enough to merit an arrest. And consent searches look particularly ineffectual, as the hit rate drops from 23 percent overall to just 7 percent when counting only those contraband hits leading to arrest. In all, the benefits of conducting searches of motorists (at least as part of a larger strategy to apprehend criminals) appear relatively circumspect, while there are good reasons to think that the costs are quite substantial.

Type I and Type II Errors

How could we have developed a system where police officers conduct hundreds of thousands of searches, often without probable cause, with low hit rates, and especially low rates of finding significant amounts of contraband? It seems unavoidable to conclude that one reason is that we simply do not assign any cost to "type I errors". A type I error is the false rejection of a null hypothesis. If the null is the idea that a particular citizen is law-abiding, wrongly concluding that they may be a criminal is a type I error. A type II error is the opposite: wrongly accepting the null, when it should have been rejected. In this context, a type II error means wrongly letting a criminal go free after failing to recognizing their criminality. Correctly identifying criminals from law abiding citizens, and treating them accordingly is of course crucial to any sense of justice.

It would seem that when an officer conducts a fruitless search, the traditional interpretation is simply that it was a good outcome for the driver, that they perhaps suffered a momentary inconvenience, but that no further consideration of the matter is warranted. If we must "kiss a lot of frogs" before we "find our prince" then all those individuals who were, in retrospect, wrongfully targeted for investigation simply have to pay a small price for the collective benefit to society of the few hits that result from this practice: we want to avoid making "type II errors" by letting drug dealers roam the streets with impunity, knowing they will not be searched if stopped at a traffic stop. The fruitless search simply has no importance; it is weighted zero, never entering any calculation of efficiency.

Indeed, type II errors are serious problems. For example, in 2003 the Washington DC area was shaken by a series of sniper attacks, and DC area police ran the tags of the perpetrator John Muhammad's car "at least nine times in 23 days" so clearly he was attracting attention. In fact Muhammad was detained in a traffic stop just hours after one of the attacks. Muhammad, later executed in Virginia for the crimes, calmly provided his license and registration to the officer while his young accomplice was hidden in the trunk of the car. The registration was valid and the officer, instructed to be on the lookout for the wrong type of car, conducted no search. Tragically, a search in this case would have led to the discovery of Muhammad's accomplice as well as the weapon, putting a stop to the violence which eventually claimed seventeen lives; seven of the victims came after the traffic stop in which Muhammad avoided being searched (see Dwyer 2003).

Type I errors, the opposite of the example above, are assumed in law enforcement and in the courts to have no inherent cost. Citizens should not mind a momentary detention by a well-meaning officer tasked with the difficult job of disrupting criminal behavior that may be about to occur. This all makes perfect sense when we take a legal perspective on the matter: the police have a difficult job and we all benefit when they use their judgment to investigate situations which appear suspicious. Furthermore, we cannot expect them to be prescient: some percent of the time the "suspicion" that a citizen evokes in the eyes of the officer will prove, on investigation, to be without merit. The investigation itself is not a sanction, just a check. But, as Tracey Meares has explained in various publications (Meares 2009; Meares, Tyler, and Gardener 2016) and backed up by various works by Tom Tyler, Jeff Fagan, and others (Tyler, Jackson, and Mentovich 2015; Tyler, Fagan, Geller 2014), these interactions, coming over and over again with the same group of "citizen-suspects" cannot be expected to be without consequence. The data collected by law here in North Carolina do not allow one to tell if an individual was previously stopped or searched by police. However, given the demographic targeting that we have documented, it is not hard to imagine that many young men, particularly of color, would likely have been stopped and searched multiple times. While any single one of those might well be a trivial matter, a series of them would be different. And, as Meares, Tyler, Fagan and others have emphasized, the interpretation of an encounter with the police (or the court system) depends dramatically on the perception of how fair the procedures were. Where an individual feels they were unfairly targeted for relatively harsh treatment, while similarly situated others were not, frustration, anger, and alienation are logical results.

In Chapter 8 we will document that in areas where racial disparities are high, black voting rates in local elections are depressed. As several others (see for example, Burch 2013; Lerman and Weaver 2014) have argued, police-initiated citizen contacts can generate political alienation and a reduced sense of full citizenship. As Epp and colleagues showed (2014), this can also lead to reduced willingness to cooperate with the police, a point we will also document in Chapter 9. Citizens who feel that they have become suspects withdraw from the police and government in general. So, while type I errors have no legal bearing in the courts, they may have a substantial impact in the court of public opinion and be an important explanation of why some individuals, and some entire communities, feel alienated from and mistrustful of the police. Considering the surprisingly low numbers of searches that lead to arrest, we believe police leaders should reconsider the rates at which they use traffic stops to conduct criminal investigations. The numbers suggest very little value.

How Accurate Are Individual Officers in Finding Contraband?

Collectively, police have a contraband hit rate of 29 percent (or 12 percent, looking only at arrest-worthy contraband). In this section, we look at individual officers, estimating their hit rates in relation to their peers. We want to know the degree to which officers are held to a uniform set of standards and we can formulate two conflicting hypotheses in this regard. One is that officers across the state are largely consistent with one another when it comes to finding contraband. Officers conducting many searches but rarely finding contraband might adjust their behavior to have a higher threshold for searching. With training and experience, they should be better able to judge whether a person's dress or demeanor really suggests criminal activity, and their search rates and hit rates should converge to some average value. Conversely, some officers might have too high a threshold, only searching when contraband is in plain sight, for instance. These officers would have very high hit rates because they only search when contraband is all but certain to be found, but they would be too cautious, perhaps letting many contraband-carrying motorists slip past. Ideally then, officers would operate in the middle-ground, judiciously searching motorists without being overcautious and hit rates would equilibrate to some general range of acceptability. We term this possibility the "learning model," in which officers dynamically adapt their search behavior based on their success at finding contraband; a very high hit rate would be brought down by more searching, a low hit rate would be brought up with less searching. The level of searching required to find the acceptable range of hit rates would vary depending on the community that an officer patrols. High-crime areas may allow an officer to search widely and still find contraband at an acceptable rate, while, in communities where crime is rare, the search rate would need to be much lower in order to maintain the same hit rate. If the learning hypothesis is true, we would therefore expect to observe a wide range of search rates across officers (corresponding to the various neighborhoods that they patrol), but a narrow range of contraband hit rates (corresponding to widely held organizational standards).

The counter hypothesis is that each officer is an island unto themselves, free to conduct as many or as few searches as they want, regardless of

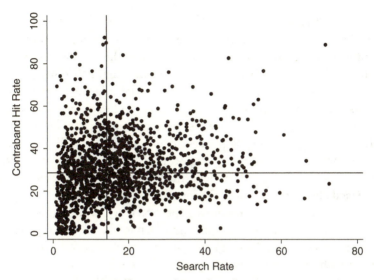

FIGURE 5.2. Comparing Officer-Level Search and Hit Rates
Note: Based on the 1,408 police officers that searched at least 100 motorists. Correlation between searches and contraband hits is 0.191. Lines show median values.

their success in finding contraband. This can be thought of as the "idiosyncratic oversight" hypothesis. If police agencies are not particularly concerned with the number of frogs it takes their officers to find a prince, then we would expect randomness. Some officers may develop nuanced search practices, others may be less particular, preferring to search randomly and in high volume. In this scenario, we would expect to observe a wide range of both search and contraband hit rates.

Figure 5.2 is a scatter plot comparing search and contraband hit rates for officers who conducted at least 100 searches. (Note that statewide the search rate is 3.36 and the contraband hit rate is 28.96, but among the officers included in the figure the mean search rate is 14.29 and the mean hit rate is 28.57. The search rate is high because we exclude officers with very low numbers of searches, but the contraband hit rate is only marginally affected by this filtering.) Evidence from the plot strongly favors the idiosyncratic oversight hypothesis over the learning model. A huge range of values is evident across both axes, indicating great variability in the propensity of officers to conduct searches and their success at finding contraband. Some officers search more than 20 percent of the motorists they stop and still manage to find contraband more than 40 percent of the time, while others search at similarly high rates with much less success. There certainly does not appear to be a range of acceptable contraband hit rates to which officers gravitate and from this we can infer a lack of statewide standards when it comes to searching. Police will continue searching at high rates even if those searches are relatively unsuccessful.[4]

This is exactly the pattern we would expect a heavy reliance on investigatory traffic stops to generate, as these stops are less about enforcing traffic laws than maximizing police–citizen encounters. If finding contraband is actually of secondary importance to demonstrating a strong police presence, then police departments would not be particularly concerned about low hit rates. Of course, we should also note that police chiefs may simply lack the information necessary to hold their officers accountable for idiosyncratic searching. While the state mandates that each agency collect and submit data from the SBI-122 form, the data is not returned to the agencies in any aggregated or useful format. Thus the SBI-122's enormous potential as a management tool is lost. Armed with officer-level statistics, North Carolina's police chiefs could have informed discussions with their officers about standards for searching motorists. Those with extremely high hit rates might be asked why they only search when they are virtually certain of finding contraband, such as when it is plainly visible. Similarly, those with very low hit rates might be counselled that they are inconveniencing large numbers of citizens with little to show for it. Is that because they need more training on how to recognize those carrying contraband, or what might be the reason such a high percent of their searches bear no fruit?

Finding Contraband on Black and White Drivers

We turn now to examining how contraband hit rates break down by race. Of particular interest are the discretionary search types because these give us a window into officers' decision-making. The last chapter showed that blacks are much more likely to experience these types of search, so now we want to know if they are also more likely to be found with contraband.

Hit Rates for Black and White Drivers

Table 5.5 shows the rate at which different searches result in contraband for black and white drivers. The first row, labeled "All Searches," reveals that taking all searches together police are equally likely to find contraband on blacks as compared to whites. However, reading down the

TABLE 5.5. *Percentage of Searches that Result in Contraband*

	Total Searches	% Total	% White	% Black	B-W Ratio
All Searches	689,657	28.96	30.45	30.13	0.99
Consent	304,768	22.98	27.17	21.20	0.78
Probable Cause	153,894	55.36	60.27	53.29	0.88
Incident to Arrest	209,148	19.29	19.73	20.86	1.06
Protective Frisk	20,254	17.35	17.15	19.38	1.13
Warrant	1,593	38.92	39.81	41.14	1.03

table makes clear that different types of search deviate sharply from this baseline ratio.

Crucially, a major divide is evident between discretionary and procedural searches. Officers are 22 percent less likely to find contraband on black drivers following consent searches and 12 percent less likely after probable cause searches. On the other hand, searches that are incident to arrest and warrant searches are essentially race neutral and blacks are more likely to be found with contraband after protective frisks. This indicates that officers are either worse at making probable cause assessments as to whether black motorists have contraband or have a lower threshold for what qualifies as cause when interacting with a black driver. Either possibility suggests that black and white drivers are treated in a disparate manner not justified by any difference in criminal behavior. For consent searches, which are by far the most disparate, either of the former possibilities are in play, but we also cannot rule out the possibility that black drivers are more likely to acquiesce to being searched. (Chapter 9 looks at how recent changes to police protocol surrounding consent searches in Fayetteville, Durham, and Chapel Hill affected the racial dynamics of these searches.)

Beyond looking at the type of search that took place we can also consider data relating to the basis of, or justification for, each search. One of the possible justifications officers can record is if they made an "observation of suspected contraband" and making such an observation can form the basis of probable cause. Out of the almost 690,000 searches that took place, the basis for 146,003 was that an officer observed what they took to be contraband. However, it appears that officers are frequently mistaken in these observations. In fact, 47 percent of the time these searches fail to recover any contraband at all. When officers are correct and do find contraband only 22 percent of the time does it lead to an arrest. And again, we observe a racial difference: officers are mistaken in their

TABLE 5.6. *Stops, Searches, Contraband Hits, and Arrests by Race*

	White	Black	Hispanic	Total	B-W Ratio	H-W Ratio
Stops	11,623,064	6,261,948	1,515,192	20,026,586		
Searches	186,959	242,882	42,912	480,509		
Search and Contraband	66,770	80,823	9,399	159,370		
Contraband and Arrest	22,038	31,584	3,523	57,839		
Search Rate	1.61	3.88	2.83	2.40	2.41	1.76
Hit Rate	35.71	33.28	21.90	33.17	0.93	0.61
Hit-Arrest Rate	11.79	13.00	8.21	12.04	1.10	0.70

Note: Excludes searches incident to arrest. Search rate is per 100 stops. Hit rate and hit-arrest rate are per 100 searches.

observations 44 percent of the time when searching white motorists and 49 percent of the time when searching blacks. This means that almost half the time when an officer decides to search a black driver because they believe they have seen contraband in the car they are wrong and no contraband is recovered. The numbers here are not encouraging for either whites or blacks, as they point to a process that is prone to errors. Moreover, that officers are somewhat worse at making these observations when interacting with black drivers once again gives the impression of an elevated (and unwarranted) level of suspicion of minority motorists.

Racial Difference in Search, Hit, and Arrest-Worthy Hit Rates
We noted above that most contraband hits are small amounts, so small that the typical hit does not lead to arrest. Depending on the type of contraband, arrest rates were as low as 30 percent (alcohol), or as high as 52 percent (weapons). Drug contraband resulted in arrest just 40 percent of the time (see Table 5.3). Table 5.6 breaks these patterns down by race. It shows the number of white, black, and Hispanic drivers stopped, searched, found with contraband, and then arrested following the discovery of contraband in a search.

As in Table 5.3, we exclude searches conducted "incident to arrest" in this table. For white drivers, 11.6 million stops have led to about 187,000 searches, a search rate of 1.61 percent of stops. These searches, in turn, have led to contraband 67,000 times, a hit rate of 36 percent. The arrest-worthy contraband hit rate is lower, however: just 22,000 arrests have followed those contraband hits, or slightly less than 12 percent of all searches. That is, if we think of arrest as the discovery of enough contraband to validate the officer's suspicion in conducting the search, this is a relatively rare outcome. Over 88 percent of searches of white drivers are, in the language we used above, type I errors. These are unsuccessful searches. Certainly if we are on the hunt for a "prince" we would want to arrest him when he was finally discovered. Otherwise, why kiss so many frogs? The data clearly reveal the fact that it is an extremely inefficient way to find significant amounts of contraband.

Black drivers are searched at over twice the rate of white drivers, and have contraband in just 33 percent of these searches. They are arrested following 13 percent of the searches, a similar rate to white drivers. Hispanics are searched at a rate almost as high as that of blacks, but are much less likely to be discovered with contraband, and particularly unlikely to be arrested following a search: just 8 percent of searches of Hispanic drivers lead to arrest following the discovery of contraband.[5] We explore this dynamic in more detail in Chapter 8. For now, the point is clear: "kissing a lot of frogs" is an understatement. Traffic stops rarely yield contraband, and when they do, it is in such small amounts that the most common outcome is a ticket. Just 12 percent of searches lead to the discovery of a large enough amount of contraband to merit arrest.

Agency-by-Agency Variation

Taken together, NC police show some alarming tendencies, namely a propensity to search blacks at a much higher rate than whites, even as they are less likely to find contraband on blacks (at least when there is discretion involved). But as prior analysis has demonstrated, there can be great variability beneath the aggregate state-level statistics. Some police agencies may be less disparate than others, and it is even possible that the worrisome disparities revealed in Table 5.5 are being driven by only a few outlying agencies. To investigate this possibility, Figure 5.3 breaks down the black–white percent difference ratio by the twenty-five police agencies with the most traffic stops.

As expected, there is considerable variance across the top-25 agencies. Clearly, however, when it comes to discretionary searches, the vast majority of the state's largest agencies are worse at finding contraband on blacks. Given that most of these agencies are also searching blacks at much higher rates than they do whites (see Chapter 4), we can take this differential in contraband hit rates as evidence of unjustified racial disparity. Officers from many of the most active agencies are either

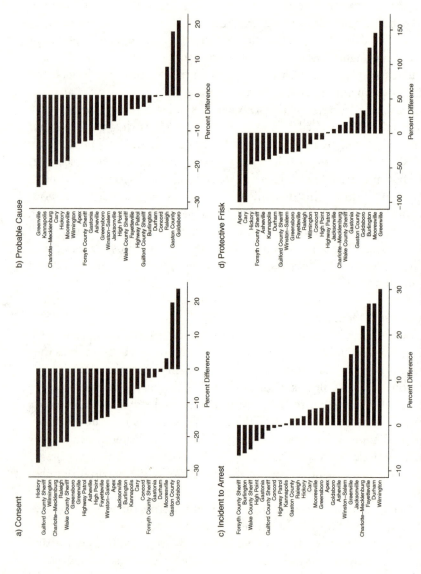

FIGURE 5.3. Percent Difference in the Likelihood of Finding Contraband

Note: Figure shows the percent difference in the likelihood of finding contraband on black versus white motorists.

more suspicious of black drivers, or use a lower search threshold when interacting with blacks.

Protective frisk searches split the agencies almost evenly, with about half being more likely to find contraband on blacks and half more likely to find it on whites. Searches that take place incident to arrest (the search type affording officers the least discretion) appear more likely to result in contraband on black motorists, at least among the top-25 agencies. So it is predominantly when officers must make a decision about whether or not to conduct a search that blacks are disadvantaged. Most importantly, the figure tells us that the statewide evidence of racial disparity from Table 5.5 is not being driven by a handful of bad apple police agencies. The problem is system wide. Twenty-two out of twenty-five agencies are worse at searching blacks with consent and twenty-one are worse at searching blacks with probable cause. This paints a bleak picture of the ability of officers to determine when a black driver should be searched.

Trends over Time

Figure 5.4 shows trends in the differential use of discretionary searches and the success of these searches at recovering contraband from 2002 to 2016 between black and white drivers. For consent searches, we see a gradual decline in search differential starting in 2007, which becomes a much steeper decline in 2014. So, over this period, consent searches are being applied more equally with regard to race. Of course, even in 2016 black motorists are about 40 percent more likely than white drivers to experience a consent search, but this is down from a peak of 160 percent more likely in 2007. Furthermore, notice that in every year the police are relatively worse at finding contraband on blacks, so the results from Table 5.4 are robust with respect to time. There does, however, appear to be cause for some cautious optimism. The decline in search differential starting in 2014 is matched by a similar decline in the percent difference of finding contraband on black and white drivers. Specifically, the percent difference in contraband drops by half, from 30 percent less likely to find contraband on black drivers to 15 percent less likely, between 2014 and 2016. It would appear that a reduced focus on using consent searches to investigate black drivers resulted in more racially equitable policing, a trend that we very much hope continues.

What caused this abrupt change in police behavior? We can only speculate by noting that attention to the NC DOJ traffic stops database (and the dramatic racial disparities that it revealed) was building in local and national media outlets starting around 2012. For example, a 2013 article

a) Consent

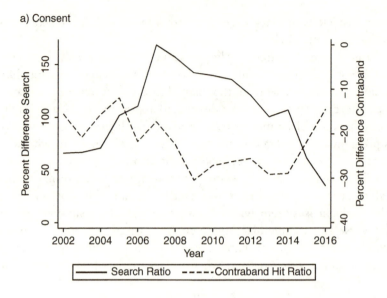

b) Probable Cause

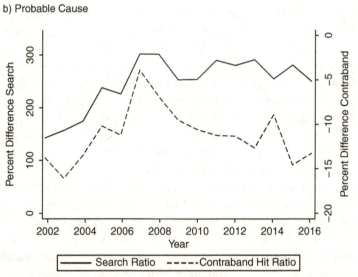

FIGURE 5.4. Percent Difference across Race in the Likelihood of Searches and Contraband

in the *Raleigh News and Observer* was titled "Traffic-stop numbers show racial bias across North Carolina" (Wise 2013). *The New York Times* dedicated significant attention to the North Carolina data in a long-form investigatory article titled "The Disproportionate Risk of Driving While Black" (LaFraniere and Lehren 2015). In particular, there has been a push from community groups across the state demanding that police agencies reform their consent search policies (a trend that we look at in more detail in Chapter 9). It is possible that these efforts, by bringing attention to a problematic police practice, have succeeded in effecting a change in police behavior, even in agencies that have not officially revised the way they carry out consent searches. In fact, Patricia Warren and Donald Tomaskovic-Devey (2009) find that such effects have taken place in NC previously. Their study compares coverage of "driving while black" in the 1990s and early 2000s with racial disparities in searches conducted by the NC Highway Patrol. They find that as levels of coverage intensified, and the NC Highway Patrol was put under greater scrutiny, racial disparities became marginally less pronounced.

Unfortunately, any gains toward equality for consent searches have not carried over to probable cause. In 2002, officers were about 110 percent more likely to search a black driver with probable cause, by 2016 the difference skyrocketed to 250 percent. These heightened suspicions of black motorists are in no way borne out by the corresponding hit rate differential. In every year, officers' perceptions of wrongdoing are less accurate when engaging with black motorists and, starting in 2007, this percent difference begins to increase, suggesting that the dramatic increase in relative suspicions of black drivers has negatively affected the ability of the police to find contraband.

Age and Gender Disparities

We continue our contraband analysis by looking at gender and age disparities. As noted previously, many of the disparities we have documented are especially pronounced among young men. We argued that this is because young black men are stereotyped as criminals and are therefore more likely to arouse police suspicions. Figure 5.5 shows percent differences in the likelihood of the police finding contraband after discretionary searches of black and white drivers of different ages and genders. Police are strikingly worse at finding contraband on young black men. Consent searches of male motorists under the age of twenty-six are 25 percent less likely to result in contraband if the driver is black; for probable cause searches the difference is 15 percent. For men, these disadvantages appear

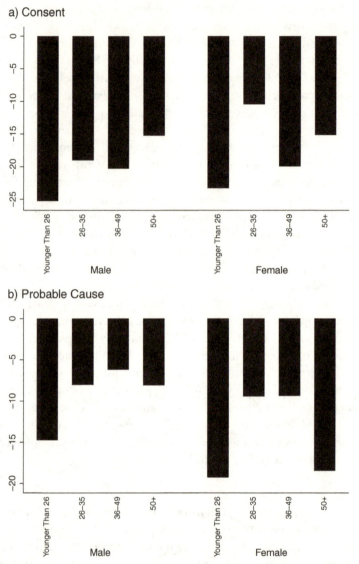

FIGURE 5.5. Percent Difference across Race in Likelihood of Finding Contraband, by Gender and Age
Note: Figures show the percent difference in the likelihood of finding contraband after consent or probable cause searches on black versus white motorists of different genders and ages.

to be slightly mitigated as they increase in age. Black men of any age are less likely to be found with contraband, but for drivers over fifty the differential in the success of discretionary searches is less than for younger drivers. For women the story is more convoluted. Of all the demographic groups in the figure, the contraband differentials are greatest for black women younger than twenty-six and over fifty who are searched with probable cause. This is perhaps because it is very unusual for white women to be searched with probable cause, so the degree to which black women are searched at all can lead to a heightened disparity.

In any case, there can be little doubt that North Carolina's young black men are the primary victims of racially disparate policing. Police suspicions of this demographic group lead them to search young black men at rates that are unjustified given the corresponding hit rates.

A Multivariate Test

Our final analysis of the contraband data is to estimate a series of logistic regressions predicting the occurrence of contraband. The idea is to provide a statistical robustness test for the previous findings. Here, we replicate as closely as possible the analysis from Chapter 4 on the predictors of search. Recall that in that chapter we found that, controlling for all the relevant factors, black and Hispanic drivers, particularly males, were much more likely to be searched. Here we look at who has contraband in the same manner. We have shown that black drivers (and young black men in particular) are less likely to be found with contraband after discretionary searches than are whites; however, we cannot eliminate the possibility that this pattern is being driven, not by race, but by other co-varying factors. So, for example, perhaps the police have lower thresholds for searching motorists who they stop at night because peering into murky backseats makes them nervous. If young black men are more likely to drive late at night, then they would be disproportionally subject to these higher nighttime search rates. This could produce the patterns we observed, but crucially it would be a race-neutral explanation. A regression framework can control for these possibilities, isolating the effects of a driver's race on the probability that contraband is found.

We proceed by estimating four models – one for consent, probable cause, incident to arrest, and protective frisk searches – using data from the top-25 agencies, which together account for 77 percent of all traffic stops. In each case, the dependent variable is dichotomous, coded 1 if contraband was found with the search type in question and 0 if the search was conducted but no contraband was discovered. So the

TABLE 5.7. *Predicting the Discovery of Contraband after Different Types of Search*

Variable	Consent	Probable Cause	Arrest	Frisk
Demographics				
Black	0.78* (0.01)	0.71* (0.01)	1.02 (0.02)	0.74* (0.07)
Hispanic	0.48* (0.01)	0.62* (0.02)	0.56* (0.01)	0.44* (0.07)
Other Race	0.70* (0.04)	0.82* (0.06)	0.68* (0.05)	1.16 (0.39)
Gender	0.91* (0.01)	1.19* (0.02)	1.52* (0.03)	1.63* (0.23)
Age	0.99* (0.00)	0.99 (0.00)	0.98* (0.00)	0.99 (0.00)
Stop Purpose				
Safety				
Speed Limit	–	–	–	–
Stop Light	1.08* (0.03)	1.03 (0.04)	1.11* (0.05)	1.10 (0.22)
Impaired	1.37* (0.08)	0.57* (0.02)	1.15* (0.04)	1.28 (0.35)
Movement	1.10* (0.03)	1.04 (0.03)	1.26* (0.04)	1.11 (0.18)
Investigatory				
Equipment	1.02 (0.02)	0.98 (0.02)	1.18* (0.04)	1.17 (0.17)
Regulatory	0.93* (0.02)	0.88* (0.02)	0.90* (0.03)	0.83 (0.12)
Seat Belt	1.24* (0.04)	1.01 (0.04)	1.44* (0.08)	1.66* (0.33)
Investigation	1.28* (0.03)	1.07* (0.03)	1.50* (0.05)	1.09 (0.16)
Other	1.12* (0.03)	0.97 (0.03)	1.04 (0.04)	0.97 (0.18)
Time				
Hour of Day	Included	Included	Included	Included
Day of Week	Included	Included	Included	Included
N	162,196	90,336	97,167	8,348

* = p-value ≤ 0.05

Note: Models use logistic regression with agency- and officer-level random effects. Coefficients are odd-ratios with standard errors in parentheses. Data is from the top-25 agencies.

analysis focuses exclusively on stops where searches occurred. That is, in Chapter 4 we already generated estimates of who gets searched. Here, we look only at those searches and ask, who gets found with contraband, given that a search has occurred? Independent variables include dichotomous variables for blacks, Hispanics, and "other" races (with whites serving as the excluded category), and gender, which is coded 1 for men. There are also controls for age, the purpose of the traffic stop, the day of the week the stop occurred, and the hour of the day the stop occurred. Additionally, we use officer- and agency-level fixed effects.[6] Table 5.7 shows the results. Coefficients are displayed as odds-ratios; numbers above 1 indicate an increased likelihood, below 1 a decreased likelihood. For example, an odds-ratio of 1.50 associated with the variable for Hispanic would indicate an increased likelihood of 50 percent for finding contraband on Hispanic drivers.

Because we use whites as the excluded racial group, the parameters associated with the variables for blacks, Hispanics, and other races should be understood as the effect of belonging to one of these groups relative to being a white driver. Thus, following consent searches, blacks are 22 percent less likely to be found with contraband than are white drivers, Hispanics are 52 percent less likely, and other races 30 percent less likely. Women are 9 percent less likely to be found with contraband than men following consent searches, but 19 percent more likely to be found with contraband after searches with probable cause. This indicates that police are relatively over-suspicious of men; that is, they are better at determining when a female driver should be searched. So, much like black drivers are viewed with more suspicion than whites and this leads to their being searched at a higher rate, men are viewed with more suspicion than women. In both cases, these suspicions compromise officers' abilities to conduct fruitful searches, rather than augmenting those abilities as *Tactics for Criminal Patrol* implies a reliance on demographics stereotypes will do. The plight of black men is particularly acute as they are the compounding case: both their sex and race work against them.

Crucial to our study are the parameters associated with being black. Earlier we showed that the police are somewhat less likely to find contraband on blacks after discretionary searches, even though blacks were much more likely than whites to experience these types of search. The models demonstrate the robustness of this finding; even controlling for many potentially confounding factors, we find that blacks are less likely to be found with contraband, especially after probable cause searches. Searches that take place incident to arrest are the only type of search where black drivers are more likely to be found with contraband than whites, but this effect is not statistically meaningful. So it is not simply the case that blacks are more likely to drive during periods of heightened police activity or to commit traffic violations that are more likely to end with a search (such as driving drunk). Instead, being black has its own unique and statistically significant effect on the likelihood that the police find contraband. It reduces it. That this effect is negative strongly implies that the police are unduly suspicious of black motorists; race is undeniably part of the traffic stop equation. Moreover, because we are using agency- and officer-level fixed effects, the pattern we observe cannot be dismissed as the work of a few statistically aberrant "bad apples," rather it appears to be a statewide phenomenon.

Finally, we draw attention to the model for protective frisk searches (the right-most model in the table). Table 5.5 showed that the police are about 14 percent more likely to find contraband on blacks following protective frisks than white drivers. However, when controlling for the circumstances of the stop, we find that the police are actually 26 percent less likely to find contraband on blacks after this type of search. This means that when the context of a stop is taken into consideration, the police are less likely to come away with contraband when searching a black driver for every type of search where there is a statistically meaningful difference between blacks and whites.

Conclusion

Every public policy comes with a set of goals and associated costs. Imagine a program evaluator asked to assess the merits of investigatory police stops as a tool in the war on drugs, weighing the pros and cons. She knows that one cost associated with this policy is the gradual alienation of minority communities as they come to see themselves as the target of unwarranted police attention. These long-simmering resentments occasionally give way to violent confrontations, as made evident by the recent events in Charlotte, Ferguson, Baltimore, and New York City. She also knows that police searches, in North Carolina at least, are often racially disparate; the police are systematically worse at searching black motorists. This alone is enough to disqualify investigatory stops as a legitimate practice, but, as a diligent evaluator, she wants to go one step further – the costs are heavy, what are the payoffs? Are investigatory stops useful in cracking down on crime? Data from North Carolina is not encouraging. Officers occasionally find contraband and sometimes that contraband is drugs or weapons, but arrest-worthy contraband is rare, occurring in only 10 percent of searches.

6

Search and Arrest Patterns by Officer and Agency

Data collected through the SBI-122 form include an anonymous identification number for each police officer. By state law this ID number is a public record, but by law it is also anonymous. We therefore do not know even such basics as the gender or race of the officer or their years of tenure on the force. Still, the ID number is an invaluable tool to investigate whether the patterns of racial disparity we have documented can be attributed to just a few "bad apples" on the force or whether they relate to widespread practices common across all officers. An officer-by-officer analysis also allows us to assess the role of discretion.

Political scientists use the term "street level bureaucrat" to describe government employees who regularly interact with the public, such as teachers, social workers, and police officers (see Lipsky 1980). As citizens we have good reason to wonder how much discretion these officials exercise when carrying out their duties. Are teachers following the curriculum? Do they grade assignments in the same manner? Of course we know that every teacher is not identical; some degree of individual variability is expected, and indeed inevitable. In the classroom we can all recall having "hard" and "easy" teachers. The degree of individual-level variability in providing a public service is an important question in any public agency. More than perhaps any other value, public institutions are expected to treat everyone equally. At the same time, we recognize that individual public servants are not robots and we want them to have some flexibility to use their judgment in doing their jobs.

Nowhere is this tension more acute than for police officers. The public does not want police officers enforcing the letter of the law, stopping every motorist who goes 1 mph over the speed limit, but we also recognize that it is inappropriate for officers to act as independent agents, making up the law on their own or enforcing it in an arbitrary manner. Two types of disparity might be of concern: one is systematic bias, where an officer is biased for or against certain types of citizens, enforcing the law differently to each. But another is purely idiosyncratic behavior. The traffic code is a complex set of rules, and some of those rules (such as those against speeding) are routinely violated by the majority of drivers, virtually every day. How many of us have not exceeded 25 mph in a residential zone or 55 on the highway? Do we always come to a complete stop at a stop sign, even when there is no traffic? What would be our response if an officer pulled us over and gave us a ticket for such a violation? They certainly have the legal authority to do so, but we expect some discretion to be used. Knowing the degree to which individual officers differ in their likelihood of issuing a ticket versus a warning, for example, can give us some insight into the degree to which police agencies are able to get their officers to follow agency-wide norms. The degree of variability in outcomes from officer to officer is a good indicator of discretion.

In this chapter we show that there is a lot of discretion. Officers show tremendous variability in their responses to seemingly similar situations. Not only do we focus on officer-to-officer differences here, but we also show sharp variability in basic patterns of behavior from agency to agency. The State Highway Patrol searches about 0.6 percent of the drivers pulled over; in many other jurisdictions, that number is over 10 percent. In order to understand who gets searched, and who gets arrested, we need to understand what drives these agency- and officer-level differences. As it turns out, these are huge determinants of traffic outcomes.

Looking at individual officers also allows us to engage directly with the "bad apple" explanation for racially disparate policing. This is the idea that disparities in the rates at which black and white motorists experience punitive police actions are driven by a small number of officers whose aberrant behavior is driven by racial animus and not reflective of officially sanctioned police protocol. If the disparities we have identified can be attributed to the extreme behavior of a few officers, then this should be made clear by the officer-level analysis we undertake in this chapter, which is designed to identify outlying officers. While we certainly identify a number of officers who do show higher than average levels of disparity, we also show that this is only one of two causes of the disparities we observe. Institutional practices and norms widely shared among most officers are the other.

Officer Discretion

Imagine you are a police officer pulled over on the side of the highway to work a speed control operation. As motorists drive by on their daily commute, you tag them with your radar gun, which tells you their speed. The limit is 55 mph, but almost everyone is driving faster than that, so where do you draw the line? Should you stop a motorist going 60 mph? What about someone driving 64 mph, or 70? You know that legally you can stop anyone going even 1 mph over the speed limit, but time constraints (and common sense) make such an approach impractical. Further, your supervisor or your training may have given you guidelines, and those may have included instructions that certain forms of traffic violations, such as driving with traffic even if over the speed limit, do not merit a traffic stop. Still, the law allows you to make that stop. So enforcing the traffic laws inevitably means operating in a legal gray zone; when everyone is breaking the law, officers must decide for themselves whom to stop. You may have orders one day to focus on keeping the traffic moving, so perhaps you sit back and wait for a truly egregious speeder, someone driving fast and recklessly. Or perhaps instructions have come down to be less tolerant and to stop as many people as you can before your shift is over. Maybe it is an order by the supervisor, perhaps it is based on differences in approach by different officers, perhaps it depends on your mood, or maybe it depends on the time of day or road conditions. There may be less incentive to pull over a speeder during a busy morning rush hour where traffic is moving smoothly but where many drivers are speeding. On the other hand, someone speeding faster than traffic safely allows during a rainstorm might be cause for more concern. The point is that some level of discretion is inevitable: we do not expect a robotic or automatic enforcement of every traffic law; if we did, traffic would come to a halt.

Officer discretion does not end when the stop is made. Having pulled someone over, you now must decide if you want to issue them a warning (verbal or written), write them a ticket, or search their vehicle. When you find a small amount of contraband, such as alcohol in the car of an underage driver, do you make an arrest? Or maybe a conversation with the parents seems to make more sense.

The NC DOJ dataset records 99,750 officers as having made a traffic stop in North Carolina between 2002 and 2015. Of these, only 20,887 made at least 100 stops, but these officers together represent 96 percent of all the traffic stops in the database.[1] It is easy to imagine that given such a range of individuals, there will be great variance in enforcement behavior, with some officers behaving more leniently and others much more strictly. But officers are not lone actors; rather their behavior derives at least in part from institutional training and expectations. If these expectations are rigidly enforced, then we would expect officers to behave more or less the same, controlling for the circumstances. So we are curious about how these countervailing forces – individualism versus institutionalism – resolve themselves. Do officers display coherent enforcement behavior or act idiosyncratically?

Figure 6.1 begins to answer this question by plotting the distributions of outcome rates by officer.

Note that the figure includes only officers with at least 100 stops to avoid drawing conclusions on the basis of small numbers. If there is an overarching institutional standard to which officers gravitate, then we would expect a large clustering of observations at some point along the x-axis. For example, perhaps citing around 60 percent of motorists and letting the remaining 40 percent go with a warning is common practice. In that case, we would expect the "Citations" distribution (the top-left panel in the figure) to spike at 60, which we could then consider the equilibrium point – a level of ticketing that best conforms to institutional standards for officer behavior.

However, the distributions provide scant evidence that any such behavioral equilibrium exists. Instead each distribution reveals a wide range of officer behavior, with some officers citing fewer than 20 percent of the motorists they pull over and others citing 100 percent. Recall that we are looking only at officers with at least 100 stops, so the patterns that emerge are not the result of statistical flukes (for example, an officer that stopped only five people and ticketed them all). Still, while the distributions show too much officer-level variation to suggest any firm institutional standard, there is some evidence of behavioral norms at work. The citations distribution has a very steep left shoulder, as there are few officers who are extremely lenient, issuing citations in fewer than 20 percent of stops. Instead, the distribution comes to a moderate peak around 45 percent. For "light penalties" (no action stops, verbal, and written warnings, taken together) the distribution peaks around 58 percent, but observations drop off rapidly moving further along the x-axis. Taken together, the steep left shoulder of the citations distribution and steep right shoulder of the light penalties distribution suggests that officers are encouraged (either through institutional directives, cultural norms, or both) not to be overly lenient. Arrests and searches are

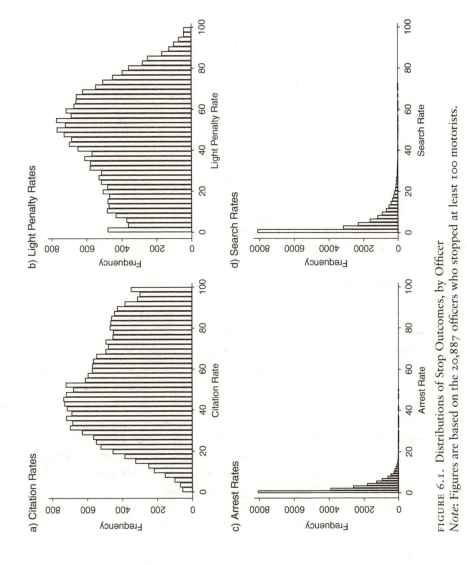

FIGURE 6.1. Distributions of Stop Outcomes, by Officer

Note: Figures are based on the 20,887 officers who stopped at least 100 motorists.

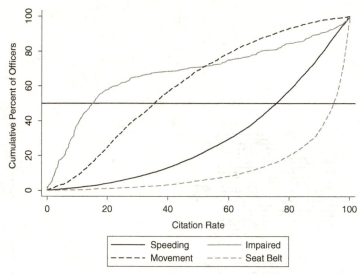

FIGURE 6.2. Citation Rates for Four Types of Stop, by Officer
Note: Each density plot includes every officer who has stopped at least 100 drivers for the indicated purpose. The numbers included are 9,306 for speeding, 230 for driving impaired, 2,465 for safe movement, and 2,860 for seat belt violations.

rare; many officers with at least 100 stops have never conducted either activity.

Of course, one explanation for the lack of clear-cut institutional standards may be that officers within in the same police department have different jobs. An officer working an overnight shift might stop a lot of drunk drivers, who will be dealt with more harshly. On the other hand, an officer working speed control may be more inclined to be lenient, simply writing out a lot of tickets but only rarely searching and arresting motorists. Controlling for this possibility is difficult without any information about the patrols that officers are assigned to work, but we can gain some insights by controlling for the type of stop. Thus Figure 6.2 dives deeper into the citations data, with cumulative frequency plots for citation rates following stops for speeding, driving impaired, safe movement, and seat belt violations. This allows us to look at the rates at which different officers issue citations for drivers pulled over for the same reasons.

A cumulative density plot shows how many observations occur at different values along the x-axis, which in this case is measuring citation rates. For instance, the line for speeding slopes gently upward, indicating a relatively even distribution of observations across various citation rates. By the time we research the end of the x-axis (where an officer issues a citation after 100 percent of stops), we have accounted for all of the officer-level observations, and thus each line culminates in the right-uppermost point of the plot.

Note that the line for each type of stop (speeding, driving impaired, safe movement, and seat belt violations) has a different slope, so clearly the type of stop is important in determining what happens next. If we look at the point corresponding to 50 percent of the officers (indicated in the plot with a horizontal line), we can see what "typically" happens when a driver is pulled over for one of the four reasons laid out in the graph. Speeders and those without seatbelts are more likely to get a ticket than those with DWI or safe movement stops. The graph does not indicate it, but this is because the DWI drivers are more likely to be arrested. In any case, if every police officer followed the same pattern of behavior, the cumulative frequency distribution would jump immediately from zero percent of officers giving a ticket for a certain kind of stop to 100 percent doing so. If there were no norms at all, and officers ranged evenly from zero to 100 percent in their likelihood of giving a ticket, then the graph would move in a straight, diagonal line from lower-left to upper-right. In other words, the slopes of the lines are an indication of how closely all officers across the state follow the same norms. And the graph makes clear that there is a lot of discretion: officers vary dramatically in the likelihood that they will give a ticket for drivers pulled over for the same reason.

We have documented that there is a wide range of behavior among individual officers. As we discussed, there is no reason to expect that all officers (or all agencies) should be identical. A great deal of variability is associated with each traffic stop, and the SBI-122 form simply does not cover that range of circumstances. Still, the wide range of search rates, for example, could mean that the vast majority of searches could have been conducted by just a few officers. The wide variability across officers in traffic stops outcomes that we see across the dataset raises the possibility that any racial differences in these same outcomes could hypothetically be due only to a few "rogue" or "bad apple" officers. Just a few such officers systematically targeting minority drivers could generate disparities across the board, even if most officers are treating drivers equitably with regards to race. We assess that possibility in the following section.

Blaming Bad Apples

Eric Garner was killed by New York City police officers on July 17th, 2014 after he was put in a chokehold while being arrested. Footage of the incident revealed that Garner repeated "I can't breathe" eleven times before finally passing out. He was subsequently taken to a hospital and an hour later was pronounced dead. After a Staten Island grand jury failed to indict the officer who had administered the fatal chokehold, protests swept the nation with thousands taking to the streets in New York, Boston, and Washington DC. Garner's last words of "I can't breathe" were immortalized by the emerging Black Lives Matter movement.

Following Garner's death, the New York Police Department (NYPD) came under intense scrutiny and Bill Bratton, the Police Commissioner, appeared to acknowledge a need for some changes. During a meeting of NYPD chiefs, Bratton showed a video montage of police brutality and stated:

The reality is at this moment – that there's some in this organization – who shouldn't be here. They're not the right fit at the NYPD in 2014. There are a few – and a very few in a very large organization – who just don't get it. They don't understand that when they take that oath of office and put that shield on, that they commit to constitutional policing, respectful policing, compassionate policing. (Parascandola, Moore, and Siemaszko 2014)

These comments adhere closely to the bad apple line of defense, which is to acknowledge some shortcomings but to lay the blame at the feet of a few deviants, rather than admit systemic failures. For as long as people have been taking issue with police misconduct, police chiefs have been blaming bad apples. In this section, we take these claims seriously and test for them statistically. We have documented substantial disparities in the way that black and white motorists experience justice on the roadways, and, statistically, it is possible that these trends are being driven by a small number of highly deviant officers. If this is the case, then we would expect to observe that most officers search, arrest, and ticket black and white motorists at similar rates, but that a few treat black motorists much more harshly. Conversely, it is possible that the problem is systemic. In that case, we would expect to find that black motorists are treated more harshly (perhaps only slightly so) by a great many officers. This possibility can be thought of as the implicit bias or systemic cause hypothesis. It is important to know: are racial disparities driven by "bad apples," by institutional patterns, or both?

Our investigation into bad apples begins with scatter plots showing the relationship between the number of whites and blacks stopped by every officer in our dataset. Recall that according to the 2010 Census about 69 percent of North Carolina residents are white as compared to 22 percent black. So, given these population statistics, we would expect that the average officer will have more interactions with white drivers; if traffic stops were proportionate to population share, then any given officer would be expected, on average, to pull over 3.14 whites for every black encountered.[2] Figure 6.3 shows that officers do indeed pull over more whites than blacks, though the ratio is not equal to that of the population.

Specifically, the "average rate" lines show that officers stop 1.73 whites for every black for safety purposes and 1.16 whites for every black for investigatory stops.[3] The solid black line shows the "population stop rate," where a dot would fall if an officer stopped whites and blacks at the same rate as they exist in the population. In both plots, the average rate line falls well to the right of the population rate, indicating that even though whites are more likely to be stopped, blacks are stopped in numbers that far exceed their representation in the population. Moreover, a side-by-side comparison reveals that while whites are more likely to be stopped in both cases, the grey average line hews much further from the solid black line in the investigatory plot, indicating a greater disparity between the population rate and the stop rate. Although blacks are greatly outnumbered by whites in the population, they are stopped almost as often for investigatory purposes. When stops focus on traffic safety, they come closer to the population rates.

Figure 6.4 shifts the focus to searches, once again dividing the data by safety and investigatory purposes. Chapter 4 showed that statewide blacks are searched at a higher rate than whites, but that these disparities were most pronounced for investigatory stops. Now we see the full effect of that differential. In the plots below, we show the average search rate and compare it to the average stop rate from Figure 6.3. If officers searched blacks and whites at equal rates, then the search rates per officer would be identical to the stop rates. We find that this is far from the case. As the note to the figure indicates, following an investigatory stop an average of 0.28 whites are searched for every one black motorist; for safety stops the ratio is 0.80 to 1, but this still deviates greatly from the average stop rate.

So far, we can say that the evidence points toward broad systemic differences common to many police officers, rather than to a "bad apple"

a) Safety

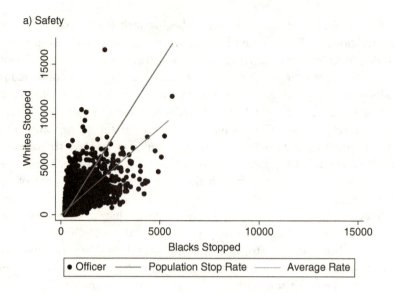

b) Investigatory

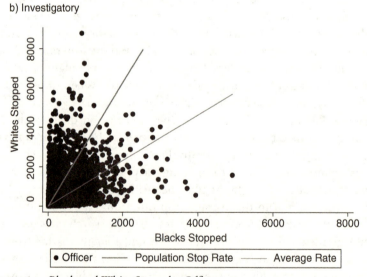

FIGURE 6.3. Black and White Stops, by Officer
Note: Officers stop 1.73 whites for each black for safety stops and 1.16 whites for each black for investigatory stops. The population share is 3.14 whites for each black. N = 20,887 officers who stopped at least 100 motorists.

a) Safety

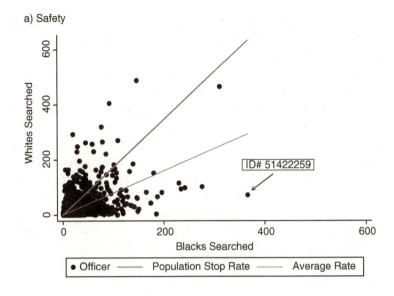

b) Investigatory

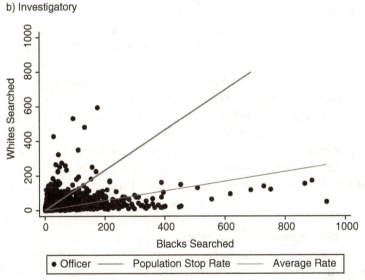

FIGURE 6.4. Black and White Searches, by Officer

Note: Officers search 0.80 whites for each black after safety stops and 0.28 whites for each black after investigatory stops. N = 4,123 officers with at least 100 stops and a minimum of 10 searches of whites and 10 searches of blacks. The safety plot excludes one officer with greater than 800 searches of whites for visual clarity.

hypothesis. Notice that the vast majority of officers are clustered in the lower-left of the graphs and that for investigatory stops, where disparities are concentrated, these dots tilt toward the x-axis. However, Figure 6.4 does show a number of outlying officers. Take, for example, officer #51422259 who, following safety stops, has searched almost 400 blacks but only around 100 whites. This officer made over 9,000 stops for the Charlotte-Mecklenburg Police Department between 2004 to 2016, 74 percent of which featured black drivers. At the same time, we see a few officers at the upper-left of the graph who searched around 400 whites but fewer than 200 blacks. Looking at the investigatory stops shows a similar pattern: a few officers do indeed seem to search vast numbers of blacks but few whites, but then again there are a number at the upper-left of the graph as well, who are much more likely to search whites than blacks. All this could be driven by factors such as operating in areas where there are simply more drivers of one race or another.

Looking at the broad patterns apparent in Figures 6.3 and 6.4, there is no question that blacks are much more likely to be pulled over than their share in the population (or the driving population), and that, once pulled over, if the stop is for investigatory reasons they are much more likely to be searched. These are broad patterns that emerge from our assessment of every officer across the state who has conducted a minimum of 100 traffic stops. This means that the disparities we have documented are suggestive of systemic or institutional patterns. Although bad apples might very well exist and we have certainly found some officers who stand out as unusually disparate, they do not appear to be driving the overall trends.

But before we discount the "bad apple" hypothesis, let us control for what drivers the individual officer pulls over and see what happens, on average, for that particular officer, to white and black drivers. For this, we simply need to look at the racial mix of drivers pulled over, per officer, as well as the racial mix of those the officer searches. One possibility that we want to take seriously is that officers might direct attention to motorists that look "out of place," for example, a young black man driving in a predominantly white part of town. If this is the case, then officers assigned to patrol white neighborhoods should be more likely to search black drivers, as the few black drivers they encounter appear all the more suspicious for their relative scarcity. Conversely, officers who work in mixed or black neighborhoods should be somewhat less suspicious of black drivers and therefore less inclined to search them. Counterintuitively, this would suggest that the officers who conduct the fewest stops of blacks as a proportion of their total traffic stops should have the highest black search rates.

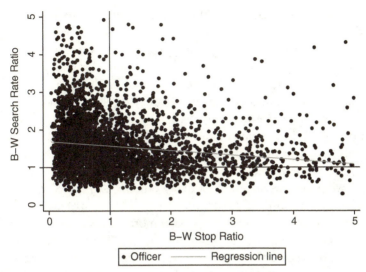

FIGURE 6.5. Black–White Stop and Search Ratios, by Officer
Note: Based on 4,123 officers with at least 100 stops and 10 searches of black and white motorists. Excludes 28 officers with B-W search ratios above 5 and 126 with stop ratios above 5 for the purposes of visual clarity. Including these outlying officers does not substantively change the results. Slope of regression line is statistically significant at -0.120 with an adjusted R-squared of 0.023.

Figure 6.5 tests this idea using a scatter plot to show the relationship between black-white stop and search ratios. Imagine for example an officer who has pulled over eighty white motorists and twenty black motorists. We would calculate this officer's black-white stop ratio as 0.25, indicating that they have stopped four times as many white drivers. This number determines the officer's location along the x-axis in the figure. Now imagine that out of those twenty black drivers, the officer in question searched ten, while searching only ten out of eighty white drivers. The officer's search rate for blacks is 10 divided by 20 (50 percent) and 10 divided by 80 (12.5 percent) for whites. The black-white search ratio can then be calculated as 50 divided by 12.5 (4), which determines the officer's position along the y-axis. The figure shows the stop ratio compared to the search ratio by race for 4,123 officers who have pulled over at least 100 drivers and searched at least ten white and ten black motorists (the same threshold we use in Figure 6.4).

As expected, the figure reveals an inverse relationship between stop and search ratios, but only a slight one; the slope of the regression line is -0.12. Officers who stop a greater proportion of black drivers are less inclined to search them disproportionately compared to white drivers. On the other hand, officers who stop mostly white drivers (to the left of the line indicating the 1.0 equality line for stops) are more inclined to search those blacks whom they do stop. Note that many individual officers (those at the extreme left of the graph) rarely seem to encounter any black drivers. But on average when they do they are more likely to search them (some are five times as likely). A few officers, toward the right of the graph, encounter many more blacks than whites. The level of disparity in their search rates, on average, is slightly lower. Note, however, that in the figure the regression line never crosses the horizontal equality line; if we do not exclude any outlying officers then the regression line crosses only when officers stop almost ten times as many black motorists. This means that officers must stop many more blacks than whites before whites begin to look "out of place." If it is true that the traffic stops an officer makes reflect the racial make-up of the area in which they are patrolling, then it would seem that whites in a black area do not appear to raise the same suspicions as blacks in a white area.

Finally, if we could count "bad apples," how many would we find? When police chiefs use the term bad apple, they are often referring to officers who act on the basis of racial cues or outright racial animus, officers "who just don't get it," as Commissioner Bratton put it in the quote above. We have no way of knowing what is in an officer's mind when they search a motorist, so instead we must settle for identifying officers who are much more likely to search black drivers as compared to white drivers. Recall that Figure 6.1 shows that officers differ dramatically in the rates at which they search drivers in general: most officers search very few, but some search more than 10 percent of the drivers they pull over. Figure 6.6 looks separately at safety and investigatory stops and simply plots every officer in the state meeting a threshold of at least fifty stops of white drivers, fifty stops of black drivers, and an overall search rate above the state average (3.36), showing the percent of black and white drivers searched. Three lines appear on each graph: a dark solid line representing the equal search rate, and two gray lines indicating the 1:2 rate and the 2:1 rate; officers above or below those rates have more than double the search rate of one race than the other. We use a hollow dot for officers who are twice as likely to search blacks (these officers appear at the lower-right of each graph) and for officers who are twice as likely to search whites (grouped at the upper-left of the graphs).

Looking first at the plot for safety stops, we see that 857 officers (out of the 2,820 who meet our threshold requirements) are twice as likely

a) Safety

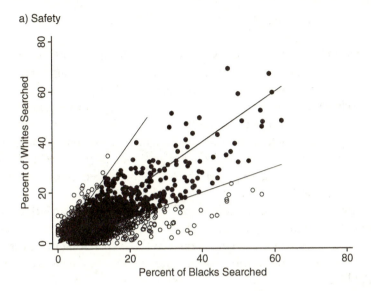

b) Investigatory

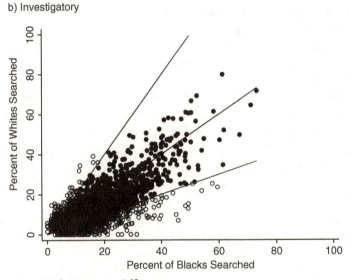

FIGURE 6.6. High Disparity Officers

Note: Among safety stops, the figure includes 2,820 officers with a minimum of 50 white stops, 50 black stops, and a search rate above the state average of 3.36. The hollow circles indicate high disparity officers. Of these officers, 857 search blacks at more than twice the rate that they search whites; 201 officers search whites at more than twice the rate that they search blacks. For investigatory stops, the figure includes 4,423 officers with a minimum of 50 white stops, 50 black stops, and a search rate above the state average of 3.36. The hollow circles indicate high disparity officers. Of these officers, 1,330 search blacks at more than twice the rate that they search whites; 156 officers search whites at more than twice the rate that they search blacks. Because investigatory stops have higher search rates in general, the two parts of the figure are scaled differently.

to search blacks, compared to 201 officers who are twice as likely to search whites. The plot for investigatory stops tells a similar story; 1,330 officers are twice as likely to search blacks and 156 are twice as likely to search whites. Overall, 37 percent of the officers in the safety stops figure fall outside of the 2:1 bounds: 30 percent below the lower bound (searching more blacks), and 7 percent above the upper bound (searching more whites than blacks). For the investigatory stops, 33 percent fall outside of the 2:1 bounds, 30 percent below, and 3 percent above. That is a lot of bad apples!

It is clear that some officers search whites at higher rates than they search blacks. But the graphs also show that the black search rates tend to be much higher than the white search rates, even among those officers with 2 to 1 search disparities. For investigatory stops, the median search rate of black drivers by officers who search blacks twice as often is 10.16, while for whites the comparable statistic is 8.52. For safety stops, the median search rate of blacks among the high disparity officers on the black side is 9.13 compared to 6.34 for whites. Glancing at the figures, it is clear not only that there are many more officers disproportionately searching large percentages of blacks as compared to whites, but also that those search rates are more extreme.

Do the data presented in Figure 6.6 support the bad apple hypothesis? They certainly do identify a number of officers, about one-third of the total, who have very high (greater than double) rates of searching one race rather than the other race. And the vast majority of these outlier officers show a propensity to search blacks more than whites, rather than the reverse. So, on first glance, that is a lot of bad apples. But the data also show a systematic tendency across all the officers to search blacks at a slightly higher rate, on average. If we were to draw a regression line through the two parts of Figure 6.6, it would show that the typical officer searches 0.60 and 0.73 percent of white drivers for every one percent of black drivers they search, for safety and investigatory stops, respectively. This relationship is highly significant statistically and reflects the central tendency of all the officers, not just those we have identified as outliers. In other words, there is a general pattern of 30 to 40 percent difference, and in addition to this, there are bad apples, at least insofar as we have defined them.

Racial disparities in traffic stops come both from widespread institutional practices and norms as well as from the actions of a minority of officers with much higher than average racial disparities in their actions. We have identified these "outlier officers" here by a conservative methodology: those who have stopped a minimum of fifty whites as well as fifty blacks and who have a relatively high search rate, compared to other officers. Even with this method, we have identified over 2,000 outliers, about one-third of the total. It is hard to call one-third of the total a set of "bad apples." Rather, these are officers who fall not very far from the norms which are enforced and encouraged throughout their agencies. Of course, as we have stressed throughout this chapter, very few norms seem to be enforced very closely, at least with regards to what happens after a stop. Rates of ticketing, warning, searching, and arrest differ dramatically from officer to officer. We should therefore not be surprised that racial differences differ dramatically in the same manner. But we cannot put the bulk of our findings on racial disparities at the feet of just a few officers; these reflect widespread practices. In the next section, we show similar dramatic differences not from officer to officer, but across the many different independent police agencies charged with enforcing the law throughout the state.

Bad Apple Agencies

Imagine if a police department did nothing to discourage (or perhaps even implicitly encouraged) the use of racial profiling by their officers. The result could be an entire department of officers who are much more likely to target black motorists. In fact, it is possible that the huge number of "high disparity" officers that we identified in Figure 6.6 could come disproportionately from only a handful of police agencies. Then the problem would be much more circumspect; instead of a statewide issue, attention could be focused on bringing these few deviant agencies in line with statewide standards.

Before replicating Figure 6.6 for agencies rather than for officers, let us first review the wide variation at which the various police departments search the drivers their officers pull over. Figure 6.7 presents a histogram similar to that presented in Figure 6.1 showing the number of agencies with various search rates. Recall that here we are looking not at individual officers, but at the rate of search across entire departments. Table 6.1 presents the highest and lowest search rate departments across the state.

If clear from the early parts of this chapter that individual police officers across the state have great discretion, these data make clear that agencies do as well. For example, according to the data, five agencies search less than 1 percent of drivers. The State Highway Patrol stands out as having

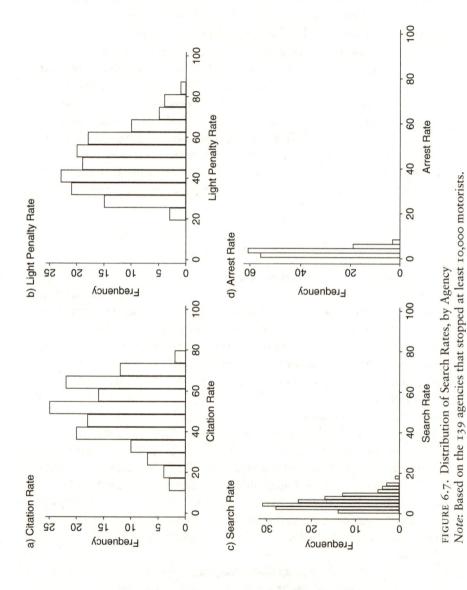

FIGURE 6.7. Distribution of Search Rates, by Agency

Note: Based on the 139 agencies that stopped at least 10,000 motorists.

TABLE 6.1. *High and Low Search Rate Agencies*

Part A. High Search Rate Agencies

Agency Name	Total Stops	Search Rate
Rutherford County Sheriff's Office	10,940	18.74
Burke County Sheriff's Office	11,296	14.59
Iredell County Sheriff's Office	37,809	14.57
Halifax County Sheriff's Office	18,804	14.21
Davidson County Sheriff's Office	31,937	13.56
Wilson County Sheriff's Office	22,901	13.00
Johnston County Sheriff's Office	31,304	12.97
Alamance County Sheriff's Office	33,772	12.69
Lincolnton Police Department	12,499	11.71
Haywood County Sheriff's Office	10,331	10.95

Part B. Low Search Rate Agencies

Agency Name	Total Stops	Search Rate
SHP – Motor Carrier Enforcement Section	104,772	0.20
NC State Highway Patrol	8,745,844	0.62
Elizabeth City Police Department	61,434	0.84
Fuquay-Varina Police Department	34,267	0.87
Youngsville Police Department	14,902	1.18
Blowing Rock Police Department	15,602	1.42
NC DMV, License and Theft Bureau	68,369	1.47
Tarboro Police Department	41,313	1.72
Morrisville Police Department	32,929	1.72
Appalachian State University Police Department	17,668	1.74
UNC Chapel Hill University Police Department	28,095	1.79
Total for the state	20 million	3.41

made almost 9 million stops (43 percent of total stops between 2002 and 2016) but having an extremely low search rate; the Highway Patrol appears to be a "ticketing machine" in the sense that they pull motorists over in high volume but are not particularly concerned with finding contraband. On the other hand, officers from Rutherford County Sheriff's Office searched close to 19 percent of all the drivers that they stopped. Of course, in some cases, low or high search rates make sense according to the jurisdictional nature of the agency; the Motor Carrier Enforcement Section is not designed to uncover illegal contraband and it is unsurprising that the NC DMV's License and Theft Bureau conduct few searches.

Given that there is great variability in search rates by agency, it is possible that racial disparities could also be driven by a few "bad apple" agencies. To explore this possibility, we replicate Figure 6.6 at the agency level. So rather than calculating search rates for individual officers, we calculate them for entire agencies, with all the stops and searches conducted by officers employed by an agency assessed collectively. The results are shown in Figure 6.8 and are presented in the same format as Figure 6.6.

For safety stops, forty-three out of 255 agencies are twice as likely to search black drivers, ten are twice as likely to search whites. Investigatory stops show a similar pattern. So, once again, we seem to have a great many bad apples. For safety stops, 17 percent of agencies search blacks twice as often as they search white motorists; for investigatory stops, 16 percent of agencies are at least twice as likely to search black drivers. Comparably, only 4 and 2 percent of agencies search whites twice as often. The figures make clear a broad pattern that most agencies tend to search blacks more often than whites, though not always. Just like with officers, it seems that we need to take seriously both the "institutional practice" and the "bad apple" hypothesis.

Finally, we take a closer look at the relative usage of safety and investigatory stops by police agencies. Search disparities are especially pronounced for investigatory stops, so we want to know how heavily police agencies rely on these types of stop. To that end, we calculate the percentage of total stops that are either safety or investigatory. For example, if an agency conducted 10,000 stops and 7,000 are safety stops, then 70 percent of that agency's stops are related to safety and the remaining 30 percent are for investigatory purposes. Figure 6.9 plots the cumulative densities of percentage investigatory stops for white and black drivers.

Figure 6.9 reveals that very few agencies make less than 20 percent of total stops for investigatory purposes. Gradually, the cumulative density increases moving along the x-axis until the proportion of total stops that are investigatory reaches approximately 30 percent, at which point the density curve climbs upward rapidly. This indicates that for the vast majority of policy agencies investigatory stops make up between 30 percent and 60 percent of total stops; we gain a lot of observations along a short stretch of the x-axis. The density curve then levels off after 60 percent when it reaches almost 100 percent. This means that very few agencies conduct greater than 60 percent of stops for investigatory reasons. The cumulative density functions for safety stops are simply the inverse of what is shown in the figure, since by definition stops which are not investigatory are safety-related.

a) Safety

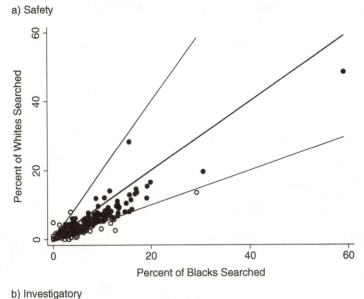

b) Investigatory

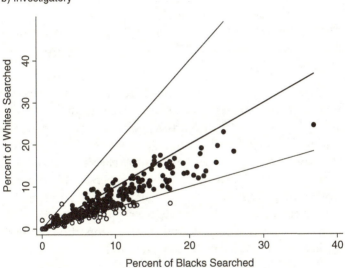

FIGURE 6.8. High Disparity Agencies

Note: For safety stops, the figure includes 255 agencies with a minimum of 50 white stops and 50 black stops. The hollow circles indicate high disparity agencies. Of these agencies, 43 search blacks at more than twice the rate that they search whites; 10 agencies search whites at more than twice the rate that they search blacks. For investigatory stops, the figure includes 249 agencies with a minimum of 50 white stops and 50 black stops. The hollow circles indicate high disparity agencies. Of these agencies, 39 search blacks at more than twice the rate that they search whites; 5 agencies search whites at more than twice the rate that they search blacks.

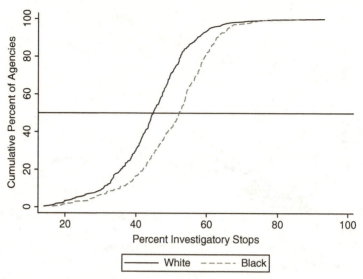

FIGURE 6.9. Percentage of Investigatory Stops, by Agency
Note: Based on the 271 agencies with a minimum of 50 stops of whites and 50 stops of blacks.

Taken together, the density curves for black and white drivers provide a stark visual depiction of the degree to which investigatory stops are disproportionately focused on North Carolina's black community. The curve for black drivers is well to the right of the one for whites. Looking at the horizontal line at 50 percent, which reflects the median or typical police agency, white drivers see about 40 percent investigatory stops and therefore 60 percent safety-related ones. The line for black drivers is moved about eight percentage points to the right, which means that in the typical agency blacks see a significantly higher proportion of their traffic stops for investigatory reasons, as compared to traffic safety.

Conclusion

Analysis in this chapter has revealed two things about North Carolina police officers. First, we discovered that there do not appear to be any firm institutional standards to which officers gravitate. Instead officers display widely divergent enforcement behavior; some issue tickets after almost every stop, others almost never do so. In fact, this finding was not surprising. In any given year, thousands of officers patrol the motorways and there are limits to what institutional training can achieve in promoting uniform behavior. Moreover, some degree of officer discretion is undoubtedly a good thing; an enforcement strategy that works well in one community may be a bad fit for another. For example, officers patrolling poor neighborhoods may be more inclined to be lenient when it comes to vehicular equipment violations, knowing that for most drivers a citation would be a substantial burden. Still, we wonder about the oversight most officers receive after being sworn into the force. As noted previously, while police agencies are required to collect and submit data gathered with the SBI-122 form, the information is not re-disseminated to the agencies in a manner conducive for executive oversight. Thus a powerful management tool, one that would help police chiefs address wayward behavior, is squandered.

Our second finding was that the bad apple line of defense has very little justification in North Carolina. This is not to say that police agencies do not have bad apples; any sizeable organization has some employees that do their jobs poorly. But blaming racial tension between police departments and minority communities on the deviant behavior of a few officers misses the point. Racial disparities in searching and the use of investigatory traffic stops are to blame for these tensions, and they result from the collective behavior of a great many police officers, not a deviant few. Indeed many entire departments have highly disparate patterns. Thus the major take-away from the chapter is that the problems we have documented are systemic, the result of widespread institutional standards that pressure officers, either explicitly or implicitly, to direct undue attention to minority drivers.

7

Profiling Hispanics, Profiling Blacks

Investigatory traffic stops are the fighting edge of the crackdown on crime and, as our analysis has shown, they are used disproportionately on black drivers. In this chapter, we focus on Hispanic drivers because the particular forms of disparity apparent between how black and white drivers are treated on the roads may not be the same for Hispanics. While both black and Hispanic drivers may face similar targeting because of a profile associated with the war on crime, Hispanic drivers also face issues related to immigration status. This has a very different set of implications as far as age and gender are concerned. Women may be targeted, and older drivers as well if an officer is seeking to look into a driver's immigration status. Logistic regressions from Chapter 4 suggested that Hispanic drivers suffer from many of the same forms of disparity as we have noted for black drivers, compared to whites. Hispanics are more likely to be ticketed, searched, and arrested than whites. We also saw that Hispanics are far more likely than either blacks or whites to be subjected to fruitless search: contraband hit rates are particularly low for Hispanic men. In this chapter, we take a closer look at Hispanics to see how these disparities break down by age, gender, officer, and search type. We do this as a single chapter because many of the patterns we observed in comparing black and white drivers will be repeated here, with some key differences. The key distinction is the fact that, among Hispanic drivers, there may be two types of police investigatory interest: criminal behavior, and immigration status. The first produces patterns similar to what we have already observed, but the second typically is not a concern among black drivers.

Profiling Criminals, Profiling the Undocumented

Stereotypes about "criminal aliens" have long been a part of the American cultural ethos. Hispanic immigrants in particular have been singled out as violent, and, paradoxically, as both lazy and job-stealing (Martinez 2002; Bender 2003; Warner 2005). These stereotypes persist despite the fact that studies consistently show that new immigrants are less likely to commit serious crimes than native-born citizens (Simes and Waters 2014; Dingeman and Rumbaut 2010). A result of deep economic and cultural misgivings about recent immigrants is that the US justice system is designed to treat non-citizens much more harshly. Perhaps the most flagrant example of this is a statutory requirement passed by Congress in 2009 that US Immigration and Customs Enforcement (ICE) maintain a mandatory minimum of at least 34,000 detention beds on a daily basis. That is, ICE is required to keep at least 34,000 suspected illegal immigrants behind bars at all times. This type of bed-quota would be unthinkable if applied to US citizens. As the American Immigration Council puts it, "clearly, such a concept has nothing to do with fighting crime or protecting the public. But when it comes to the detention (and deportation) of immigrants, very different standards of justice are at work" (Ewing, Martinez, and Rumbaut 2015, 3).

While the police are typically not involved in immigration issues, which are a federal function, there has been pressure for states and local police agencies to cooperate with ICE, in particular since the 1996 passage of the Immigration Reform and Immigrant Responsibility Act (IRIRA). This law enabled local police departments to enter into Memoranda of Agreement (MOA) with the federal government to enforce national immigration policies, under section 287(g). Agencies with these 287(g) agreements may turn over suspected illegal aliens to federal officials. As of 2017, several agencies in North Carolina were signatories, mostly for their county jails, meaning that those sent to jail may be turned over to federal authorities, but others theoretically should not be (see United States Immigration and Customs Enforcement 2017). All this has meant that many local law enforcement agencies have become involved in monitoring citizenship status as well as road safety. Further, undocumented drivers often lack a valid driver's license, which of course can lead to citation or arrest.

State legislatures have put forward their own approaches to illegal immigration, which often rely heavily on local law enforcement to find and arrest immigrants (Boushey and Luedtke 2011; Chavez and Provine

2009). Between 2006 and 2008, approximately 2,400 anti-immigration bills were introduced in forty-four state houses (Huerta-Bapat 2017). Consequently, the aggressiveness with which law enforcement police for immigration status is highly variable, by state and even by community.

At one end of the scale is Arizona, which generated headlines (and lawsuits) in 2010 when the legislature passed the *Support Our Law Enforcement and Safe Neighborhoods Act* (S.B. 1070), requiring police officers to attempt to determine motorists' immigration status following a traffic stop. Critics argued that this provision of the law was tantamount to legalizing racial profiling, as the police would undoubtedly be more likely to suspect Hispanic motorists of being illegal immigrants (Lach 2012). But, in *Arizona v. United States* (2012), the Supreme Court disagreed, ruling that the "papers please" component of the statute was constitutional. Together with the *Whren* decision, the *Arizona* ruling paves the way for police to use investigatory traffic stops in an effort to find illegal immigrants. *Whren* had focused more on criminal suspicion, but in *Arizona* the focus was clearly on citizenship status.

Concerns over illegal immigration appear to be growing, and since the election of President Trump in 2016 we can expect it to continue to be high. There is a robust relationship between economic hardship and harsh attitudes toward recent immigrants (Jaret 1999; Chavez 2008). The 2008 recession and somewhat lackluster recovery (at least throughout rural America) made Hispanic immigrants a go-to target for a resurgent populist movement, as made evident by the election of Donald Trump who campaigned on an explicitly anti-immigration platform, promising to build a wall between the USA and Mexico. These tensions are certainly present in North Carolina, which saw its Hispanic population more than double between 2000 and 2010. Today, around 10 percent of the population is Hispanic. This rapid growth has created consternation among both political parties. Beverly Perdue, the Democratic governor from 2009 to 2013, included cracking down on illegal immigrants as part of her campaign messaging. These sentiments were reflected in House Bill 318, called the *Protect North Carolina Workers Act*, which was signed into law by Republican Governor Pat McCrory in 2015. A key provision was to eliminate "sanctuary cities" by prohibiting local municipalities from turning a blind eye to potential illegal immigrants. Hispanic advocacy groups had urged the governor to veto the bill (Santiago and Burns 2015). One popular enforcement strategy in the effort to arrest illegal immigrants has been the establishment of roadblocks (vehicle checkpoints) in predominantly Hispanic neighborhoods (Capps et al.

2011; Nguyen and Gill 2015). And, of course, this kind of target enforcement is legal under the *Whren* and *Arizona* rulings. Vehicle checkpoints are a particular focus in the 1999 legislation mandating data collection in North Carolina traffic stops, and we will explore their use here.

Immigration status notwithstanding, Hispanics are also ethnic minorities. Johnson (2004, 7) reminds us that "the vast majority of today's immigrants to the United States – as many as 80 to 90 percent each year – are people of color. Consequently, an attack on immigrants disproportionately affects people of color." Even without the shadow of immigration hanging over them, Hispanic drivers might attract disproportionate attention from the police simply by virtue of their minority status, just as blacks do.

However repurposed, the challenges and accompanying flaws of investigatory traffic stops as a policing strategy remain the same. Just as there are not many drug dealers on the motorways there are not so many illegal immigrants as compared to legal residents. More importantly, separating lawbreakers from innocent drivers by sight remains an exercise in guesswork. This means that many Americans of Hispanic descent will be needlessly inconvenienced, humiliated, and alienated by the police. And with that greater possible police scrutiny, even legal residents may pay a heavy cost: after all, increased police scrutiny to any one group in the population is not consistent with the constitutional provision of equal protection, and they may see the police as a hostile rather than allied force, similar to what we have seen among African-Americans, unfortunately. Certainly, this is the predominant assumption among the Hispanic community; a national survey conducted shortly after the 2012 *Arizona* ruling found that 79 percent of Hispanic voters thought that SB 1070 would make it more likely that legally present Hispanics would be stopped by police (Kelley, Fitz, and Wolgin 2012). The same survey showed that 68 percent of Hispanics thought the law would make it less likely for immigrants to report a crime or volunteer information to the police. Epp, Maynard-Moody, and Haider-Markel see this as a distinct possibility, noting that:

As new laws encourage police to hunt for illegal immigrants and the use of investigatory stops expands to target Latinos, these unjust and antidemocratic patterns, unless deliberately checked, are likely to only become more widespread ... The vast majority of the people asked for papers will be citizens or legal residents. These innocent targets of record requests will resent the question and the implication that they look like less than a full, respected member of society. (2014, 157)

Readers will note that many of the figures and tables in this chapter look familiar. This is because we have simply replicated analyses from previous chapters, but with Hispanics instead of blacks. Findings are troubling – we show that Hispanics are subject to harsher outcomes at rates that often exceed even what we found for blacks. When it comes to contraband, discretionary searches of Hispanics are woefully less productive; officers are almost 50 percent less likely to find contraband on Hispanic than white drivers after consent searches. This is perhaps not surprising, given research that recent immigrants are less likely to be involved in serious crime, but police appear to be operating under different assumptions, as Hispanics are much more likely than whites to experience a search. It seems that whites really are a privileged class when it comes to driving on the roadways; minorities – black or Hispanic – are subject to much higher rates of punitive treatment, such as fruitless search. While the searches may not be designed to be punitive, when we see patterns where unsuccessful searches are so much more common among minority drivers than among white drivers, it certainly might look unfair to those minority drivers. And whether designed to be a punishment or not, it looks like one from the receiving end. After all, no one would want to experience this level of police suspicion, and it is not equally applied to similarly situated white drivers.

A Distinct Profile of Stop Purposes Compared to White and Black Drivers

We showed in Chapter 2 that traffic stops fluctuated annually from a low of just over 1 million in 2005 and 2006 to a high of over 1.75 million in 2010 and 2011. Hispanic drivers regularly constituted about 8 percent of that total (see Figure 3.2). Table 7.1 shows the reasons why the three sets of drivers are stopped, separately for male and female drivers. Note that we include checkpoint stops here.

The first columns show the absolute numbers of drivers stopped, by purpose. Looking at the percentage columns allows us to see the relative likelihood of stop, the "stop profile" for the six different demographic groups. For white females, 49 percent of the stops are speeding, 17 percent regulatory, and no other stop purpose reaches 10 percent. For Hispanic males, by contrast, just 31 percent of the stops are for speeding, with regulatory and investigation stops relatively common as well. In Table 7.2 we show the relative frequency of stop by stop purpose for Hispanic drivers compared to black and white drivers, respectively. The

TABLE 7.1. *White, Black, and Hispanic Traffic Stops Compared*

A. Females

	Numbers			Percents		
	White	Black	Hispanic	White	Black	Hispanic
Speed Limit	2,102,874	999,107	131,169	48.71	40.24	35.82
Stop Light / Sign	216,510	126,424	22,017	5.02	5.09	6.01
Driving Impaired	28,188	8,786	2,279	0.65	0.35	0.62
Safe Movement	217,744	119,824	24,024	5.04	4.83	6.56
Equipment	316,323	253,310	32,872	7.33	10.20	8.98
Regulatory	743,258	583,644	60,919	17.22	23.51	16.64
Seat Belt	322,781	148,251	18,589	7.48	5.97	5.08
Investigation	169,562	107,128	30,933	3.93	4.31	8.45
Other	166,046	112,729	26,010	3.85	4.54	7.10
Checkpoint	33,852	23,796	17,383	0.78	0.96	4.75
Total	4,317,138	2,482,999	366,195	100.00	100.00	100.00

B. Males

	Numbers			Percents		
	White	Black	Hispanic	White	Black	Hispanic
Speed Limit	3,209,845	1,309,759	386,084	42.73	33.28	30.90
Stop Light / Sign	326,413	186,853	59,792	4.35	4.75	4.79
Driving Impaired	74,249	32,688	29,806	0.99	0.83	2.39
Safe Movement	414,610	228,580	92,083	5.52	5.81	7.37
Equipment	582,540	447,089	124,203	7.75	11.36	9.94
Regulatory	1,076,220	786,953	175,568	14.33	19.99	14.05
Seat Belt	837,181	332,180	79,388	11.14	8.44	6.35
Investigation	573,720	331,979	144,783	7.64	8.43	11.59
Other	336,832	229,117	106,286	4.48	5.82	8.51
Checkpoint	80,253	50,724	51,453	1.07	1.29	4.12
Total	7,511,863	3,935,922	1,249,446	100.00	100.00	100.00

TABLE 7.2. *Relative Frequencies of White, Black, and Hispanic*
Stops, by Purpose

	Ratio Compared to:			
	White Drivers	Black Drivers	White Drivers	Black Drivers
Stop Purpose	Male	Male	Female	Female
Seat Belt	0.57	0.75	0.68	0.85
Speed Limit	0.72	0.93	0.74	0.89
Regulatory	0.98	0.70	0.97	0.71
Stop Light / Sign	1.10	1.01	1.20	1.18
Equipment	1.28	0.88	1.23	0.88
Safe Movement	1.34	1.27	1.30	1.36
Investigation	1.52	1.37	2.15	1.96
Other	1.90	1.46	1.85	1.56
Driving Impaired	2.41	2.87	0.95	1.76
Checkpoint	3.85	3.20	6.05	4.95
Total	1.00	1.00	1.00	1.00

Note: The ratios in Table 7.2 are calculated by dividing the percentages in Table 7.1. In the first cell, 6.35 of Hispanic male drivers were stopped for Seat Belt Violations compared to 11.14 percent of white male drivers; that ratio is 0.57.

numbers are the simple ratios of the percent of Hispanic drivers stopped for a given purpose divided by the percent of white or black drivers pulled over for that same reason. So, if 5 percent of Hispanic drivers and 5 percent of white drivers were pulled over for a particular stop purpose, the ratio would be 1.00. If the numbers were 5 percent of Hispanic drivers, but 10 percent of white drivers then the ratio would be 0.50. By looking at the ratios in this way, we can see the relative profile of traffic stops for the six groups: black, white, and Hispanic males and females.

Values allow one to see the relative focus of Hispanic traffic stops as compared to those of white or black drivers. The data are sorted by the first data column. Numbers below 1.00 show that Hispanics are relatively less likely to be stopped for that purpose; numbers above 1.00 indicate an increased likelihood for Hispanic drivers to be pulled over for that reason, compared to white or black drivers, respectively. Since the data are sorted by the relative frequency of Hispanic drivers being stopped for that purpose compared to white male drivers, we can look down that column and clearly see that investigations, other, driving impaired, and checkpoint stops appear to be particularly associated with Hispanic males, as they are each at least 50 percent more common among them than among white males. Driving impaired stops are more than twice as common, and checkpoint stops are almost four times more common. (Note that in checkpoint stops, no data is collected if no action is taken.) Looking at the second column, the numbers are in a relatively similar order, suggesting that the profile for Hispanic males differs from that of black males in much the same way as it does for white males. Seat belt and speeding stops are relatively rare among Hispanic males compared to either white or black males. For regulatory stops, Hispanics have almost the same rate as whites, but 30 percent less than black male drivers. Hispanic males are 28 percent more likely to be stopped for equipment violations than white males, but 12 percent less likely than black males.

Considering female drivers, Hispanic women are relatively unlikely to be stopped for seat belt or speeding stops, but relatively more likely to be stopped for checkpoints and investigations. For checkpoints, their rate is five or six times higher than for white or black female drivers. Nguyen and Gill (2015) report anecdotal evidence of police checkpoints appearing in areas frequented by Hispanic drivers (such as outside Spanish-speaking church congregations) after the adoption of 287(g) programs that encouraged local law enforcement to crack down on illegal immigration with the backing of federal authorities. Checkpoint stops are irregularly recorded by officers using the SBI-122 form, and, as discussed in Chapter 2, we drop them from our analyses for this reason. However, Tables 7.1 and 7.2 make clear that these can be seen as a highly selective enforcement tool that generates adverse outcomes among Hispanic drivers three to six times more commonly than among white or black drivers.

Comparing Stop Outcomes

After a Hispanic driver is stopped, what happens next? Figure 7.1 shows the rates of different outcomes for male and female Hispanic and white drivers of different ages. (The corresponding figure comparing black and white drivers was discussed in Chapter 4.) Once again, there is a stark divergence in outcomes across ethnic, age, and gender lines.

Looking first at the figure in the top-left for "no action taken," we see that both Hispanic and white men are much more likely than women to be let go with no enforcement action, not even a verbal warning. This suggests that men are pulled over with less justification than women and then subsequently released when officer suspicions prove unwarranted. Among males, the youngest Hispanic men are more likely than young white men to get "no action" but the trend reverses among men twenty

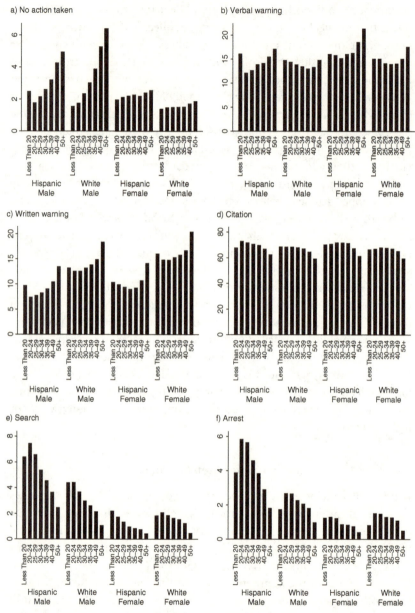

FIGURE 7.1. Outcome Rates by Ethnicity, Gender, and Age Group
Note: Based on 614,689 instances of no action; 3,279,478 verbal warnings; 2,782,438 written warnings; 13,116,223 citations; 442,918 arrests; 689,657 searches.

and over; for women Hispanics are consistently more likely to be released with no action.

Hispanic men and women receive verbal warnings at about the same rate as their white counterparts and appear slightly less likely to receive written warnings. Citations are distributed almost evenly across ethnic lines, although older drivers appear slightly less likely to be ticketed and Hispanic men and women slightly more likely than their white counterparts. Recall that in Chapter 4, we found that blacks were marginally less likely to be ticketed; here we see little difference.

Looking at searches and arrests, however, we see a return to the clear patterns we saw in Chapter 4 in comparing whites to blacks. Hispanic male drivers are much more likely to be searched, and arrested, than whites, and again we see a powerful gender dynamic. Hispanic and white females are about equally likely to experience a search, but Hispanic men are much more likely than white men. We see the same pattern in the last plot, which looks at arrest rates. Hispanic men are much more likely to be arrested than women or white men; at many age groups, the disparity is greater than two to one. For women, again the reverse is often true, except among the youngest age group. Just as Table 7.2 made clear a specific "profile" of those traffic stops associated with Hispanic drivers, so here we can see distinct patterns of outcomes. These differ substantially by age and gender. Note that the crime profile would account for a focus on young men of color, but the immigration profile would apply equally well to women. However, an investigation into a person's immigration status need not involve a search or arrest; a "papers please" request can be enough.

Figure 7.1 shows that Hispanic men are more likely, but women are less likely to be searched than whites of the same age. However, this analysis grouped all search types together. In Table 7.3, we break searches down into their component types: consent, probable cause, incident to arrest, protective frisk, and warrants.

Hispanics are more likely to be subjected to each type of search, with the exception of warrant searches where the rate is equal. Disparities are particularly pronounced for searches that take place during an arrest and it appears that officers are more inclined to feel that a protective frisk is necessary to safely engage with Hispanic drivers. When it comes to discretionary search types, Hispanics are about 47 percent more likely to be searched with probable cause than white drivers and 81 percent more likely to be searched with consent.

TABLE 7.3. *Type of Search by Ethnicity*

Search Type	Searches	% Searched of Total			H-W Ratio
		All Stops	White	Hispanic	
Consent	304,768	1.51	1.09	1.97	1.81
Probable Cause	153,894	0.76	0.43	0.63	1.47
Incident to Arrest	209,148	1.03	0.78	2.03	2.60
Protective Frisk	20,254	0.10	0.07	0.16	2.29
Search Warrant	1,593	0.01	0.01	0.01	1.00
Total Stops	20,235,746	–	11,714,896	1,546,805	–
Total Searches	689,657	3.41	2.38	4.81	2.02

Hispanics are less likely to be searched for discretionary reasons than black motorists (Table 4.1 from Chapter 4 presented the analogous black–white comparison). This makes sense if we remember that Hispanics are subject to investigatory stops for different reasons than blacks. When an officer makes an investigatory stop for a black driver, it is typically to find contraband or evidence of criminal activity. Unless the contraband is in plain sight, this requires a search. For Hispanics the goal of such stops may be to assess immigration status, which does not require a search, only a "papers please" request by officers. So the lower rate of discretionary search for Hispanics may reflect the different goals of investigatory stops when leveraged against Hispanic and black drivers. Of course, officers are still far more likely to search Hispanics for discretionary reasons than whites, highlighting the extent to which white drivers are insulated from search-motivated police stops.

Contraband

As we discussed in Chapter 5, contraband is an important piece of the traffic-stops puzzle. In most cases, we are unable to determine if a traffic stop or subsequent action was justified; there are no guarantees that different races or ethnic groups violate traffic laws at the same rate. However, contraband affords us a window into the merits of police actions. The purpose of searching a motorist is to find contraband, so if officers are much less likely to find contraband on minorities, then this suggests that officers are overly suspicious of minority drivers. Such evidence suggests bias, either implicit or explicit, may be at work.

Table 7.4 shows the percentage of searches that result in contraband for white and Hispanic drivers.

TABLE 7.4. *Percentage of Searches that Result in Contraband*

	Contraband hits	% Total	% White	% Hispanic	H-W Ratio
All Searches	199,725	28.96	30.45	18.71	.61
Consent	70,042	22.98	27.17	14.20	.52
Probable Cause	85,193	55.36	60.27	48.86	.81
Incident to Arrest	40,355	19.29	19.73	14.36	.73
Protective Frisk	3,515	17.35	17.15	10.47	.61
Warrant	620	38.92	39.81	25.93	.65

Looking first at the top row labeled "All Searches," we see that overall Hispanics are 39 percent less likely to be found with contraband following a search. Fewer than 20 percent of searches of Hispanic drivers yield contraband, as compared to 30 percent of white drivers. This is a huge disparity; by comparison blacks were equally likely to be found with contraband overall as whites (see Table 5.5). Apparently, officers are much worse at divining which Hispanic drivers may be harboring contraband; their unsuccessful search rate is consistently much higher for each kind of search. Consent searches are the most disparate; Hispanics are 48 percent less likely to have contraband. This low value may stem from a pattern where innocent Hispanic drivers are more likely than whites to agree to be searched when asked or because Hispanics are simply less likely to be carrying contraband. We lack the data to distinguish between these possibilities, although there is no evidence that white drivers are prone to refuse a search when asked. Looking at procedural searches gives us some idea, however, that the reason is most likely the simple fact that Hispanics are less likely to carry contraband than whites: protective frisk searches and searches incident to arrest yield much lower contraband hit rates for Hispanics. Since these searches are conducted without regard to an officer's suspicion of carrying contraband, but for their own safety or as a routine matter after the decision to arrest has been made, they reveal something different than probable cause and consent searches.

We showed in Table 5.6 that "arrest-worthy" contraband hits are significantly lower for Hispanic compared to white or black drivers. In fact, a total of only 3,523 Hispanic drivers have been arrested following contraband discovered in a search, an 8.21 percent success rate. This compares to 12 and 13 percent for white and black drivers, respectively. As we discussed, all of those numbers are low, but the law enforcement value of searches of Hispanic drivers is even lower than for those of the other races. Fewer than 200 Hispanic women have been arrested in North Carolina since 2002 for contraband hits following from a search.

The fact that Hispanic drivers are less likely to have contraband does not seem to stop officers from searching them much more than white drivers. If we look at Tables 7.3 and 7.4 together, we can see this clearly. Hispanic drivers are subjected to consent searches 81 percent more often than white drivers (from Table 7.3), but these searches yield contraband only half as often (Table 7.4). Probable cause searches are 47 percent more common among Hispanic drivers, but these yield contraband 19 percent less often. The data clearly indicate that officers are overly suspicious of Hispanic drivers. Figure 7.2 plots the percent difference in the usage of discretionary searches on Hispanics and whites and the relative success of these searches at finding contraband over time.

In Chapter 5, we showed that officers have become increasingly likely to search blacks with probable cause relative to whites (the percent difference increased from 110 percent to 250 percent between 2002 and 2016). For Hispanics the trend is not nearly so dramatic. The relative usage of consent and probable cause searches is relatively stable, fluctuating from a 50 percent to a 0 percent increased likelihood for consent searches and between 40 percent and 70 percent for probable cause searches. Most important is that in almost every year Hispanics are more likely than whites to experience these types of search and less likely than whites to be found with contraband. Note that as police officers have used consent searches more equitably, the relative differential in finding contraband has dropped. That is, they have become relatively more successful at finding contraband on Hispanics during this period. This is similar to what we saw in Chapter 5 and suggests that racially equitable searching improves contraband hit rates for searches of minority drivers, at least for consent searches. The data for probable cause searches show the opposite: a gradual reduction in the disparity of finding contraband at the same time as there is increasing disparity in the use of probable cause searches for Hispanics. In any case, in no year are hit rates higher for Hispanic drivers than for whites, and in no year are search rates lower.

Officer Discretion

In the last chapter, we examined the "bad apple" hypothesis that a small number of highly deviant officers are responsible for black–white disparities. Although we found that such statistically deviant officers exist, we also discovered that a great many officers are more likely to search

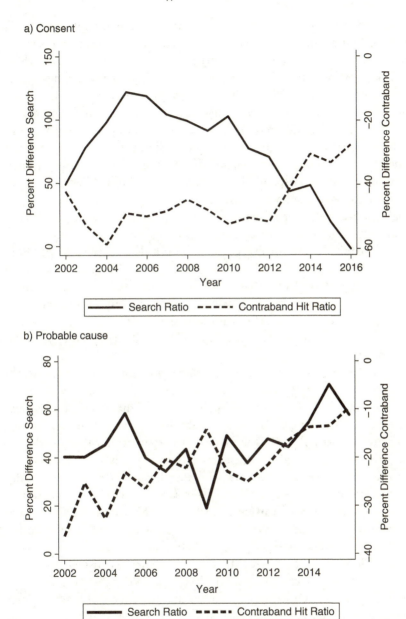

FIGURE 7.2. Percent Difference in the Likelihood of Search and Contraband

blacks than whites. Thus there is support for the bad apple hypothesis only insofar as there are officers whose behavior is so racially disparate that they stand out among their peers, but the larger claim that these few officers are responsible for the statewide (or agency-wide) disparities does not withstand scrutiny; these disparities result from a system-level propensity to search blacks at higher rates as well as from bad apples.

What about for Hispanics? Perhaps some officers are assigned to "immigration patrols" where they focus specifically on finding and arresting undocumented immigrants. Those officers might have greatly elevated rates of searching Hispanic drivers relative to whites. Alternatively, we could find, as we did with black search disparities, that having much higher search rates for Hispanic drivers is standard practice. To explore these possibilities, we start by simply plotting the search rates for white and Hispanic drivers for every officer with at least fifty stops of white drivers, fifty stops of Hispanics, and an overall search rate above the state average of 3.36 percent. (That is, we exclude officers with too few stops of white or Hispanic drivers to calculate a robust search percentage, and we also exclude those officers with low search rates.) Figure 7.3 shows the results for safety stops in the upper panel and investigatory stops on the lower.

As in Chapter 6, officers that are either twice as likely to search whites or twice as likely to search Hispanics are indicated with a hollow circle. Looking first at the figure for safety stops, we find that many officers meet this level of disparity. Of the 830 officers that we include in the analysis, 417 are at least twice as likely to search Hispanics. In other words, the majority of officers with sufficient stops and searches of Hispanics to ensure statistical robustness are searching Hispanics at a dramatically higher rate as compared to white drivers. On the other hand, only thirty-seven officers are at least twice as likely to search whites. Far from being limited to a few bad apples, it appears that it is standard practice for officers to be much more suspicious of Hispanic drivers.

The last chapter showed that black–white disparities are more pronounced for investigatory stops, but here, looking at Hispanics, we find the opposite. Of the 1,366 officers that meet the threshold requirement, 286 search Hispanics at double the rate they search whites, but 252 are twice as likely to search a white driver. To be sure, there are still a lot of high disparity officers (and more on the Hispanics side of the equation) but they are more evenly balanced than we have seen before. The data in this section suggest that officers treat Hispanics more harshly than white drivers when stopping them following a safety-related traffic

a) Safety

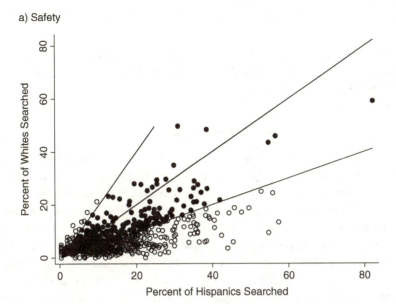

b) Investigatory

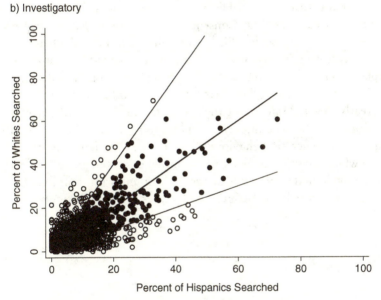

FIGURE 7.3. White and Hispanic Search Rates Compared
Note: The safety figure includes 830 officers with a minimum of 50 white stops, 50 Hispanic stops, and a search rate above the state average of 3.36. The hollow circles indicate high disparity officers. Of these officers, 417 search Hispanics at more than twice the rate that they search whites; 37 officers search whites at more than twice the rate that they search Hispanics. The investigatory figure includes 1,366 officers with a minimum of 50 white stops, 50 Hispanic stops, and a search rate above the state average of 3.36. The hollow circles indicate high disparity officers. Of these officers, 286 search Hispanics at more than twice the rate that they search whites; 252 officers search whites at more than twice the rate that they search Hispanics.

stop. Following an investigatory stop, search rates for both whites and Hispanics are significantly higher, but not as disparate in their focus on one racial group or the other.

Conclusion

Racial disparities are not isolated to black motorists. This chapter makes clear that Hispanics are also subject to much higher rates of search than are white drivers. In this, Hispanic drivers, particularly males, suffer from the same kind of targeting that appears to occur with black males. It is notable how poor officers are at divining, before they search them, which Hispanic drivers may be in possession of contraband. Although Hispanics are much more likely to be searched, they are much less likely to be found with contraband, and this search–hit rate discrepancy is even larger than what we found for black motorists. That is, the police appear to be far too suspicious of Hispanic drivers, at least in comparison to white or black motorists. Consent searches appear particularly problematic, as they are far less likely to result in contraband when used on Hispanic drivers. We also find that, once again, the notion that a few bad apple officers are to blame for the heightened disparities is not supported by the data. In fact, we find that hundreds of officers search Hispanics at greatly elevated rates compared to whites. In other words, heightened suspicions of Hispanic motorists appears to be a statewide norm, rather than an idiosyncratic behavioral trait of a few deviant officers. It is a norm which seems particularly unsupported by any empirical evidence of greater likelihood of Hispanic drivers to be found with contraband. Their searches are more likely than those of whites to come up empty.

8

Black Political Power and Disparities in Policing

When it comes to driving in North Carolina, the difference between being black and white is stark. As we have shown, black drivers are much more likely to be searched and arrested, but less likely to be found with contraband. Having documented these disparities, we consider their cause. How has driving to work, a simple and mundane act for white Americans, become a more fraught and risky endeavor for black Americans? One reason that investigatory stops have become so widespread may be that they are targeted toward minority groups who lack the political power to be heard. Thus, regardless of the degree to which the war on crime is motivated by explicit racial animus, its political feasibility is borne of the fact that those citizens paying the highest costs are underrepresented among government policymakers. That is, the whole approach is made possible because of political inequalities. This, at least, is our hypothesis, and in this chapter we offer various tests to see if it rings true. We find that in municipalities and counties where the black community makes up a larger share of city council seats or if the sheriff is black, racial disparities in traffic stops are less acute, controlling for potentially confounding factors.

Our idea is not necessarily that the police explicitly target the black community and other minority communities within their jurisdiction for any reason in particular. Rather, the idea is that if such disparities were strong, and the affected community had the political power to complain, the disparities would be pushed downwards through political pressure and demands on government. On the other hand, in communities where minorities represent just a small share of the population, a small share of the voting public, and hold little in the way of political resources, disparities against them may not lead to visible and politically relevant complaints. Without power, disparities can continue with impunity and with little relative attention. With power, disparities are lower, because if they were to grow this would lead to attention, complaints, concern, and action to reduce them. At least that is the set of ideas we test here.

Political Power

For a group to have political power, it must be able to exercise some influence over the political process. We see three ways through which power is manifested: presence, voice, and representation. We expect that all three of these variables, separately but especially in combination, will be associated with the degree of disparity in policing. The lower the degree of power of a subset of the community, the greater the disparities we may expect to see.

First, a group has some power merely due to its presence in the community. Numbers matter, and small minorities are easier to target for harsh treatment than larger groups. Elected officials aim to represent the interests of their communities. Bureaucratic agencies are attuned to the publics they serve. No local political leader would normally be expected to support policies that alienate a majority of the population. For smaller minorities, it may be easier to justify or ignore some issues. (Note that this could be because of overt or subconscious hostility but it need not be; the group might simply be ignored, and since it is ignored, actions that affect it adversely may not even come to the attention of government leaders.) As a group's presence grows, they are harder to ignore, and their political power grows. Because law enforcement is part of local government, the presence and relative size of different groups in the population should influence its policies and practices. We would expect the same in schools or other local bureaucracies.

Presence without voice may not lead to the desired political response. To be heard, a group must have voice, and in our system voice may be represented as the share of voters. Voters express their voice and determine who is elected or reelected. Citizens or other residents who are present, but who do not vote or engage with government, can expect their interests to be less well represented. Thus, we define voice as the share of the voters who come from each racial group. Therefore, while the two are highly related, we look separately at the population share of white and black citizens as well as their respective shares in the electorate.

Finally, descriptive representation matters. Scholars have previously found a link between the share of seats in a legislature controlled by women and attention to issues of particular concern to women (Bratton 2005; Bratton and Ray 2002; Cammisa and Reingold 2004). The same has been found with regards to blue-collar workers (Carnes 2012, 2013), racial minorities (Canon 1999; Grose 2011), and LGBT representatives (Hansen and Treul 2015). Cities with no black or minority representation on the city council, within the mayor's office, or in other elected bodies may see less attention to issues of racial equity.

Closely associated with our own interest in policing, but not focused on traffic stops, Salzstein (1989) and Stucky (2011) both investigated the linkage between having black elected officials and the relative rates at which black men are arrested, across a number of cities. On average, these studies suggest that the presence of a black mayor or a majority-black city council decreases the black arrest rate. Our idea is similar: if there is substantial black political representation, it will be more difficult for racial disparities to go un-noticed, un-addressed, and un-remedied.

Taken together, community presence, political presence (voice), and presence in government (representation) make up the political power of a given group. As presence, voice, and representation increase, a group's influence over policy grows. Policing strategies that would cause considerable outrage if directed toward powerful groups can be carried out with less scrutiny when targeted toward the powerless.

Controlling for Alternative Possibilities

We believe that the link between political power and policing outcomes is relatively straightforward. As minority groups gain political power they can put pressure on police departments to deemphasize policing strategies that result in highly disparate patterns of search and arrest. But the politics of race can be complicated and alternative theories suggest more convoluted dynamics than we have postulated.

For instance, a number of social scientists have proposed that majority groups will implement social controls directed at minority groups to maintain dominance, which is known as racial threat theory. To maintain dominance in the face of increasing competition for power, elected officials and those organizations tasked with maintaining order will implement policies that advantage the majority while disadvantaging or even demonizing the minority (Blalock 1967; Blauner 1972; Horowitz 1985; D'Alessio and Stolzenberg 2003; Stucky 2011). Clearly, one group charged with social control is the local police department. So, under the racial threat hypothesis, police departments adopt policies and institute norms that maintain the current balance of power (Stucky 2005, 2011). Racial threat theory suggests that these efforts at social control should intensify as minority groups become more visible in the community, both socially and politically. When minorities are very small in numbers, there is no threat at all. The theory suggests that majority response (or hostility) should be at its greatest as the minority group grows to a substantial share of the population. Different scholars have used different definitions of exactly what is the maximum threat level. After all, once the minority share is above 50 percent, they are no longer a minority at all and the theory should suggest that its effects should be reversed.

Minority-threat theories typically have been tested in locations where the majority population is white, and provide little guidance on how measures and tests of the racial threat hypothesis should apply in majority–minority environments. In North Carolina, many local communities are majority non-white. As a result, we propose that rather than racial threat being the cause of discrepant outcomes, it is the extent to which a community incorporates its minority members.[1]

Another frequent explanation for discrepant patterns in policing is that police officers simply look for people who are out of place; at the institutional level, this might look like an order to investigate "fish out of water." We saw some evidence of a one-way application of the fish-out-of-water idea in Figure 6.5; officers encountering small numbers of blacks compared to whites were more likely to search the black drivers. Officers encountering few whites, however, were more likely to search those whites only when encountering whites was extremely rare. However, our analysis in this chapter does not look at municipalities with extremely low numbers of white or black drivers because of concerns about the reliability of any calculations based on low numbers of drivers being stopped, especially since we are interested in what proportion of them are searched, an event that is relatively rare, statistically speaking. More generally, the "fish out of water" explanation can blend into the "powerless minority" explanation that we explore here. We do not assess the situations where blacks (or whites) are almost invisible in a given town, but we certainly do explore those towns where one group or the other might be only 5 or 10 percent of the population. This is consistent with our main research focus, in fact.

Finally, we control for three important demographic variables in all of our models: the level of crime, poverty rate, and population size. Crime matters because traffic stops have been used as a tool in the wars on crime and drugs: neighborhoods with high rates of crime may lead to a more aggressive police presence that uses all available tools at its disposal. Readers should note, however, that levels of crime are correlated with race in North Carolina as elsewhere, because both higher levels of crime and greater numbers of black residents are found in some cities. Therefore, by controlling for crime, we estimate the impact of race beyond the impact associated with crime. Poverty matters because it affects policing in many ways. People in poverty may drive cars with equipment or registration problems that generate more traffic stops. As these factors are not about race, we want to control for them in our analysis. Levels of poverty are of course correlated with race in North Carolina as elsewhere. Similarly, we control for the population size in each municipality. Large municipalities feature many differences from small towns, including in the structure of their police departments (e.g., their institutionalization and bureaucratic structure), the ability of political leaders to respond to local neighborhood concerns, and sheer physical scope, making policing considerably more complex, and potentially more geographically distinct, in larger cities as compared to small towns. Our findings below, therefore, should be interpreted not with caution, but with an awareness that any race effect we find is over and above whatever part of that effect that might be due to poverty, crime, or population size.[2]

Hypotheses

We formulate two observable implications to test in this chapter. Understanding that our conception of political power relates individually (but especially in combination) to its three components, our expectations are very simple.

> H1: Higher levels of political power drive racial disparities in traffic stop outcomes towards equal treatment of groups.

Additionally, following from our discussion of investigatory versus safety-related stops in much of this book up to this point, we expect the disparate use of investigatory stops to play a role. We expect that investigatory stops are the primary mechanism by which black drivers are targeted, as compared to whites. Specifically, in those towns where the ratio of black drivers pulled over for investigatory stops as compared to white drivers is higher, we take this as an indicator of targeting. As a result, we expect it to be related to higher disparities. This leads to our second hypothesis, which is:

> H2: The ratio of black drivers to white drivers pulled over for investigatory traffic stops is positively related to racially disparate outcomes in traffic stops.

We test each hypothesis with regards to a) searches, b) "light outcomes," c) citation rates, and d) arrest. This progression moves from the start to the end of the traffic stop. For each, we will conduct two tests: first, we examine whether they hold true when studying municipalities; second, we examine whether they hold true for sheriff's offices.

Hypothesis Testing using North Carolina Municipalities

In our first test of these hypotheses, we focus on the political power of a city or town and on how the use of investigatory stops influences the behavior of the associated police department. To test our hypothesis that the political power of the black community conditions levels of disparity in traffic stops, we build an index capturing the wholistic definition of political power. We review each aspect of our political power index – presence, voice, and representation – as they relate to the rates at which white and black drivers experience various traffic stop outcomes. Additionally, when predicting the racial disparity in outcome, we include the black-white investigatory stops ratio. In each model, the logged population of a city, the proportion of the city living in poverty, and the level of crime are included.

We focus on traffic stops between 2008 and 2016, and we include only cities and years where at least 100 black drivers and 100 white drivers were stopped. This simply drops out agencies and years where too few traffic stops occurred to support robust conclusions. Our restriction to the period since 2008 is because voting turnout and crime statistics were not systematically available before 2008. Finally, in this section, we limit our attention to municipal police departments, omitting state agencies and specialized agencies such as hospitals and universities. In the following section, we examine county sheriff's departments; this is a parallel analysis, because the dynamics of city government and directly elected county sheriffs differ. In the end, we have eighty-six North Carolina municipalities, and 497 agency-year observations that meet these criteria. The analysis for sheriff's departments includes sixty-six offices meeting our numeric thresholds and 334 agency-year observations.

We use the black-white investigatory stops ratio to measure the relative focus in each department on investigatory versus safety traffic stops.

TABLE 8.1. *Summary Statistics of Traffic Stop Black–White Ratios*

	Minimum	1st Qu.	Median	Mean	3rd Qu.	Maximum
Searches	0.17	1.36	1.76	1.93	2.24	9.90
Light Outcomes	0.53	0.93	1.00	1.01	1.08	1.75
Citations	0.62	0.92	0.99	0.98	1.04	1.38
Arrests	0.26	1.19	1.56	1.72	2.06	5.92
Investigatory Stops	0.83	1.08	1.17	1.18	1.27	1.96

Recall that traffic stops are deemed investigatory stops if the declared stop purpose is due to equipment violations, regulatory, seat belt, investigation, and other. Traffic stops are deemed safety-related if the declared stop purpose is speeding, stop sign or light violations, driving under the influence, or unsafe movement. This distinction matters, because police departments can allocate only a finite amount of time to investigatory and safety stops. To focus greater attention on investigatory stops and to the war on crime, an agency must divert attention from ensuring safety on the streets.

For each outcome we calculate a black-white ratio.[3] As a reminder, if the calculated value is 1, then black and white drivers see equitable treatment. Values below 1 indicate that white drivers see that outcome more than black drivers, while values above 1 indicate that black drivers see that outcome more than white drivers.[4] Table 8.1 presents summary statistics for these variables. Similar statistics have been presented in earlier chapters; the statistics in Table 8.1 relate only to the 497 agency-year observations that met out threshold for inclusion in forthcoming regression models.

Looking at the means, searches are 93 percent more common for black drivers than whites, light outcomes and citations are almost equally likely, and arrests are 72 percent more likely among black drivers, on average. The investigatory stops ratio, defined as the number of investigatory stops divided by the number of safety stops, ranges from 0.83 to 1.96 with a mean of 1.18. Black drivers are 18 percent more likely to experience investigatory stops rather than safety stops, compared to whites. The minima, 25th percentile value, median, 75th percentile value, and the maxima show the full range of each variable across all the agency-years. Searches have a minimum of more than five times more likely among white drivers, to ten times more likely among black drivers. Arrests range from four times more likely among whites than blacks to almost six times more likely among blacks. With a good range of variability for each variable, we test if our theory about political representation can explain this variance.

Building and Evaluating a Measure of Political Power

We build a measure of black political power based on the three aspects of political empowerment that we discussed earlier in the chapter: 1) presence; 2) voice; and 3) representation. We operationalize each in the following ways: 1) percentage of the population that is black; 2) percentage of the voting population that is black; and 3) percentage of the local elected government that is black. Here we will discuss how each is measured, what each variable looks like, and why in isolation each only captures a portion of the broader concept we want to measure: political power.

Presence is the share of the population. By representing a larger or smaller share of the population, a given group plays a bigger or smaller role in determining the goals of elected officials and city government. As a result, as a group's presence grows, then their political power grows. To measure presence of the black community in a city or town, we calculate the proportion of the population of a city or town that is black. Population numbers come from the 2010 census. To provide a sense of what this variation looks like, let us turn to four North Carolina cities. In Cary, the population is 8.89 percent black, and 73.05 percent white; Cary is a moderately large urban town adjacent to the state's Research Triangle. In Durham, which is one of the three cities that comprise the Research Triangle, the population is 42.24 percent black and 42.57 percent white. A similar racial composition is found in Fayetteville (45.70 percent white and 44.83 percent black), which is home to one of the large military bases which are common in the state of North Carolina. In contrast to these three cities, Kinston has a minority white population comprising 28.56 percent of the community, and a majority black population comprising 69.01 percent of the community. Across all the communities in our study, the black share of the population ranges from 6.56 percent to 69.08 percent; the mean is 28.56 percent. Cary and Kinston therefore represent something close to the extremes, and Durham and Fayetteville represent situations of close to equal balance, therefore with a higher black share than average across the state.

We measure voice by looking at voter turnout numbers. This is a key factor in translating numbers into power, of course. To measure political participation, we look at voting statistics by race in each city for municipal elections from 2007, 2009, 2011, and 2013.[5] Share of voters from 2007 is used for 2008 and 2009; share of voters from 2009 is used for

2010 and 2011; share of voters from 2011 is used for 2012 and 2013; share of voters from 2013 is used for 2014 and 2015; and finally share of voters from 2015 is used for 2016. This is done to leverage the time element present in the dataset; disparate treatment in a future time period cannot cause voter turnout in a previous time period. For each election, we calculate the proportion of voters who are black in a given city in a given election. This measure captures the strength of the black voice within the electorate. The minimum black vote share in a community in our sample is 0.16 percent, the maximum is 96.90 percent, the mean is 20.53 percent, and the median is 14.90 percent.

To measure descriptive representation, we gathered information on the race of the mayor and city council members for each city in our analysis between 2013 and 2014. To provide a contextual sense of the type of variation that exists in North Carolina, we can turn to the four cities in our running example. In Cary, where the black population accounts for less than 10 percent of the community, 0 percent of the council is black. In Durham and Fayetteville, the black proportion of each city council is 29 percent and 50 percent respectively; in each city the black community comprises approximately 44 percent of the population. In Kinston, where the majority of the population is black, only 33 percent of the city council is black.[6]

We use factor analysis to construct a latent dimension of black political power in a given community based on the three variables described. One factor was estimated; this factor explains 73 percent of the variance across the three variables.[7] The result is a variable measuring black political power that ranges from -1.06 to 2.74 with mean 0.06 and median -0.15.

To put this constructed measure in context, we can turn once again to the four cities that have been our ongoing examples. On average during this time span, Cary has a black political power index score of -0.77; as a reminder Cary has a small black population that makes up a negligible proportion of voters and has no black local elected officials. In nearby Durham, which has a large black population that makes up a greater share of the voting population but holds only 29 percent of the local elected seats, the black political power index, on average, is 0.96. In Fayetteville, which has a similar demographic make-up but where a greater share of the local elected officials are black, the political power index, on average, is slightly higher than that of Durham at 1.15. Finally, in majority black community of Kinston, the Black Power Index is near its maximum at 1.91.

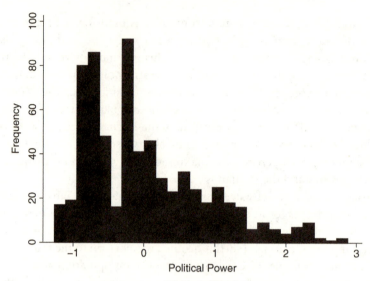

FIGURE 8.1. Black Political Power

Figure 8.1 shows the distribution of the black political power variable. The x-axis presents the calculated value. The y-axis presents the number of municipalities in a given range of values.

By definition the index ranges from low to high political power with a mean of approximately zero and a standard deviation of one. There is a skewed distribution toward low levels of power and low levels of incorporation, with a few instances of high power and high incorporation. In most cities, the black community has little power. In a few cities, it has a lot.

Measures of Context

To operationalize the context within which municipal police agencies operate, we account for the size of a city, the level of poverty, and the level of crime. Population size and the percent of the population in a city living below the poverty line come from the 2010 census. The log of the population is used in the analysis. The level of crime comes from the annual FBI report on crime in the United States.[8] Only those crimes classified as a felony one crime are included. These are violent crimes: murder and non-negligent manslaughter, rape, robbery, aggravated assault, property crime, burglary, larceny-theft, motor vehicle theft, and arson. The crime level is estimated per 100 people.

TABLE 8.2. *The Effect of Political Power on the Disparity of Traffic Stop Outcomes*

	Searches	Light Outcome	Citation	Arrest
Political Power	−0.225**	−0.039**	0.033**	−0.041
	(0.102)	(0.012)	(0.010)	(0.067)
Investigatory Stops Ratio	0.929**	0.148**	−0.138**	0.592**
	(0.338)	(0.042)	(0.032)	(0.278)
Log(Population)	0.101	0.016**	−0.016**	−0.027
	(0.064)	(0.008)	(0.006)	(0.041)
Crime per 100	−0.001	−0.000	−0.000	−0.001
	(0.001)	(0.000)	(0.000)	(0.001)
% Below Poverty	0.456	0.231*	−0.125	1.403*
	(1.089)	(0.132)	(0.106)	(0.718)
Intercept	−0.165	0.647**	1.327**	1.156**
	(0.718)	(0.087)	(0.070)	(0.482)
R^2 Within	0.01	0.01	0.02	0.000
R^2 Between	0.14	0.24	0.27	0.097
R^2 Overall	0.08	0.12	0.15	0.033
Num. obs.	497	497	497	497
Num. groups: City	86	86	86	86

Note: Entries are regression coefficients, with standard errors in parentheses.
Note: ** prob. < 0.05 * prob. < 0.10.

Analysis

We fit four hierarchical linear models[9] with varying intercepts by city. Our variables are used to predict one of the four traffic stop outcome variables: search ratios, light outcome ratios, citation ratios, or arrest ratios.[10] Additionally, as explained in the expectations section above, we control for the log of the population, the percent of the population below poverty, and the crime rate.

Table 8.2 shows the results of the regressions predicting the black-white outcome ratios. Following from our hypotheses, we expect that the coefficients for our political power should push the predicted outcome to equality. For search rate ratios, light outcomes rate ratios, and arrest rate ratios, this should be a negative coefficient; while for citation rate ratios, this should be positive. And indeed this is exactly what we find: For each one unit increase in the political power index, the search rate ratio goes down by -0.225; the light outcomes ratio declines by -0.039; and the citation ratio increases by 0.033 (each of which is statistically significant at the .05 level). Further, we confirm our expectations relating to the black-white ratio of investigatory stops. Where such stops are focused more on black drivers, the light outcomes, searches, and citations ratios are more disparate, in line with our expectations.

Political power is strongly and significantly related to three of the four outcomes reviewed, though its effect on arrest ratios does not reach statistical significance. The investigatory stops ratio predicts each outcome in the expected direction. We can explore the impact of political power as well as the relative focus on investigatory stops among black and white drivers by looking at simple plots. Figure 8.2 shows how the outcome rate ratio is expected to change across the range of potential values that the political power variable may adopt. Four lines are also presented: the equality (or baseline) ratio of 1.0 indicating no racial differences as a dashed grey line; the regression line, which is the predicted value from the regression in Table 8.2, as a solid black line; and the 95 percent confidence interval around the regression line as dashed black lines. Four figures are presented in identical format. These are the search ratio, light outcomes ratio, citation ratio, and arrest ratio. On the x-axis is the black political power index and on the y-axis the relevant ratio.

In each part of Figure 8.2, we see the expected relationship. For searches, light outcomes, and arrests, the regression line declines; there is a negative relationship between power and the relevant ratio. The regression lines slope downward as political power increases. In Figure 8.2a, focusing on searches, the regression line never crosses the equality line, but the confidence interval does include 0 at the highest levels of political power. The regression line declines from a value over 2 to very close to 1. The expected search rate for blacks declines from over twice that of whites to virtually the same. In Figure 8.2b, light outcomes, the regression line crosses the equality line, and is statistically distinct from 1 at the lowest and highest levels of political power. Regarding the relative rates at which black and white drivers are given a citation, in Figure 8.2c, equality comes more quickly as political power moves up. It may seem strange to suggest that a measure of black political power is that blacks get tickets just as often as whites. But if officers are pulling over cars for speeding, a ticket may be just what the driver deserves. Figure 8.2d shows that the arrest ratio is consistently above 1 (equality), and does not change much as political power changes.

Figure 8.3 presents four identically formatted comparisons of the same outcomes with the other independent variable of interest: the percent of investigatory stops. The four parts of Figure 8.3 again show each individual policy agency-year, with the regression line showing how the three

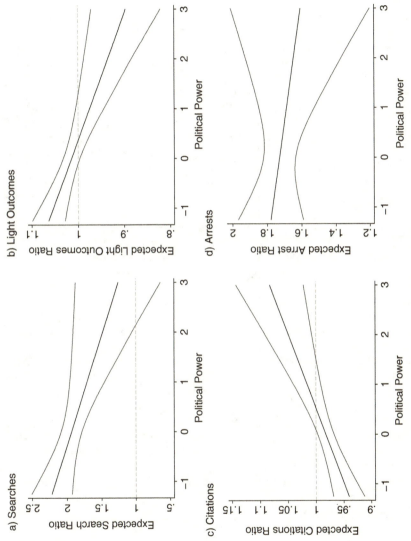

FIGURE 8.2. Effect of Black Political Power on Traffic Stop Outcomes

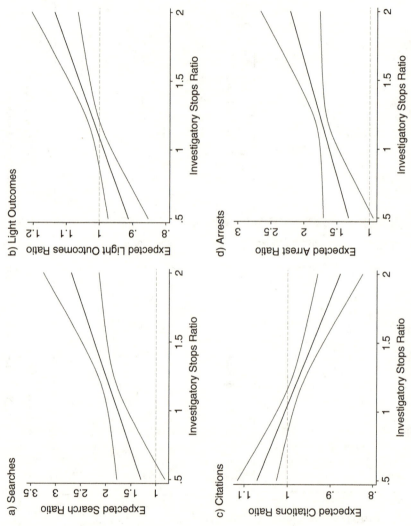

FIGURE 8.3. Effect of Investigatory Stops Ratio on Traffic Stop Outcomes

variables of interest (the light outcome ratio, search ratio, citation ratio, and arrest ratio) vary as the percent of investigatory stops moves from low to high. Here, our theoretical expectations are that as the percent of investigatory stops increases, racial disparity in outcomes should also increase. And the figures confirm these expectations.

Light outcomes and searches increase in their relative focus on black drivers as we move from low to high on the investigatory stop ratio, and the citation ratio declines. For light outcomes and citations, there is only statistical evidence of racial difference in outcomes on average with all other values held at their means when the investigatory stop ratio is near its extreme values. For searches, the relationship is substantively stronger. Low levels of the investigatory search ratio are associated with less disparity in searches, but still a positive one. As investigatory stops increasingly focus on black drivers as compared to whites, however, the search rate disparity goes up substantially.

Across the controls from Table 8.3, only those for population size reach statistical significance at the 0.05 level, and this in two of the models only (light outcome ratios and citation ratios). As the population increases, other things held constant, the light outcome ratio decreases and the citation ratio increases. Additionally, the percent living below poverty appears to not be associated with the search ratios or citations ratios. However, it is weakly statistically significant at the 0.10 level as it relates to light outcome ratios and arrest ratios. Crime per 100 in the population does not appear statistically significant for these ratios.

A Second Test Using North Carolina County Sheriffs

In addition to testing these hypotheses using municipal police departments, we can test whether political power of the black community and discretion influence disparities in county sheriff's departments. County sheriff's departments differ from municipal police departments in two significant ways that shape the analysis. First, county sheriffs are directly elected every four years in partisan elections. This means that rather than testing the indirect electoral connection filtered through the elected local government, we can directly test the effect of a potential electoral connection. Second, sheriff's departments have jurisdictions over the unincorporated areas of a county. Sheriffs also run county jails and serve court papers throughout the county, including in metropolitan areas. For routine traffic stops, however, it is fair to think of sheriff's departments operating in the parts of a county not within the jurisdiction of a municipal police

TABLE 8.3. *Summary Statistics of Traffic Stop Black–White Rate Ratios*

	Minimum	1st Qu.	Median	Mean	3rd Qu.	Maximum
Searches	0.28	1.06	1.34	1.53	1.78	11.26
Light Outcomes	0.55	0.90	0.97	0.98	1.03	1.86
Citations	0.31	0.93	1.02	1.06	1.17	2.90
Arrests	0.11	0.95	1.30	1.43	1.75	6.02
Investigatory Stops	0.64	1.02	1.11	1.13	1.21	1.98

department. Practically, this means that county sheriff's departments work in the rural areas of the state, not in the urban centers.

We will keep in mind the rural / urban difference while looking at sheriffs as well as the fact that they are directly elected. Sheriff's departments have lower search rates on average than police agencies (see Baumgartner, Christiani et al. 2017), possibly reflecting their direct election status.

Data and Measures

The county sheriff's department analysis spans from 2008 through 2015, and includes every county sheriff's department that made at least 10,000 stops in a given year where at least 100 white drivers were stopped and 100 black drivers were stopped. Additionally, the Gaston County Police Department and Gaston County Sheriff's Department are excluded, because they patrol overlapping areas; Gaston County is the only county in North Carolina that has a county police department. Sixty-six sheriff's departments meet this threshold for a total of 334 agency-year dyads being used in the analysis. (There are 100 counties in North Carolina, and 100 county sheriffs.) As in the previous analysis, the dependent variables in each regression are the black-white outcome rate ratios. Additionally, to operationalize discretion, we once again use the investigatory stop rate ratio. Summary statistics for these variables are presented in Table 8.3.

As in the previous analysis, each of the outcome rate ratios have a wide range of values. Among county sheriff's departments that meet our threshold for analysis, black drivers are on average 53 percent more likely to be searched and 13 percent more likely to be arrested; they are, on average, about equally likely to see a light outcome or receive a ticket. In each case, these are lower disparities on average than among the municipalities.

The two major differences between county sheriff's departments and municipal police departments in North Carolina are: 1) the sheriff is directly elected by those residing in the county; and 2) sheriff's departments mainly patrol the unincorporated areas of a county. As a result, the measures for presence, voice, and descriptive representation that we use to calculate our index of black political power are almost the same as before but must be slightly adjusted.

Presence is measured as the proportion of residents in the unincorporated areas of a county that are black. As before, this information comes from the 2010 census. Black proportion of the population ranges from 0.67 percent to 59.62 percent, with a median of 13.20 percent and a mean of 17.34 percent. Voice is measured as the proportion of those voting in a county that are black (note that we use the entire county here, as the whole county votes). As before, this information comes from the North Carolina Board of Elections. As before, election turnout from 2007 is used for 2008 and 2009; turnout from 2009 is used for 2010 and 2011; turnout from 2011 is used for 2012 and 2013; and turnout from 2013 is used for 2014 and 2015. The proportion of the voting population that is black ranges from 0.46 percent to 60.40 percent, with a median of 17.94 percent and a mean of 21.00 percent. Descriptive representation is measured as the race of the sheriff. This is measured on a yearly basis. However, little change occurs during our window (2008–2016), because sheriffs serve four-year terms and there is little turnover. There are 317 agency-years with white sheriffs and thirty-two with black sheriffs.

Once again, these three aspects of political power are used to estimate a latent factor of political power using factor analysis.[11] The resulting factor ranges from -1.30 to 2.85, with a median of -0.33 and a mean of -0.01. Figure 8.4 presents the distribution of scores.

Three control variables are included in the regressions. These are: the log of the population residing in unincorporated areas of the county, a random intercept by agency, and the partisanship of the sheriff. There are 181 agency-years with Democratic sheriffs and 162 with Republican sheriffs. Finally, in the previous set of regressions, we also included control variables for the percent living below poverty and the crime rate, but this information is not available at the county level.

Analysis

Table 8.4 presents the results of the regressions. As before, a separate regression is fit for each outcome ratio, and in each case a hierarchical linear model is estimated with agency-level random intercepts. As a reminder, we hypothesized that as political power increases, disparities should decrease; and as the investigatory stops ratio increases, then disparities should increase. Table 8.4 presents the results of these regressions.

TABLE 8.4. *Predicting Disparities in Traffic Stops Outcomes, Sheriff's Departments*

	Searches	Light Outcome	Citation	Arrest
Political Power	−0.152*	−0.031**	0.110**	0.029
	(0.088)	(0.015)	(0.033)	(0.071)
Investigatory Stops Ratio	0.385	0.093**	0.020	0.014
	(0.270)	(0.043)	(0.087	(0.238)
Republican Sheriff	−0.064	0.000	−0.028	0.036
	(0.148)	(0.026)	(0.055)	(0.120)
Log(Population)	−0.216**	−0.029*	0.060	−0.119
	(0.102)	(0.019)	(0.041)	(0.080)
Intercept	3.464**	1.187**	0.408	2.694**
	(1.139)	(0.207)	(0.447)	(0.906)
R^2 Within	0.012	0.002	0.002	0.004
R^2 Between	0.062	0.158	0.210	0.050
R^2 Overall	0.031	0.066	0.084	0.016
Num. obs.	334	334	334	334
Num. groups: County	66	66	66	66

Note: * indicates statistical significance at the 0.10 level and ** indicates statistical significance at the 0.05 level.

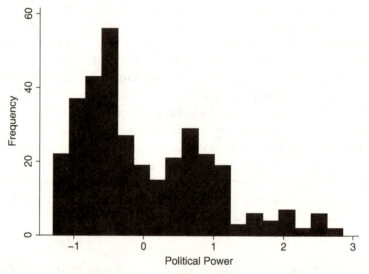

FIGURE 8.4. County Political Power Factor Scores

Table 8.4 reinforces our findings looking at municipal police departments for political power, but shows mixed results – as expected – for the role of investigatory stops. As political power of the black community increases, the disparities decrease for searches and light outcomes and increase for citations: they converge towards equality in each case. These results are statistically significant at the 0.05 level for both light outcomes and citations, and at the 0.10 level for searches. Unlike in the municipalities regressions, only in the light outcome regression is the investigatory stops ratio variable statistically significant at any level.

As before, we present the graphical representations of the relationship between our key variables of interest and the expected outcome rate ratio. Figure 8.5 presents the relationship between black political power and traffic stop outcomes. The solid sloping line indicates the predicted rate ratio, the horizontal line indicates equality, and the curved dashed lines show the 0.95 confidence interval.

In Figures 8.5a and 8.5b, we see the regression line decreasing as political power increases. While the expected search rate ratio never touches or dips below the line of equality, it comes close at the highest levels of political power. Conversely, the expected light outcome rate ratio almost immediately crosses the equality line. Additionally, the expected relationship is seen in Figure 8.5c, which shows the relationship between levels of political power and the citation rate ratio. The line increases across the range of values, and crosses the equality line at low values of political power. However, for both the light outcome rate ratio and citation rate ratio this relationship does not become statistically significant until the political power variable is almost 0.

Figure 8.6 presents the relationship between the investigatory stops rate ratios and the expected traffic stop rate ratio outcomes. As in the previous figures, the solid sloping line indicates the expected rate ratio, the horizontal line indicates equality, and the curved dashed lines show the 0.95 confidence interval.

While the investigatory stop rate ratio variable is only statistically significant in the light outcome rate ratio regression, the hypothesized substantive effect is observed for both the expected search rate ratio and the light outcome rate ratio. The slope increases across the range of values. For the search rate ratio, the line is always above equality. For the light outcome rate ratios, the line crosses equality when values of the investigatory stops ratio are high. In the citations rate ratio regression and associated Figure 8.6c, the relationship is essentially flat. The regression line is essentially indistinguishable from equality.

Finally, the control variables present the expected results given the differences between county sheriff's departments and municipal police departments. Party of sheriff is not statistically significant in any

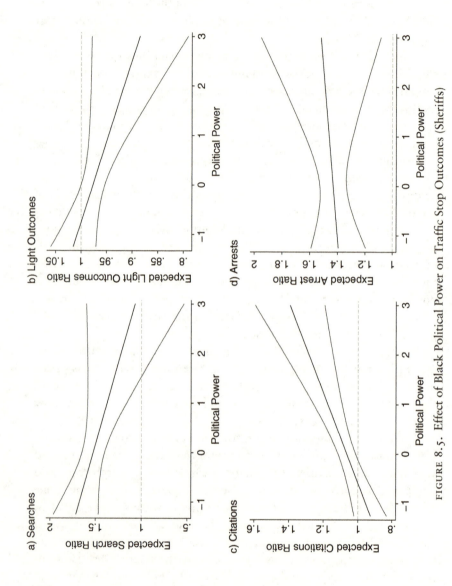

FIGURE 8.5. Effect of Black Political Power on Traffic Stop Outcomes (Sheriffs)

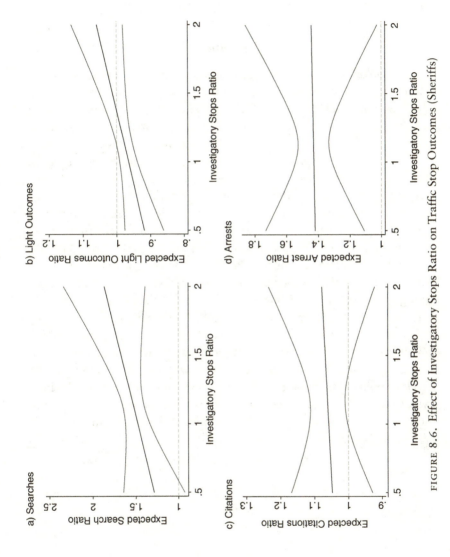

FIGURE 8.6. Effect of Investigatory Stops Ratio on Traffic Stop Outcomes (Sheriffs)

regression, and appears to have a negligible substantive effect. However, the log of the population in the unincorporated areas is statistically significant at the 0.05 level in the search rate ratio regression and at the 0.10 level in the light outcome and citation regressions. This means that racial disparities may be higher in the smaller counties than in the larger ones.

Conclusion

Having looked systematically at three types of variables: who gets stopped for investigatory compared to traffic safety stops, who experiences which types of outcomes after a traffic stop, and who has political power, we showed that these all fit into a coherent picture. Power matters. It changes the behavior of the police. On that note, the results we have presented in this chapter may be troubling or inspiring depending on how one interprets them. On the one hand, we have documented some very significant (and, we think, troubling) disparities in policing. On the other hand, we have shown these to be potentially related to two factors over which local leaders may have some control. Of course, this control can be used either to exacerbate and continue the pattern of racial disparity that we see, or to reduce it. Political power can be affected through voting and organization. (It can also be suppressed by voter alienation and gerrymandering, and our analysis suggests some of the substantive effects to which such policies may lead.) Investigatory stops targeting minority drivers can certainly be changed by the actions and leadership of police executives. This suggests that there may be administrative reforms that police leaders can undertake, with or without the presence of high levels of political power for the minority population in their jurisdictions, which can have a significant impact on racial disparities in traffic stops outcomes. We look precisely at this question in the next chapter.

9

Reforms that Reduce Alienation and Enhance Community Safety

David Easton (1965) famously described the political process as the "authoritative allocation of values." Implicit in this definition is the notion that governments have the authority not only to make laws, but to enforce them as well. This is a familiar concept: if we break the law, there are consequences. Of course, very often those consequences are initiated by local law enforcement. This places police officers in a particularly important position as representatives of government. Few would deny that the state can compel its citizens to do things, or that this arrangement is necessary. But as much as possible, we would like to avoid thinking about it because prisons, handcuffs, tear gas, and police dogs are unpleasant reminders of the state's coercive power. It is there nonetheless, and it is a key element of government.

Police-initiated contact with citizens, especially young men, can be highly alienating if the officer's actions cause the citizen to believe that they are a suspect. To be a suspect after participating in a crime is one thing; to realize one appears suspicious to the authorities for no particular reason other than appearance, or place of residence, is quite another. Therefore, police interactions with citizens are a key place where socialization occurs, and where individuals develop their attitudes toward the government. It can alienate or it can reassure (see Tyler, Fagan, and Geller 2014, discussed in Chapter 1). The police can come to be seen as allies, as they are for many of us, or they can be seen as a threat. Most of us are familiar with reassurance in our interactions with police, but a segment of the population is greeted with greater suspicion by the police. While sometimes this suspicion is warranted, it sometimes is not. It is of course impossible for the police to target their suspicions accurately in every case; after all, they are suspicions, not certainties. Problems of community trust are not created, however, at random or by one-off incidents, such as a single or occasional discussion with a citizen who turns out to be uninvolved in the issue being investigated. Problems come when members of certain groups within the community come to feel that they are repeatedly being subjected to unfair treatment. To such individuals it signals that the government views them as a criminal, no matter what they may do, or that the police are telling them they are not free even though legally they have the right to be so. Alienation, anger, and resentment are natural responses if the suspicion is unwarranted.

Thus, we have particular cause for concern when it appears that the police are treating people disparately, based on any criteria other than criminality, because the damages from excessive police attention are compounding. In the short term, being pulled over and having a vehicle searched is inconvenient, but when one and members of one's social network experience this type of enforcement action on a regular basis, it becomes clear that the government views one with suspicion. Over time, suspect citizens may begin to return the sentiment. Surveys and public opinion research show that those experiencing disparately negative treatment (or see those that they identify with experiencing such treatment, such as family members and friends) are more likely to have negative feelings toward the police and government more generally (Rothstein and Stolle 2008; Intravia 2016; Thibaut and Walker 1975; Tyler and Folger 1980; Tyler, Casper, and Fisher 1989). This of course has a racial component; indeed a strong one. As we noted in Chapter 4 when reviewing racial differences in traffic stop outcomes, a 2014 poll found 71 percent of whites expressing a "great deal" or a "fair amount" of confidence that the local police would treat blacks and whites equally, but just 36 percent of blacks say so (see Drake 2015). White Americans are twice as likely to put faith in the fairness of the police as are black Americans.

Considerable research has shown that people who feel that they are operating within an unjust system perpetuated by government agencies are less likely to engage with that system. They are less likely to vote, less likely to contact elected representatives, less likely to contact government agencies, and less likely to cooperate with government agents (Lerman and Weaver 2014; Tyler and Jackson 2014; Boeckmann and Tyler 2002). They may even avoid things many of us take for granted, such as being involved with our children's schools. Many may avoid engaging with welfare or unemployment offices even to request aid to which they may be entitled; in short, such individuals can pull away from government in all its forms. Thus, there may be strong negative effects on the very quality of democracy, on the fabric of social life, when suspicion is the basis of police–citizen interactions. Further, having a subset of citizens go through these experiences reduces the quality of democracy for all of us.

Mutual suspicion is at best mildly counterproductive but its consequences can be much more severe. Minority communities need government services as much as any other community, and governmental legitimacy requires the support and participation of its citizens. Further, police investigations rely on citizen cooperation. Epp et al. (2014) document an extreme example of mutual mistrust where feelings of alienation within a community were so deeply rooted that residents would not cooperate with police investigations in any capacity, even for crimes with many eyewitnesses such as drive-by shootings. A 2016 *New York Times Magazine* story explored the case of a gang shooting in a New York housing project that left a mother dead in the cross-fire, and the difficulties of the police in finding any witnesses to help, though the event had been witnessed by many (see Mueller and Baker 2016). Desmond, Papachristos and Kirk (2016) described a sharp reduction in 911 calls from black neighborhoods following racially charged incidents in Milwaukee, but no effect in more affluent white areas of the city; they attribute this lack of engagement with the police, even calling for assistance with a crime, to highly publicized racial incidents that make black residents feel the police may not be trusted. Crime investigations require not only freedom from intimidation by criminal gangs, but also trust in the authorities; some communities have neither.

Finally, while we have focused on the effects of a lack of trust on citizens, we might also point to the costs of such a system for government officials, including police officers themselves. Who wants to work in an area where one is mistrusted and viewed with suspicion, especially if one's motivation is to provide a public service at considerable personal sacrifice and danger? In fact, the few surveys that have targeted police officers suggest that they dislike working in communities that distrust them (Morin et al. 2017). Thus, there appears to be a real marketplace for reform, as both citizens and police officers stand to benefit from changes that could foster greater cooperation.

In the previous chapter, we saw that the political power of the black community within a city influences levels of policing disparity. As the power and political visibility of the black community increases, disparate policing decreases. Additionally, we saw that disparities in the use of investigatory stops and racial disparities in traffic stop outcomes go hand in hand. However, that analysis did not put forward any concrete policy recommendations nor did it connect disparate treatment to citizen behavior. Here we push this line of inquiry further by examining how various policy reforms might influence disparities in treatment. Specifically, we discuss two potential avenues for decreasing disparities: a focus on safety rather than investigatory stops and implementing mandatory use of written consent forms for consent searches. The first aims to reduce overall and real levels of disparate treatment, while the second aims to reduce the use of a practice seen as ad hoc by citizens. We show that if agencies focus on traffic safety, rather than using traffic stops as a supplemental investigatory tool, then racial disparities in outcome ratios trend toward equality. Additionally, implementing a written consent form, rather than requiring only verbal consent, reduces usage rates for consent searches, with positive community effects. We conclude by summarizing these findings into a simple recommendation: use traffic stops for their original purpose – traffic safety.

Finally, we assess an important concern with these possible reforms: would less aggressive policing increase violence or crime? Through an analysis of the city which implemented the most dramatic shift in its policing practices, Fayetteville, we show not only that crime continued its long decline during the period of reform, but that, adjusting for the crime rate, citizen calls for service actually increased as the reforms took hold. Thus, community cooperation with the police was enhanced, leading to safer and better outcomes for all.

Focusing on Traffic Safety

Throughout the book, we observe that members of the black community in North Carolina are subject to higher rates of surveillance, arrests, and searches than their white counterparts. Additionally, in Chapter 4 we saw that harsh outcomes were disproportionately directed toward black drivers following investigatory stops. This leads to our first question: by focusing on investigatory stops, are there simple reforms that might decrease these disparities?

Psychologists provide some guidance in this area, demonstrating that if discretion in uncertain situations decreases, then implicit biases will play a smaller role (Glaser et al. 2014; Glaser 2014; Chaney and Saltzstein 1998; Keiser et al. 2002). That is, where decision-makers have more discretion, implicit biases have more room to come into play; where decision-makers are constrained to follow clear rules, bias is reduced. Furthermore, researchers have shown that people are less reliant on stereotypes and heuristics when they are given stricter guidelines for how to make decisions. Conversely, as uncertainty, ambiguity of the rules, or discretion in decision-making increases, then people are more likely to rely on heuristics and stereotypes in making up their minds. In the context of policing, the association between being black and criminality appears to be so deeply ingrained in the American cultural ethos that officers may subconsciously single out black drivers for extra surveillance. Thus, minimizing discretion may reduce reliance on these cultural heuristics (Eberhardt et al. 2004; Williams and Eberhardt 2008; Bonilla-Silva, Lewis, and Embrick 2004; Hetey and Eberhardt 2014; Rattan et al. 2012; Eberhardt et al. 2006; Eberhardt, Dasgupta, and Banaszynski 2003; Gilliam and Iyengar 2000). So, we expect that if the purpose of traffic stops is explicitly defined and discretion is limited, then disparate treatment should be lower.

We have repeatedly drawn a distinction between safety stops and investigatory stops, and we continue to rely on this distinction here. Safety stops are those aimed at enforcing the rules of the road to decrease the likelihood of an accident. The stop purposes falling into this category are: speeding, running a stop sign or stop light, unsafe movement, and driving while intoxicated. Investigatory stops are those aimed at allowing an officer a look inside of a car. The other defining characteristic of investigatory stops is a relatively higher level of discretion afforded to officers when making these stops. (In other words, we assume that officers can exercise greater discretion when deciding whether or not to stop a driver for a regulatory violation than they can for drivers making unsafe movements.) The stop purposes falling into this category are: equipment violations, crime investigation, not wearing a seatbelt, violating a regulation (e.g., expired license tags), or stop purposes recorded as "other." While the first two in this list are permissible primary reasons to stop a vehicle in almost every state, the last three are not. For example, seventeen states do not allow a seatbelt violation to be a primary reason for a traffic stop.[1] Additionally, some even within North Carolina have taken active steps to decrease their department's reliance on regulatory stops. As Fayetteville's former chief of police said, "I'm not a big fan of regulatory stops. And I'll tell you why: Regulatory violations generally don't kill or maim people" (originally quoted in Barksdale 2014).

Let us note at the outset that police officer discretion is apparent in almost all traffic stops: most of those technically guilty of speeding are not pulled over, after all. Thus, our distinction between safety stops and investigatory stops does not provide a firm distinction between lower and higher discretion on the part of the officer; discretion is always there. But on average, if a police chief indicates to his or her force that officers should focus on traffic safety, and not use the traffic laws as a pretext to investigate citizens for possible, but unclear, violations of other types of laws, then this will have the effect of reducing discretion and getting the force focused on safety on the roads. So we ask a simple question, even if it imperfectly reflects our goals: what would be the degree of racial disparity in traffic stop outcomes if the police made only traffic safety stops, not investigatory ones? We can easily simulate what this world would look like simply by excluding all the investigatory stops from our analysis and re-running some of our previous analyses without them.

Eliminating Investigatory Stops Reduces Bias

A total of 9,498,866 investigatory stops were made during the period of this study, accounting for 47 percent of all stops. Of these, 5,124,463 were of white drivers, and 3,332,380 were of black drivers. Recall from Chapter 4 that the statewide black-white outcome rate ratios following an investigatory stop are 1.09 for light outcomes, 0.91 for citations, 2.11 for arrests, and 2.25 for searches. Thus, blacks were 9 percent more likely to be released from a traffic stop with no action or a warning, 9 percent less likely to get a ticket, 111 percent more likely to be arrested, and 125 percent more likely to be searched. The arrest and search numbers make clear that investigatory stops are adding substantially to the racial disparities overall, since these are considerably higher than for other forms of stops.

What happens to these ratios if the three types of investigatory stops that are not permitted in many other states are excluded? These comparisons can be seen in Table 9.1. The second column in the table presents the outcome rate ratios if all stops that occurred in our dataset are included, while the third column presents the ratios if only safety stops occurred. The fourth and fifth columns present two ways to measure the change between the two scenarios: the fourth column presents the raw difference; the fifth column presents the percent change in ratios between the scenario where all stops that were made are included and the scenario where only safety stops that were made are included.

As can be seen, the rate ratios in all cases become more racially equitable; they all move closer to one. The light outcome rate ratio decreases

TABLE 9.1. *Comparing Outcome Rate Ratios between All Stops and Safety Stops*

Outcome	All Purposes	Safety Purposes	Difference	Percent Change
Light Outcome	1.10	1.03	–0.07	–6.61
Citation	0.93	0.98	0.05	5.24
Arrest	1.68	1.29	–0.40	–23.67
Search	2.15	1.76	–0.39	–18.30
Total	18,059,297	9,602,454	–	–

Note: Totals in the last row are of white and black drivers only.

by 0.07, the arrest rate ratio decreases by 0.40, and the search rate ratio decreases by 0.39. Conversely, the citation rate ratio increases by 0.05, bringing the outcome ratio closer to equality. So, simply by eliminating certain types of stops (stops that are not permissible in many other states) racial disparities are substantially less pronounced. Most notably, the arrest and search outcomes are reduced by about 20 percent, a substantial movement toward equality of treatment.

What about controlling for potentially confounding factors? Is there still a reduction in racial disparities when investigatory stops are eliminated from the data? To find out, we compare odds-ratios from a series of logistic regressions predicting the likelihood that black drivers experience various outcomes, including and excluding investigatory stops from the data. Table 9.2 presents a summary of the results. (These models replicate the analysis from Chapter 4, with controls for stop purpose, gender, ethnicity, age, time of day, day of week, agency, and for all but the search model whether contraband was found; see the online appendix to this chapter for full results. Only stops made by the top twenty-five agencies, determined by the number of stops made over the time span, are included in the analysis.) The first column shows the odds-ratios associated with being black, using every possible stop in the dataset. The second column in the table presents the odds-ratios using only those stops made for safety reasons. The next two columns show the change in the estimated impact of being black, first as an absolute change, then as a percentage of the original coefficient.

Recall, that white drivers are the excluded category, meaning that the odds-ratios associated with being black should be interpreted as the relative increase (or decrease) in the likelihood of a stop outcome as compared to white drivers. The standard errors for the coefficients and

TABLE 9.2. *Comparing Odds-Ratios from Logistic Regressions between All Stops and Safety-Related Stops*

	All Stops	Safety Stops Only	Change in Odds	Pct. Change in Odds
Search	1.94 (0.01, 0.16)	1.73 (0.01, 0.37)	−0.21	−11
Light Outcome	0.98 (0.00, 0.11)	1.02 (0.00, 0.11)	0.04	4
Citation	0.99 (0.00, 0.11)	0.98 (0.00, 0.12)	−0.01	−1
Arrest	1.43 (0.01, 0.28)	1.09 (0.01, 0.38)	−0.34	−79
N	6,627,813	3,202,414		

Note: All coefficients are statistically significant at the 0.05 level.
Note: Entries in parentheses are the standard errors associated with the coefficient and then the R^2s associated with each model.
Note: Each model includes fixed effects for agency, and only contains stops made by the top 25 agencies in North Carolina. The full models can be seen in the appendix to this chapter.

pseudo R^2 values produced from each regression are in parentheses next to each odds-ratio; they are formatted as standard error first and pseudo R^2 second. To see the full regressions, see the online appendix associated with this chapter.

Clearly, the trends documented in Table 9.1 are robust to this multi-variate specification. Going from the regressions that include all possible stops to those including only safety stops, the odds-ratios associated with black drivers decrease for the search and arrest regressions. In fact, for arrest, the 43 percent disparity almost completely disappears. For searches, it is reduced from a 94 percent increased likelihood to 73 percent. In the case of the citation and light outcome regressions, odds-ratios come very close to one (for both models) indicating that these outcomes are implemented at approximately the same overall rates for white and black drivers. Additionally, in every case except for the light outcome regression a greater amount of variance is explained. (For example, the proportion of the variance explained goes from 16 to 37 percent for searches, and 28 to 38 percent for arrests.) This means that relatively objective factors that can be included in the model do a better job of explaining these outcomes, with correspondingly less room for idiosyncratic officer discretion. Where discretion is lower, bias can be expected to be lower as well, as discussed above.

Written Consent Forms

One simple reform to reduce bias in policing is to focus efforts on traffic safety; not to use the myriad violations of which most drivers are routinely guilty as an open invitation to conduct a police investigation. Since most citizens do not routinely appear suspicious to the police, most of us are unaware that the police might use a technical violation as an excuse to pull us over. But this clearly occurs, and good policing may sometimes demand it. Still, if our goal were to reduce racial disparities, a simple reform would be to reduce officer discretion in pulling people over. Of course, police are accustomed to and value that discretion, but as we discussed above, the greater the discretion the greater the room for implicit bias and inaccurate stereotyping.

Another plausible reform, and one implemented in several North Carolina communities, has been to publicly mandate that an officer receive a person's written, rather than verbal, permission, before conducting a consent search. A consent search is one where an officer asks an individual permission to conduct a search. The introduction of the mandatory use of written consent forms changes the typical dynamic in such a situation by requiring signed written consent on a form that explicitly lays out the citizen's absolute right to withhold consent. As a city councilman said in Durham, North Carolina: "If I have to sign something, then I am more cognizant of what my rights really are" (originally quoted in Gronberg 2014). This is particularly true when the form explicitly informs the driver of those rights.

As we will see in the section below, demanding a signature on a form that informs the citizen of their right to withhold consent to be searched typically reduces the number of consent searches by well over 75 percent. While this is of course part of every American's freedom to be free from "unreasonable search and seizure" under the Fourth Amendment, in the power relationship of an officer interviewing a citizen, the vast majority of individuals will give consent when asked. And if not, and the officer says they gave consent, then in court the matter will be addressed by the word of the officer versus the word of the suspected criminal. Asking for written consent reduces the numbers of searches dramatically. Practically speaking, if the search yields nothing, the officer may simply let the driver go. If it yields a cache of drugs or other contraband, then in court the question of whether the driver gave consent will cause the jury to weigh the sworn testimony of an officer with that of a criminal defendant found in possession of serious contraband. Most juries will give credence to the officer in that case. Illegal search defenses can be successful but there is no guarantee that they will be, especially when the defendant at trial has other credibility issues such as previous convictions.

We want to note immediately that officers may ask for consent even when they have probable cause to conduct a search. Legally speaking, when an officer has probable cause to suspect that a person may be involved in a crime, the officer need not seek consent. Practically speaking, in some cases where an officer may have probable cause, he or she may prefer the less confrontational tactic of asking permission to search. "Is it ok if I look in the trunk?" might be an easier way for an officer to handle a situation than a more forceful tactic. When consent searches become more difficult because of a written consent form, some officers or departments might show a slight increase in probable cause searches; this would be evidence of a "substitution effect." Exactly what proportion of consent searches have been done where an officer also had probable cause, we cannot say. In the analysis below we will look carefully for any possible substitution effect where probable cause searches increase at the same time as consent searches decline. If substitution were occurring, it should offset only a proportion of the initial number of consent searches.

Several benefits follow from the use of written consent forms. First, in court testimony there can be little disagreement about whether the citizen really did provide consent if their signature is on file on a form that also asks for the password to their cell phone and clearly indicates their freedom to refuse the search. Second, as we will show below, written forms dramatically reduce the overall number of consent searches and with that, they reduce the overall number of searches. A third benefit is that citizens are not made to feel as though they may have been fooled or tricked. If there is probable cause, the officer has the clear legal authority to conduct the search. If there is no probable cause, but he or she seeks to do a search anyway, then the only way to do so is to obtain permission. This can be done, of course, and it routinely is as we shall see below. But it may be a powerful contributor to feelings of alienation among community members who feel targeted. Most Americans are unlikely ever to experience a request for a consent search following a traffic stop, but some face the prospect much more commonly than others. And they may rightly feel that while they have the theoretical right to refuse, according to the Constitution, in reality they cannot. Reducing the use of such searches can reduce the reason for any such individual to be alienated from the police and the government.

Implementation in Fayetteville, Durham, and Chapel Hill

Several cities in North Carolina have begun using written consent forms for traffic stops. However, only a few have made their use mandatory. Other departments, including those in Asheville, Charlotte, Greensboro, Raleigh, and Winston Salem, have the forms available to officers, but do not make their use mandatory (Wise 2014). We focus on three cities that have implemented the mandatory use of written forms for consent searches in this section: Fayetteville, Durham, and Chapel Hill. In each city, the introduction of the reform was explicitly directed at improving trust between the police department and the community it serves. In some cases, this was one in a number of reforms, while in others it is the primary (public) reform. For a copy of the form used in Durham, see Appendix D. Other forms are similar in content.

We focus on the implementation of the written consent form in these cities for three reasons. First, there is enough time before and after the implementation of the reform to evaluate its effect on search rates, crime rates, and citizen-initiated police contact. Second, the implementation of the reform was well documented by local news sources, press releases from the local government, and press releases from local activist groups. Third, the story of implementation is different in each case. Before discussing the impact of the policy shift, we will discuss the context in which the mandatory use of the forms in each city was implemented.

Fayetteville

The first of the three cities to implement the mandatory use of a written form in traffic stop consent searches was the Fayetteville Police Department. Controversy over racial profiling in the police department increased over the course of 2010 and 2011, capturing the attention of local groups, local elected officials, local news, and the police department (see Barksdale 2010, 2011). The peak of the controversy ran from September 2011 through February 2012. This prompted the city council to hire a consultant to evaluate the extent to which racial profiling was occurring and provide recommendations on how to address it. The consultant found no evidence of explicit racial profiling, but did find evidence that black drivers were subject to more warrantless searches than white drivers (WRAL 2012a, b, c, d).

To address this, the consultant recommended a number of policy changes. Of these, the immediate attention of the city council and police department were directed at consent searches. The council initially attempted to ban the use of consent searches in Fayetteville. However, after a dispute with the police department, a confrontation with the city manager leading to his resignation, and a court injunction, the city council scaled back its call for reforms. Rather than a full halt to consent searches, the council and the police department agreed on the mandatory use of written consent forms, beginning in March 2012 (WRAL 2012b, c, d). Later that summer, the police chief throughout this controversy, Tom Bergamine, retired. Almost a year later (February 2013) a new chief, Harold Medlock, came into office with the explicit mandate to rebuild trust in the community. With the new leadership, notable changes in police strategy and behavior took place (Barksdale 2014; WRAL 2012a, 2013).

It is difficult to overstate the controversy associated with these events in Fayetteville. The outgoing city manager accused the city council of "throwing the police department under the bus" (see Barksdale 2012a). The head of the North Carolina Police Benevolent Association declared he would ask for a federal investigation "into what he described as a conspiracy to undermine the Fayetteville Police Department," further elaborating that he thought the city was "awash in crime, calling it a 'cesspool of corruption and anti-police hatred'" (Leskanic 2012). The city council effectively demanded a moratorium on consent searches pending the outside evaluation of the policy department's practices. This moratorium was in place for months before the formal adoption of the written consent form in March 2012. The city manager and the police chief denied accusations and the city was left with a confrontational situation until both departed and new leadership was put in place. In our analysis below we will therefore test for effects during three periods: 1) the turbulent period from September 2011 through February 2012 when the consent moratorium was in place; 2) the March 2012 reform mandating written consent searches; and 3) the February 2013 appointment of Harold Medlock as the new Chief of Police.

Durham

While the implementation of the written consent form was at times turbulent in Fayetteville, it moved forward steadily toward implementation and use. This was not the case in Durham, where the Police Department adopted an antagonistic stance towards the reforms, and where greater endemic problems were discovered. A number of groups, including neighborhood activists such as SpiritHouse, ministers, the FADE coalition (Fostering Alternative Drug Enforcement), and the Southern Coalition for Social Justice (SCSJ) brought the attention of the city council and mayor to potential racial profiling in the police department and widespread community mistrust of the police (see Bridges 2017). To address these allegations and concerns, Durham's mayor, William V. Bell, commissioned the city's Human Relations Commission to evaluate whether claims of racial profiling held weight and to make recommendations on how to address these issues if found to be valid. The examination of the department found explicit racial bias, and made a series of recommendations to the mayor, city council, and police department, and was published in April 2014 (WRAL 2014a, b). One story that emerged from this period that would result in a court case was the warrantless search of Keith Ragland, an African-American man with a disability (WRAL 2015a). While many reforms were proposed and to varying degrees adopted, one implemented reform was the mandatory use of written consent for consent searches. Mandatory use of written consent forms formally began in October 2014 in Durham (Gronberg 2014; WRAL 2014a, b), but the roll out of the reform began in September 2014 when the official policy change was announced. (Note that the story with which we began this book, the confrontation between Officer Kelly Stewart and Mr. Carlos Riley, went to trial in 2015, so was directly affected by the tense relations prevalent in Durham during this time.)

Durham faced three particular challenges: 1) the mandatory use of the written consent form came as a mandate from a unified council, mayor, and city manager following months of public pressure rather than from a dialogue between them and the police department; 2) previous to the mandatory use of the forms, the default and explicitly preferred type of search to conduct following a traffic stop was a consent search rather than a probable cause search; and 3) the crime rate increased throughout the debate surrounding police trust to the implementation of reforms and beyond. The result was an antagonistic implementation of the mandatory use of written consent forms. Ultimately, this led to the police chief, Jose Lopez, taking his retirement at the end of 2015 (Bridges 2015c). His replacement, Cerelyn "CJ" Davis, took office in June 2016 with instructions to rebuild trust in the community (WRAL 2016). When analyzing the effect of the reform, we will make two comparisons: the September 2014 reform mandating written consent forms, and the June 2016 arrival of Chief Davis.

As we will see in the data for Durham, a powerful substitution effect occurred there. While Chief Lopez disagreed ("'There is no way you can substitute a probable cause for a consent search,' he said. 'You either have probable cause or you don't'"), Deputy Chief Larry Smith "said officers typically start with asking for a consent search, even if there is probable cause," further contradicting the Chief in "pointing out that probable cause 'is not an exact science,' and two officers could disagree on whether a situation rises to the level of probable cause" (see Bridges 2015d for these quotes and 2015e for coverage of a testy community meeting in Durham discussing our initial analysis of the implementation of the written consent form described in more detail below). With police leaders suggesting in public that officers can substitute probable cause when they cannot get consent to do a search, it is clear that the administrative culture in the Durham Police Department was not enthusiastic in responding to the community and city council pressure to revise procedures. And, as the data below will show very clearly, they subverted implementation of the program, at least for a time.

Chapel Hill

Finally, while Chapel Hill may be a neighbor to Durham, the implementation of the mandatory use of the written consent form could not have been more different. Through conversations with community groups and community members, the police department voluntarily decided to begin changing how they police the city. Included within the suite of changes, Chapel Hill's police chief, Chris Blue, proposed and put into action the mandatory use of written consent forms. This policy went into effect July 2015, while other reforms continue to be introduced and implemented (Grubb 2016a, b). It is fair to suggest that Chapel Hill's reforms were forward-thinking and in response to national and statewide issues rather than reactions to a particular crisis in the department or the community.

How did this change searching?

Our analysis is very simple: we count how many searches occur each month before and after the reforms. For Fayetteville and Durham, we test for the reform as well as for the arrival of the new police chief. We are particularly interested in consent searches, of course, but we also look at probable cause searches and the total number of searches. If a "substitution effect" occurs, then probable cause searches could increase by some percentage of the decrease observed in consent searches. This should be a small effect, however, as most searches are not in that "gray area" (if such an area exists) where either is possible.

Graphical Depictions of the Trends

First, we look at whether the implementation of the written consent form altered the number of searches in each city by search type. We aggregate the data by month and show the number of consent, probable cause, and total searches. If the reforms are effective, we should see an immediate decline in consent searches, little change in probable cause searches, and a decline in the total number of searches roughly equivalent to the decline in consent searches. That is, if there is little to no substitution effect, the decline of consent searches should not be offset by an increase in probable cause searches and the total number of searches will therefore decline by the same amount as the consent searches. We can see if there is a substitution effect if probable cause searches increase and if total searches decline by less than consent searches.

Figure 9.1 provides preliminary evidence that written consent reforms dramatically reduce consent searches. The moving line in each subfigure indicates the number of consent searches per month in that city. The vertical line or lines in each figure indicate the start of a reform. In Fayetteville, the lines indicate (in order from left to right) the consent search ban period, the start of the mandatory use of written consent forms, and the change in leadership. In Durham, the lines indicate (in order from left to right) the mandatory use of written consent forms and then the change in leadership. In Chapel Hill, the single line indicates the introduction of the written consent form. (Note that for Durham and Chapel Hill some months appear to be missing in the state database on which we rely; see Appendix E and the online appendix to the book for more detail. These appear as blanks in the figure.)

In both Fayetteville and Durham, there is an observable decline in the number of consent searches conducted immediately following the initial reform in each city. In Fayetteville, the sharpest decline occurs in the period of the greatest controversy between and within the city government and the police department. As the use of consent searches approached zero during this period, it then stabilized at that level when the written forms for consent were formally introduced and the new chief started. In Durham, shortly before the reform was formally introduced and after the initial controversy, the number of consent searches began drastically falling. This trend continued when the new police chief started. Finally, in Chapel Hill, a modest decline seems to have occurred, but nothing as drastic as in the other two cities, and the numbers were already very low to begin with. While the number of consent searches decreased, what happened to the use of probable cause searches in each city?

Figure 9.2 provides a preliminary look at how probable cause searches were affected in each city. As in Figure 9.1, the moving line in each

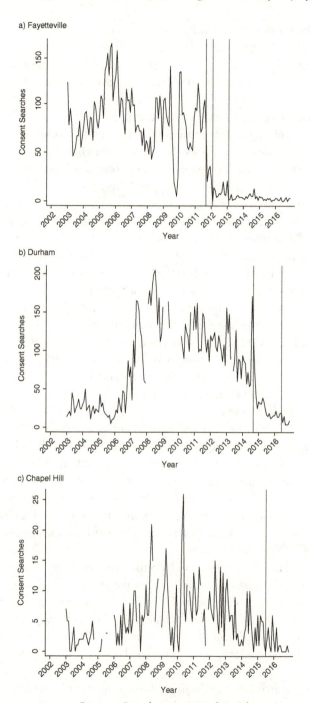

FIGURE 9.1. Consent Searches per Month in Three Cities

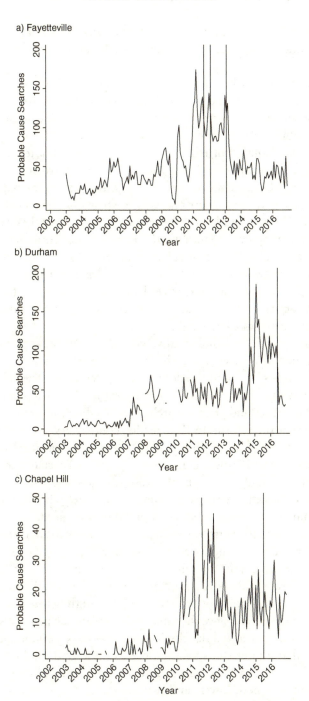

FIGURE 9.2. Probable Cause Searches per Month in Three Cities

subfigure indicates the number of probable cause searches per month in that city, and the vertical line or lines in each figure indicate the start of a reform.

In Fayetteville, while the number of consent searches drastically decreases at the beginning of the controversy and continues to decrease to almost zero after the reform went into effect, there was some substitution. Probable cause searches had previously been on the order of fewer than fifty per month, but rose to over 100 per month after the reform, declining again only after Chief Medlock took control of the department. In fact the searches rose even before the reform, perhaps adding to the atmosphere of mistrust that was so strong in Fayetteville in 2010 and 2011. The rise and later fall of probable cause searches can clearly be seen in the Figure. In Durham, the Figure makes clear that a similar but even more clearly evident substitution effect occurred. The number of probable cause searches only decreased after Chief Davis took control of the department in June 2016. Unlike either of the first two cities, there appears to be little substantive effect on probable cause searches following the ban in Chapel Hill.

Examining the trends holistically, we can observe the extent to which a substitution effect occurred, and how changes to policy concerning consent searches bled into the decision to search at all. The substitution effect here would be indicated by a constant level of searching between the periods before and after a search. This would clearly reflect a policy to circumvent the reform. In Fayetteville, controversy surrounding consent searches began at the end of 2011, the reform was implemented in March 2012, and the new chief took control in February 2013. After that point, the number of probable cause searches decreased to their historic levels, consent searches were almost completely eliminated, and the overall number of searches was correspondingly reduced.

In Durham, controversy began in late 2013 and carried through all of 2014, the reform went into effect in October 2014, Chief Lopez retired in December 2015, and the new chief took over in June 2016. The dramatic increase in the numbers of searches conducted by the Durham police from the historical norm of around 100 per month before 2007 to well over 200 in the period since then may help explain the problems of community trust that affected the city in the 2013–2015 period. In any case, it is clear that a powerful substitution effect occurred until Chief Davis arrived. Initial indications suggest that she has rapidly moved the police department to a new, lower level, with searches dropping dramatically. Note that the new levels bring the city back to where it was some ten years before. The anomaly may have been the dramatic rise in searches from 2007 to 2016.

In Chapel Hill, the story is less clear. This may be due to the fact that unlike either Fayetteville or Durham the reform was not introduced as a result of allegations or substantiated claims of racial bias. While the number of consent searches does decrease after the July 2015 reform, the overall number of searches appears unaffected. The absolute numbers are, however, very low, and quite noisy from month to month. The Chapel Hill case could be seen as one where the police department, and a forward-looking Chief, proactively sought to implement a solution before a problem is severe. We believe this model helps avoid bias, increases citizen trust, and comes at little cost in terms of law enforcement priorities. After all, probable cause searches continue as before. Apparently, the Chief agreed, as he implemented the policy change to enhance community trust, knowing that it would have little cost in terms of public safety.

Statistical Tests

In addition to looking at a graphical description of the trends, we test whether the introduction of the mandatory use of written consent forms altered the percent of stops resulting in any search, consent searches, and probable cause searches. To do this, we fit a series of ARIMA regressions, where the dependent variable in each is the monthly number of searches for each city. The use of ARIMA models allows for any natural over-time trends separate from the reforms themselves to be controlled for. Essentially, we know that decisions made in the previous month or previous months are likely to inform the decisions made in future months. (For example, the size of the department may change, or the budget may go up or down. These effects would carry forward from one month to the next.) In order to capture this idea, we test for and model any autoregressive (AR), non-stationary (I), and moving average (MA) tendencies (hence the ARIMA name). Diagnostic correlograms for each city and outcome can be seen in the online appendix to this chapter.

Beyond modeling the overtime dynamics, the models are very simple. For each city there is a binary indicator for whether the mandatory use of the written consent forms was in place; this is simply a series of zeros for the period before the reform and a set of ones for the period after the reform. Estimated coefficients for this variable (called "Written Consent Form" in Tables 9.3 and 9.4) show the change in the search rate

TABLE 9.3. *The Effect of Written Consent Forms on Consent Search Rates in Three Cities*

		Fayetteville	Durham	Chapel Hill
Reforms	Consent Search Ban	−55.47**		
		(10.07)		
	Written Consent Form	−66.48**	−32.90*	−4.07
		(22.55)	(19.26)	(4.41)
	Leadership Change	−20.64	−4.66	
		(57.93)	(68.67)	
Controls	Intercept	88.34**	−0.16	5.75**
		(4.42)	(1.18)	(1.05)
	AR(1)	0.67**	−0.41**	0.41**
		(0.06)	(0.08)	(0.06)
	AR(2)		−0.11	0.01
			(0.07)	(0.08)
	AR(3)		−0.23**	−0.11
			(0.08)	(0.09)
	AR(4)		−0.16**	0.36**
			(0.08)	(0.07)
	MA(1)	0.03		
		(0.09)		
	N	183	162	165
	Log Likelihood	−790.19	−739.58	−453.42

Note: ** prob. < 0.05. * prob. < 0.10.
Note: Standard errors are in parentheses below coefficient estimates.

associated with the reform. For Fayetteville and Durham, we include a "Leadership Change" variable, defined as zero for the period before the arrival of a new police chief and one after. Recall that Chief Medlock started in March 2013 in Fayetteville and Chief Davis in June 2016 in Durham. Finally, for Fayetteville only, we include a "Consent Ban" variable defined as one for each month during the height of the controversy (September 2011 through January 2012), and zero for all other months.

Tables 9.3 and 9.4 present the results of this analysis, in order for consent searches, probable cause searches, and all searches. The coefficients for Consent Ban, for Written Consent Form, and for Leadership Change tell us the degree to which search rates changed from before to after these events. The ARIMA components of the models need not be of concern to a reader interested in the impact of the reforms; they document that we have controlled for the time dynamics properly, avoiding false statistical inference.

Consent Searches

Table 9.3 presents the results for consent search rates. In each, only the relevant reforms were included in the models. The effects of the reforms are represented by their coefficients in the table.[2]

In Durham and Fayetteville, the written consent form reform dramatically decreases the rate of consent searches in each city at a statistically significant level, by just under thirty-three consent searches and just under sixty-six consent searches in each city respectively. In Durham this is at the 0.10 level of statistical significance, while in Fayetteville this is at the 0.05 level of statistical significance. Additionally, in both cities, change in leadership has no statistically significant effect on the consent search rate and appears to have a negligible substantive impact. This reflects what we observed in Figures 9.1b and 9.1c. In Fayetteville, there is also a statistically significant change in consent searches conducted by month during the ban of consent searches. During this period, the consent search rate decreased by fifty-five additional consent searches beyond what the natural trends in the data show. This mirrors what we observed in Figure 9.1a: a dramatic decrease during the height of the controversy, and then a continued but lessened decrease following each successive reform. Unlike either Durham or Fayetteville, there is no statistical relationship between the number of consent searches conducted by the Chapel Hill Police Department and the reform.

Probable Cause Searches

Table 9.4 presents an identical analysis for the rate of probable cause searches.[3] Here we are looking for any possible substitution effects, which would be reflected in a positive coefficient for the reform variable, reflecting an increase in the percentage of stopped drivers subjected to such a search once the mandatory written consent form policy went into place.

If the written consent form reform has a positive coefficient associated with it, then a substitution effect of some degree has taken place. If the written consent form reform has a negative coefficient associated with it, then not only did a substitution effect not take place, but changing the process for consent searches began reframing how searches were conducted. In Fayetteville, there is a statistically significant decrease at the 0.10 level when the leadership changed. Probable cause search rate decreases from the baseline by twenty-eight probable cause searches per month. Thus, in Fayetteville, both types of searches went down.

TABLE 9.4. *Probable Cause Search Rates*

		Fayetteville	Durham	Chapel Hill
Reforms	Consent Search Ban	−17.46		
		(32.60)		
	Written Consent Form	−40.66	54.84**	0.49
		(64.57)	(4.12)	(8.38)
	Leadership Change	−27.83*	−62.00**	
		(14.78)	(3.92)	
Controls	Intercept	0.53	0.16	0.02
		(0.51)	(0.14)	(0.18)
	AR(1)	0.68**	−0.24	
		(0.11)	(0.61)	
	AR(2)		0.11	
			(0.19)	
	AR(3)		0.07	0.01
			(0.08)	(0.02)
	MA(1)	−0.89**	−0.48	−0.71**
		(0.08)	(0.60)	(0.06)
	MA(2)		−0.52	
			(0.62)	
	N	182	162	153
	Log Likelihood	−754.48	−650.06	−497.58

Note: See Table 9.3.

In Durham, the opposite is found. Following the implementation of the written consent form, the number of probable cause searches conducted increased at a statistically significant level. The number of probable cause searches conducted increased by fifty-five over the baseline number immediately following the reform indicating some substitution was occurring. Judging from these numbers, in Durham, the substitution effect might be called startling. However, it is reduced after the new chief comes into office. (Her tenure includes only six months before the end of our data collection period, however; so we interpret these findings with some caution.) The number of probable cause searches decreases by sixty-two per month.

The varied evidence seen across these tests indicates that the context surrounding the reforms may influence how they are implemented. It might be easy to conclude that the Durham situation is all too common, that a reform imposed by the community on a reluctant police leadership may prove ineffectual, especially if a city is suffering from significant crime, making the police feel they can give up no tools or discretion.

However, Fayetteville presents the opposite story: there, community–police relations were perhaps even at a lower point than in Durham; in any case they were at a breaking point, as noted by the city manager resigning and accusing city councilmen and others of "throwing the police under the bus" and a spokesman for the police officers calling for a federal investigation of those who were engaged in a "conspiracy" to "undermine" the department (see above). Though it took some time, through leadership change, a commitment to building trust, and significant reforms such as written consent as well as de-emphasizing investigatory stops, the situation in Fayetteville was largely turned around. Chapel Hill may represent a middle ground where there was no widespread erosion of trust in the first place but where the chief nonetheless took proactive steps to enact the reform, hoping to build community trust. In the next section, we discuss the impact of the reforms in Fayetteville by noting the continued decline in crime and the increase in community engagement with the police.

Regaining Trust: Crime Rates and Community Engagement

In the three cases discussed in the last section, mandatory written consent forms were aimed at promoting trust and reducing alienation. In addition, we saw in the earlier section that Fayetteville went much further than only this by reducing investigatory traffic stops quite dramatically under its new (post-February 2013) leadership. If such reforms increase trust of the police and reduce feelings of alienation, then we can expect to see a statistically meaningful increase in citizen-initiated contact with the police. Additionally, there may be little cost in terms of increased crime if the aggressive traffic patrols are not effective crime fighting tools in the first place, or if the increase in community cooperation more than offsets whatever reduction in police aggressiveness the policies involve. In this section, we test these ideas and focus solely on Fayetteville, because it is the only city for which the relevant statistics are available.

We estimate the effects of reform in Fayetteville in two ways. First, we look at how the implementation of the written consent form correlates with the crime rate, measured as the number of arrests that take place in each month. The number of arrests most closely mirrors the statistics used by the FBI to estimate crime rates. Specifically, the use of arrest rates mimics the statistics made available through the Universal Crime Reporting (UCR) initiative. A concern would be if arrests begin to increase after written consent forms go into effect, as this might suggest that the form limits the ability of law enforcement to prevent crimes.

Second, we look at whether citizen-initiated contact with police increased after the form was introduced. This is measured by counting total calls for service. We normalize the number of calls by dividing by the number of arrests. Our logic there is simple: if there is less crime, there would be fewer calls for service. So our measure of calls is calls divided by arrests. If calls per arrest are increasing, this indicates a relatively greater engagement of the community in reaching out to the police, for a given level of criminal behavior. Data for these tests comes from the open data portals maintained by the city of Fayetteville, http://data.fayettevillenc.gov/.

Figure 9.3 summarizes the overtime trends in adjusted calls for service and arrests in Fayetteville aggregated by month. Calls for service data span from 2011 through the end of 2015. Arrest data spans from 2007 through the end of 2016. In each subfigure, the horizontal solid line indicates the count of the relevant measure per month. The vertical lines indicate reforms.

As can be seen in Figure 9.3, the reforms correspond with and potentially cause positive outcomes in the city. First, the number of calls for service adjusted for the number of arrests rises across the depicted time period. Trust appears to be increasing. Further, while the number of arrests peaks when the controversy over consent searches is at its height, it consistently decreases from that point forward regardless of reform and who was police chief.

To disentangle the extent to which these relationships appear to be due to overtime trends influenced by events and decisions outside of these reforms and the reforms themselves, we estimate ARIMA regressions as we did in the previous section. As a reminder, these models allow for the direct effect of the reforms to be estimated while controlling for overtime trends in the data. The dependent variable in each of the models is the adjusted calls for service and the number of arrests respectively. As in the previous regressions, the independent variables in the model are: an indicator for whether the month belongs to the controversial consent search ban period, whether the written consent form is in place, and whether the new chief has been instated.

Table 9.5 presents the results for these tests, revealing that the number of calls for service per arrest increases by 5.50 after the new chief is installed. In response to the previous two reforms, there appears to be slight but not statistically meaningful increase in calls. With one simple (but highly publicized) change in police practices, we see a statistically significant difference in how the citizenry interacts with the local

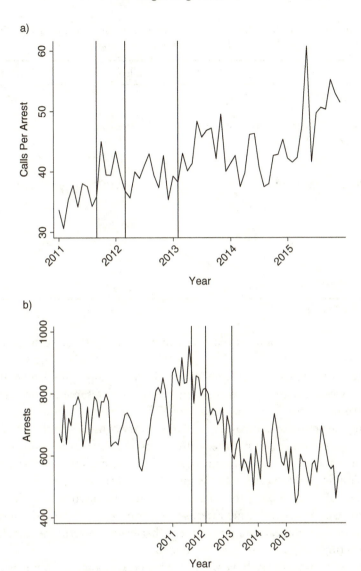

FIGURE 9.3. Frequency of Calls for Service (Adjusted for Crime) and Arrests

police. While a statistically significant relationship is found, two major confounders in this analysis should be considered. Fayetteville instituted the written consent form at almost the same time that a new police chief took over and as one in a number of reforms to increase community policing in the city. These contextual confounders suggest that the

TABLE 9.5. *Monthly Average Adjusted Calls for Service and Arrests by Policy Intervention*

		Calls for Service	Arrests
Reforms	Consent Search Ban	3.77	20.24
		(2.71)	(60.93)
	Written Consent Form	2.10	−8.88
		(3.51)	(44.31)
	Leadership Change	5.50**	−142.20**
		(2.63)	(46.10)
Controls	Intercept	37.18**	738.00**
		(3.45)	(17.81)
	AR(1)	0.88**	0.60**
		(0.19)	(0.08)
	MA(1)	−0.61**	
		(0.23)	
	N	60	120
	Log Likelihood	−168.77	−660.82

Note: See Table 9.3.

full story is more complex than we can reliably tease out with the data available to us.

Additionally, we can examine what effect – if any – implementation of the written consent form had on arrests. We observe an interesting pattern in the results of this regression. The number of arrests increased during the period of controversy and temporary consent search ban. Then they began to decrease once the written consent form was introduced and after the period of greatest controversy, but this decline is not statistically significant. However, with the installment of the new police chief, the number of arrests, our proxy for crime rate, decreased. The UCR uses arrests as a proxy for crime rates, so any concern that the written consent policy would lead to more crime, either by empowering criminals or obstructing the police, appear unfounded.

At the very least, we have preliminary evidence that the implementation of the written consent form – a specific reform to decrease the discretion of officers on the street – coupled with the compliance of the police department improves the relationship between the police and citizens. For those officers and departments wishing to better relations with the local community and decrease tensions, this might be one simple way to do so. Further, for community activists, this might be one reform to push for when attempting to address disparate treatment of various groups within a community.

Conclusion

We examined two simple solutions that might alter both real and perceived racial disparities and gave some indication of the benefits that can accrue both to the community and the police if such policies are enacted. First, we posed the hypothetical question of what would happen if no investigatory stops occurred. Then we examined how one simple reform – the implementation of the written consent form – alters police and community behavior. We first compared the mix of traffic stops by purpose, showing that de-emphasizing broken taillight and expired tag stops would have prevented millions from being stopped. Furthermore, when these types of investigatory stops are eliminated there are substantial reductions in levels of racial disparity, although black motorists are still more likely to be searched and arrested than whites. Such a reform does not work magic, after all, but it moves us collectively in the direction of less racial disparity.

Second, we asked how a single simple reform might influence search patterns and levels of trust and alienation in communities. As awareness of the traffic stops data has grown, several cities have adopted important reforms to reduce racial disparities and to repair the broken trust between the police and minority communities. Three of these are Fayetteville, Durham, and Chapel Hill. A comparison of the reforms enacted (or reluctantly accepted) in the three cities is instructive. We showed that a combination of leadership directives and simple initiatives can alter the relationship a department can have with their community. Then by focusing solely on Fayetteville, we showed that using fewer consent searches does not appear to cause an increase in crime, but it does appear to increase citizen-initiated contacts with the police, which in turn can be related to less crime. Simple administrative reforms are possible and effective for those police leaders who seek to reduce racial disparities and build community trust. Such reforms are not only good for community relations, democratic values, and trust, but they are also good for the police, as they generate more citizen contact in the fight against crime.

10

Conclusions

In 1999, when the NC General Assembly passed Senate Bill 76, mandating the collection of traffic data by law enforcement agencies, no one was sure what the data would show. Certainly, African-Americans serving in the General Assembly who had advocated on behalf of the bill suspected that the data would reveal what they (and their constituents) had known all along: that the police treat white and black motorists differently. But this opinion that racial disparities would be clearly evident was far from unanimous. Leaders of the State Highway Patrol argued that such allegations were unfounded and would be shown so by the data, which they volunteered to collect. The *Raleigh News and Observer* opined that the law was a good thing since it would either show that the allegations were unfair or, if validated, lead to immediate and effective reform. It was completely unclear at the time what degree of disparity might be uncovered, should any be found at all.

Recall from Chapter 2 that initial investigations suggesting that the drug interdiction unit of the State Highway Patrol (the "I-Team") was twice as likely to search black drivers had been greeted with alarm. Such claims were an important impetus behind the passage of the data-collection bill, which was expected to lead to either a clear demonstration that such fears were unwarranted or to immediate steps to improve the situation. Two Republican Senators, one now a member of the US House, co-sponsored the bill, and the leadership of the State Highway Patrol also endorsed it, certain that it would lead to the dismissal of baseless claims of racial disparity.

Then something curious happened. The bill was passed, expanded in 2001, and soon data was pouring into the NC DOJ. However, no state-mandated efforts to analyze the data were ever conducted. This was more than just a lost opportunity; it was, in fact, a violation of the law. The law mandated that the Attorney General's office make a report to the General Assembly every two years about the data. The question then about racial disparities in traffic stops went unanswered. How could it be that a law passed with such clear bipartisan intent was more or less forgotten by the General Assembly? There is no easy answer and the case serves as a reminder that policymaking does not end with a bill's passage. Implementation is, obviously, crucial and requires the faithful and diligent attention of lawmakers and bureaucrats. But political attention is fleeting and by the time the data were available for study, "driving while black" was no longer so high on the nation's political agenda, as the nation had gone to war in Iraq and moved on to other concerns. No official analysis was ever conducted, and none has been conducted to this date. The state has never concluded that there is a problem on the highways. Nor, of course, has it certified that there is not.

Fortunately, the data-collection process laid out in the law has continued, and the NC DOJ has been diligent in making the traffic stop data available to the public. It is therefore possible to answer the questions that preoccupied the General Assembly in the winter and spring of 1999. That is what we have tried to do with this book and our findings could not be clearer. Racial disparities are pervasive across the state; they exist in the largest urban police departments and the smallest rural agencies; they exist from the Outer Banks to the Blue Ridge Mountains; they exist in liberal college towns and conservative farm communities. The extent of the disparity is shocking. In 1999, the possibility that blacks were twice as likely to be searched by the Highway Patrol prompted lawmakers to seek answers. Today, after eighteen years of data collection have assembled over 20 million observations, we can report that a two-to-one disparity, far from being an aberration, is in fact the statewide average; many police agencies are much more disparate in their treatment of black motorists. And, as we showed in Chapter 7, these disparities are not limited to blacks; Hispanics are also much more likely to be searched and arrested than whites. Ironically, given that the Highway Patrol was singled out in the original legislation, that agency actually has much lower search rates and racial disparities than average. The 2001 expansion of the law to the vast majority of police agencies throughout the state revealed much greater disparities than within the SHP.

Another key element of our findings is that these tactics do not appear to have any readily apparent crime-fighting benefits. When contraband is discovered it is almost always in small amounts, so much so that the typical contraband "hit" does not even lead to an arrest. To boot, those demographic groups that are most likely to experience a search (young minority men) are actually less likely to be found with contraband. Hispanics in particular are much more likely to be subjected to "fruitless search" than whites or blacks. When we look at the behaviors associated with each police officer, we find no correlation between a propensity to search and the propensity to find contraband, suggesting that there are no overarching standards, that training does not produce a clear profile of when to search, and that it may well be an idiosyncratic guessing game, with each officer using his or her own judgment. Traffic stops can be used as a crime-fighting tool, but they are remarkably blunt and inefficient in that capacity. Traffic stops can certainly be a traffic safety tool, and we have shown that when officers focus on traffic safety, the racial disparities apparent in the outcomes of those stops are greatly reduced. Disparities are higher when officers use the rules of the road as a pretext to pull over those drivers who attract their attention for reasons unrelated to the safety of their driving.

The NC legislature was correct to demand the data. Many states have followed. While one can quibble, and many may be on the defensive, as a nation we know that police–minority relations have long been frayed and many scholars have documented striking differences in trust in government, participation in politics, and alienation from the police among white and minority citizens, especially African-Americans, as we discussed in Chapter 1. And with sustained attention to police violence since 2013, it is clear that these issues will not go away. It is important not to brush them off, ignore them, or allow ourselves collectively to ignore the poor state of relations between the police and the nation's minorities.

Some Individual Illustrations of the Psychological Toll of Traffic Stops

Many media reports have documented the trauma among minority drivers associated with routine traffic stops. As we wrote in Chapter 1, no one likes to be pulled over. But minority drivers may experience such events differently than white drivers, for two reasons. First, long-term historical trends likely correspond with what we have shown throughout the previous chapters of this book: odds are much greater for a minority driver to be pulled over, and even a routine traffic stop may turn into something more upsetting and even dangerous. Second, increased media attention to police violence in dealing with unarmed black motorists or pedestrians has heightened attention to such concerns, especially among minority citizens. Here we discuss three elements of the issue, using particular cases covered in the media as illustrations. One is the upsetting nature of the double-standard to which minority drivers know they may be held. Second is the lack of accountability when accusations of disparate policing or racial profiling are leveled against police agencies. And third is the ultimate paradox: while we know it "takes a lot of frogs to find your prince" and that contraband hits are very rare, on those rare occasions when large contraband caches are indeed found, defense attorneys increasingly are looking at traffic stops statistics to document extreme patterns of profiling by individual officers or drug interdiction teams. And judges occasionally force them to drop charges when the stop fits a pattern of racial profiling and/or the search may have been conducted illegally.

Routine, Expected, and Upsetting Personal Experiences with the Police

One 2017 video highlights the high emotional toll of a routine traffic stop and the fear that it can instill. The driver, Ayanna Cruver, took the video of herself in her car shortly after a stop that she found extremely upsetting, but which in retrospect she recognized as benign.

Crying and obviously distraught, Ms. Cruver explains to the camera that she was pulled over and asked to exit her vehicle, which made her fear for her safety. The officer had pulled her over after she left an Air Force Base in Louisiana where her husband had just retired after twenty-two years in service to the country. The officer explained that she had been driving under the speed limit and that such driving can be a sign that the driver may be extremely tired or perhaps inebriated. Asking her to come to the back of the vehicle, he found that she was neither. But what the officer perhaps intended as a check to make sure Ms. Cruver was healthy and in condition to drive was seen by the driver as a life-threatening danger. "I just broke down crying and I told him, I said I was so scared, and I knew he felt awful that I was that scared but I was so scared. I never thought that in that situation I would feel fearful, but I legitimately felt horrified. How awful to be stopped by the police and feel that scared." The officer calmed her down, explained that he was just concerned for her safety, and even gave her a hug, encouraging her to be safe and take care.

It blew my mind how frightened I was that a police officer stopped me ... The nature of the situation in our country right now made me feel horrified that I got stopped and asked to get out of the car. But the positive spin is that he really was just a nice officer checking to see if I was ok ... But the sad piece is that I should not have had to feel this scared. (USA Today 2017; Pitts 2017)

As columnist Leonard Pitts wrote about the video, when members of the public have been inundated with stories about motorists such as Sandra Bland, Walter Scott, or Philando Castile who each died after a police encounter beginning with a traffic stop, it makes sense that some would be concerned. A WRAL-TV investigation in 2015 includes this story about John Hunt, a middle-aged black resident of Raleigh:

Hunt was heading home to Raleigh when a Vance County sheriff's deputy got behind him. Hunt says he didn't want to stop over the crest of a hill, so he turned on his flashers until he found a safer place to pull over. He says he was shocked when the deputy ordered him out of the truck, gun drawn.

"I thought he was going to shoot me," Hunt said. "He had the gun on me the whole while and got behind the truck, instructed me to bend down on my knees. And when he did that, another officer, he took my hands, he snatched it back, and another officer came, turned to the side, pulled a gun on me, and the other officer that stopped me put the handcuffs on me."

Hunt asked, but said he wasn't given a reason for the stop. Deputies didn't ask as they searched his truck, he said. "I was afraid. I was terrified." (WRAL 2015b)

A 2015 *New York Times* story about traffic stops begins this way:

GREENSBORO, N.C. – Rufus Scales, 26 and black, was driving his younger brother Devin to his hair-cutting class in this genteel, leafy city when they heard the siren's whoop and saw the blue light in the rearview mirror of their black pickup. Two police officers pulled them over for minor infractions that included expired plates and failing to hang a flag from a load of scrap metal in the pickup's bed. But what happened next was nothing like a routine traffic stop.

Uncertain whether to get out of the car, Rufus Scales said, he reached to restrain his brother from opening the door. A black officer stunned him with a Taser, he said, and a white officer yanked him from the driver's seat. Temporarily paralyzed by the shock, he said, he fell face down, and the officer dragged him across the asphalt.

Rufus Scales emerged from the encounter with four traffic tickets; a charge of assaulting an officer, later dismissed; a chipped tooth; and a split upper lip that required five stitches.

That was May 2013. Today, his brother Devin does not leave home without first pocketing a hand-held video camera and a business card with a toll-free number for legal help. Rufus Scales instinctively turns away if a police car approaches.

"Whenever one of them is near, I don't feel comfortable. I don't feel safe," he said. (LaFraniere and Lehren 2015)

A 2015 *Charlotte Observer* reviews some of the early data reports associated with this book, reforms put into place by Charlotte-Mecklenberg

Police (CMPD) Chief Rodney Monroe, and a community leader's own experiences. That community leader, Patrick Graham, makes clear his concern for how younger members of his community can naturally be expected to develop their own feelings and expectations in interacting with the local police department:

> Four years ago, Patrick Graham says he was pulled over on Statesville Avenue, in a predominantly black part of the city. He says the officer told him he had changed lanes without signaling.
>
> Graham, an African-American who is president of the Urban League of the Central Carolinas, says he was lucky. After running Graham's license, the officer came back to the car, called him "Dr. Graham" and sent him on his way …
>
> While Graham credits Monroe and CMPD for working to establish better relationships across the city, he says he believes traffic stops remain the "most intimate contact" some minority communities will ever have with police.
>
> "If being pulled over is your only point of reference," Graham says, "that will leave a bad taste in your mouth." (Gordon 2015a)

A companion article entitled "The personal side of traffic stops" reviews the experiences of three prominent Charlotte residents, including the police chief, with their own experiences with questionable police stops (see Gordon 2015b). Rev. Tiffany Thomas explains her experience from a year before, driving with an attorney friend on the I-485 when state troopers stopped them and asked to search the car.

> Thomas' friend, a former assistant district attorney who is black, told him no. "The officer said, 'What are you hiding?' It got very tense," Thomas says.
>
> Over the next 20 minutes, the officer asked several more times for permission to search, Thomas says. "My friend said, 'You haven't arrested me. You can't hold me here any longer.'"
>
> The officer eventually let them go, but not before writing a ticket. Says Thomas, "It was ridiculous how long we were out there."

Harold Cogdell, an attorney and former local elected official, describes this encounter:

> About five years ago, Cogdell, a former elected official, says he was pulled over near Central Avenue and Sharon Amity Road. He was wearing a Brazilian soccer jersey, and he says the white CMPD officer started out talking to him in Spanish, asked him how long he had been in the country and said his windows were tinted too dark.
>
> Then he asked to search the car. Cogdell told him no. "He told me I had to wait, that he was calling in additional officers and that I might be arrested for a window-tinting violation." He said he waited about 15 minutes before one of the other arriving officers recognized him, and Cogdell was allowed to go. "This is

not something new and unusual," he says. "It's something that's been occurring for years."

Rodney Monroe, the police chief, had this encounter:

Some 30 years ago, when Monroe was with the Washington, D.C., police, he says he had strapped on his service revolver after bowling in his weekly league. Someone reported that there was an armed black man in the bowling alley.

He left with his 5-year-old daughter. On the drive home, he pulled into a fast-food drive-thru.

"Suddenly, we were surrounded by officers, guns sticking through the windows, demanding to see my hands," Monroe recalls. "My daughter was hysterical, grabbing for me, and all I can think of is keeping my hands on the wheel, that something bad could have happened if I reached for her."

Eventually, the police identified Monroe and apologized.

"Do I fault the other officers? No. Do I believe I was profiled? No. I was a black man with a gun," Monroe says. "They explained why they stopped me. And we moved on." (see Gordon 2015b)

We need not multiply the examples; they can be found in any large newspaper or media website. Whereas Chief Monroe apparently thought it was not profiling when he was targeted by armed police because he was "a black man with a gun" and Atty. Cogdell realized that his experience was "not something new and unusual" but "has been going on for years," the expected nature of these incidents does not make them any less severe. Minority drivers realize that such events can be expected; parents teach their sons how to behave in such situations; millions of Americans are raised, socialized into the idea that their encounters with the police may turn violent in a split second, so caution, respect, and submission are the safest means to emerge safely from the encounter. This discussion may seem woefully inadequate to a black reading audience, but it may seem completely foreign to a middle-class white one. Such concerns are just not present in the mainstream, middle-class, white community.

Lack of Institutional Response

In Texas, state troopers have recorded millions of highway patrol stops and statistics reveal large racial disparities in search rates (see Baumgartner et al. 2016; Schwartz and Dexheimer 2017), but never has a complaint about racial profiling been confirmed by the Department of Public Safety. *Austin American-Statesman* reporter Sean Collins Walsh reviewed thirty complaints and looked at the videos. His article begins as follows:

The Texas state troopers said they pulled over the truck driven by Guillermo "Willie" Rios because the license plate was not on the front bumper. It was on the dashboard.

But video of the ensuing traffic stop and vehicle search shows that the troopers were instantly suspicious of Rios and his passengers.

"There's not a scratch on that truck," Trooper Abraham Martinez said to his partner when they return to their patrol car, out of Rios' earshot. "Something is not right. I think all of this is a front."

The search turned up nothing, and Rios, a South Houston city councilman who also works as a contractor in the oil field, filed a racial-profiling complaint against the troopers with the Texas Department of Public Safety.

"They passed my vehicle, they look over at me, we all look Mexican, and then they pull us over," Rios recounted in a recent interview about the 2014 incident. "They treated me like a criminal right when I got out ... They pulled me over because my truck was too clean. How is that a reason to get pulled over?"

DPS investigated the allegation but did not find evidence of racial profiling. In fact, the agency has rejected every allegation of racial profiling that it has ever received. (Walsh 2016)

Walsh goes on to document several cases where drivers were pulled over on the thinnest of suspicions, including an African-American attorney refusing a search in much the same way as Charlotte Atty. Cogdell in the example above. A key issue, beyond possible racially profiling, is the reaction of the drivers. As Councilman Rios makes clear, he knows he was pulled over because of the color of his skin. Dr. Graham (in Charlotte, NC) was let off without any further investigation once the officers ran his driver's license, and one could imagine being pleased at the good outcome. But, as a community leader, his response was concern for those who might not be so fortunate, and knowledge that the initial stop was not strongly legally justified. It may not have been illegal, since officers have great leeway and in a practical sense if an officer says a driver changed lanes without signaling, and there is no video record, then there will be no finding of an illegal stop. But, Dr. Graham knew that there was no good justification for his traffic stop and it was a reminder to him of those patterns of policing that erode public trust. On the other hand, if Chief Moore suggests that his own dangerous encounter was understandable because he was "a black man with a gun" then it suggests that many police agencies do not share the same concerns about eliminating profiling incidents when confronted with them. In fact, almost every time they rule that racial profiling cannot be proven, and indeed the numbers themselves cannot be used as proof. Rather, the numbers must point to areas of concern, leading to further investigation. With the investigations being conducted by internal affairs departments loath to find evidence of profiling, it is not surprising that documented cases are rare. Durham is in fact one of the few cases where the city government has officially concluded that there was racial bias within the police department. This finding came from the Human Relations Commission, not an internal DPD investigation, as we explained in Chapter 9.

Criminal Prosecutions Gone Bad

A 2014 *New York Times* article about Durham not only noted the low state of community relations, but also the increased use of traffic stops data in criminal defense cases. In those rare instances where searches have led to the discovery of large amounts of contraband, defense attorneys have asked to see the data. As Richard Oppel explains:

The School of Government at the University of North Carolina at Chapel Hill has a new manual for defense lawyers, prosecutors and judges, with a chapter that shows how stop and search data can be used by the defense to raise challenges in cases where race may have played a role.

In one recent case, the public defender representing a Hispanic man on cocaine trafficking charges in Orange County, N.C., got a dismissal after presenting the prosecutor with evidence that Hispanics – while only 8 percent of the local population – had received more than half of the hundreds of warnings issued by the sheriff's deputy who had made the arrest. The deputy had testified that he stopped the man's truck for a minor traffic infraction. The prosecutor said multiple factors led to the dismissal.

Defense lawyers' raising the issue "is gathering steam," said Alyson Grine, a lecturer at U.N.C. who trains defenders and is an author of the new manual. Several North Carolina police chiefs, she added, have even begun to use the data to sit down with individual officers and examine their search patterns as part of routine management. (Oppel 2014)

A particularly striking case occurred along a rural stretch of I-85 west of Charlotte in a 2011 case (see Clark 2013). Three men named Gomez, Pena, and Dela Cruz were travelling from Georgia to New York when deputies from the Cleveland County Sheriff's Office Interstate Criminal Enforcement (ICE) Division pulled them over for speeding. Officers found six pounds of cocaine, so in this case they had truly "found their prince." However, Judge Nathaniel J. Poovey ruled that charges would have to be dropped, ruling that the search was conducted without consent or probable cause, that the deputies had committed racial profiling, and by turning off audio recording equipment had destroyed evidence. He described their behavior as "repugnant." Defense attorney Calvin

Coleman said that "about 70 percent of the citations issued by the Sheriff's Office Interstate Criminal Enforcement Division team during a period of several months were issued to Hispanics" though not all records had been maintained.

A third case is from Johnston County in 2014: a state trooper's decision to search a driver was ruled illegal on appeal; the search led to charges of possession of 200 to 400 grams of cocaine, which was found under the back seat of the car. An Appeals Court ruled that there had not been probable cause; the trooper had not taken the initial "no" as an answer when he asked to search a car, continuing to ask until the renter agreed, having her sign a written consent form. He had told the driver to sit in the front seat of his patrol car while he convinced the passenger, who had signed the rental car agreement, to consent to the search. In the end, the search led to the discovery of over half a pound of cocaine, but the Appeals Court threw out the conviction ruling that the driver had been illegally seized without reasonable suspicion when the trooper told him to "sit tight" in the front seat of the patrol car (see Blythe 2016).

In both the Orange County and the Cleveland County cases, traffic stop patrols had uncovered significant drug caches being transported by Hispanic drivers. In both cases, evidence was presented that deputies followed long-standing police training and practices to use the traffic laws as a way to pull a car over, perhaps just on a "hunch" and perhaps as the result of racial profiling, and then to seek to search the car. Judges in both cases were concerned with the disparate statistics showing that some individual deputies or drug interdiction teams had stopped thousands of Hispanic drivers, but few of other races in spite of patrolling areas of the state, such as Orange County (home to Chapel Hill) that have few Hispanics. Racially disparate patterns of stops, combined with legally suspect searches not clearly justified by probable cause, were the downfall of these two cases.

Most likely, more will follow as defense attorneys and public defenders become more accustomed to using the data associated with an individual officer through such websites as https://opendatapolicing.com/nc/, administered by the Southern Coalition for Social Justice, but making use of the same data we have used throughout this book. These data resources allow an attorney to look up the records of the officer involved in their client's case to investigate possible patterns of disparate behavior toward drivers of different races. If found, and particularly if combined with evidence that consent or probable cause was not associated with a search, then the evidence from that search could be thrown out. In the

Johnston County case, racially disparate statistics were not in play, but the case hinged on what constitutes "reasonable suspicion."

We have documented throughout this book several disconcerting elements about the racial characteristics of traffic stops in North Carolina. First, drivers of different races are subjected to dramatically different odds of being pulled over. Driving While Black really is a problem. Second, search rates for minority drivers are roughly twice as high as for whites. Third, these search rates are not fully justified by higher contraband hit rates. Fourth, contraband hit rates are extremely low, especially when we consider contraband finds leading to arrest, or even more so when we look only at large contraband finds. In this section, we have given more anecdotal but still important personal evidence of the stress, trauma, and emotional toll that unfair policing takes on those subjected to it. This is particularly troubling when accusations of it are so rarely found to be warranted when police departments investigate themselves. Finally, we have given examples that even when sheriff's deputies finally do "find their prince" the thousands of innocent victims of previous racially disparate traffic stops cause judges to be convinced that the stop was motivated by race, and to look hard at the admissibility of evidence, even pounds of illicit substances, that might result from searches following such fishing expeditions. We come full circle in finding that when such police practices finally do lead to what the officers are looking for – significant drug caches being transported across state lines – that the "needle in the haystack" element of the use of routine traffic laws to fight the war on crime or the war on drugs renders the evidence collected to be so suspect that charges are dropped when the evidence is ruled inadmissible. What a waste. What a tragedy.

The (Young Minority Male) Citizen as Suspect

We believe that the racial disparities documented in this book originate predominantly from an evolution in police tactics that began in the 1970s. Around that time, police departments around the country were under pressure to address rising crime rates. While police officers may solve an individual crime (in the sense that they might discover who is responsible and bring him or her to justice) they have only a marginal ability to affect the underlying societal causes of crime. There is little that the police can do to improve local economic opportunities, or the quality of public schools, or the availability of inexpensive public transportation. Nevertheless, the police are widely viewed as the solution to crime, so when crime becomes more prevalent, the burden of doing something about it falls to the men and women in blue. Their tools, however, of "handcuffs and jail time," as Alice Goffman put it (2014, 203), are woefully incomplete.

In the 1980s, the strategy was to implement a new, proactive approach to crime fighting. Rather than waiting to solve crimes after they happened, the police would work to identify criminals and to apprehend them before the crime occurred. Pedestrians were subjected to interviews and pat-downs based on "the cut of their jib" as Justice Douglas put it in his 1968 dissent in *Terry* v. *Ohio* (see Chapter 1). Drivers were subjected to even more scrutiny, especially since the Supreme Court ruled in 1996 (in *Whren* v. *United States*) that an officer may pull over a car for any violation, and the rules of the road feature hundreds of such possible infractions. Each of these became a possible pretext for an officer to pull over virtually any car on the road. This proactive style of policing was designed to show "the criminals" that the police knew who they were, what they were doing, and where they were to be found. The message was clear: we are watching you. Entire police textbooks and training programs were developed around this school of thought. A consequence is that ordinary citizens on their way to work or the grocery store became potential suspects and were subject to stops aimed not at promoting traffic safety but at apprehending felons. The new, aggressive style of proactive policing may have been well intentioned; we would all like to believe that the police could stop crime before it even occurred. (Indeed the 2002 film *Minority Report*, directed by Steven Spielberg and starring Tom Cruise, focuses on a fictional future where a special police unit apprehends criminals before they commit their crimes.)

No one wants to live in a police state, so how was this new approach to crime fighting ever viable? The answer is that it was extremely targeted. Middle-class whites were simply not affected by it and continued to enjoy a less invasive, community-oriented style of policing. It was predominantly members of minority and lower-income communities who suffered through this heightened level of police scrutiny. Of course, residents of these communities did voice their disapproval (and continue to do so) but lacked the political and economic capital to make lawmakers take notice. Chapter 8 highlighted the importance of political voice; in communities where African-Americans are better represented we generally find less acute racial disparities in traffic stops. We should note an obvious corollary to our findings in Chapter 8; where voice is low, disparities may be higher. That is, if the police alienate a targeted segment of the community, and they lose their voice, this can become a self-perpetuating and vicious circle.

Carceral Capitalism

Occasionally, the courts have issued strong sanctions against clearly documented racial profiling. Typically, however, this has been when a powerful or wealthy individual happens to be caught in the net. Such an event happened in rural Georgia when Atlanta Hawks forward Mike Scott and his brother were travelling on Interstate 85 from the Atlanta area to Virginia to attend a basketball camp. After the blue lights came on, Scott and his brother found themselves handcuffed, on the pavement, and arrested, with some marijuana, ecstacy, and cash taken as contraband. Scott, in contrast to many who may have been stopped in this rural 10-mile stretch of I-85 where the Banks County Sheriff has jurisdiction, had an NBA salary of $3.3 million in 2015 when the stop occurred. He hired a team of lawyers who documented that the deputy involved had twice been forced to resign previous law enforcement jobs, and, as a member of the "crime interdiction unit" had made over 1,400 traffic stops during 2015 and 2016, but had issued only eight tickets. Of the forty-seven arrests he had made, forty-four were minority drivers. Scott's attorneys argued that the unit was focused on criminal forfeitures. "'He's not out there to enforce the traffic laws. He's out there to shake people down for drugs and money'" argued Scott's attorney Billy Healen. The judge agreed, also noting inconsistencies in the ways the traffic stop was written up, ruling that the stop was unjustified (see Rankin 2017).

What was once a rural "speed trap" with a goal of writing large numbers of speeding tickets has become a different and even more troubling thing. Because those involved in illicit activities can have their assets seized by the law enforcement agency that arrests them, an incentive structure clearly exists to seek out people who may fit a profile. The pattern of Banks County Deputy Brent Register, who arrested Scott, fits this pattern: large numbers of stops with the vast majority of drivers released with a warning. The stops were for such violations as travelling too closely, making an improper lane change, or equipment failures. While the Deputy issued almost no speeding tickets, and did not even use a radar gun to identify speeders, his agency spent over a quarter million dollars in fiscal year 2016 in forfeiture funds. These funds paid for equipment, training, travel, and capital improvements (Rankin 2017). Between the lines in the story of the Banks County (Georgia) Sheriff's Department is the story of an agency fishing for gold with thousands of mostly unremarkable traffic stops. Once in a blue moon, one of them might lead to a financial bonanza. That is what they might have been expecting when they found some drugs in Mike Scott's car. Who knows how many other drivers have been profiled for such reasons over the years? But because it has never happened to many middle-class white drivers, the concept seems incredible. It is all too real among younger black and brown men, however.

Our North Carolina database does not indicate which traffic stops led to forfeitures such as those which were apparently driving the Banks County (GA) Sheriff's Department to stop hundreds of innocent motorists in what amounts to a fishing expedition. But we can look at various patterns in the data to identify suspicious trends. One of those is an excess in "light outcomes" such as warnings rather than tickets. And we can document that minority drivers are much more likely to see such events than white drivers.

That kind of "hidden tax on the poor" cannot be expected to generate trust. In fact, it is both illegal and deeply alienating of local communities. In their report on Ferguson, the US DOJ writes, "the confluence of policing to raise revenue and racial bias thus has resulted in practices that not only violate the Constitution and cause direct harm to the individuals whose rights are violated, but also undermine community trust, especially among many African Americans" (2015, 6). What happens when trust is eroded below a certain level? People withdraw from the community. They become alienated from government, they avoid interactions with government agencies including schools, unemployment offices, hospitals, and other institutions that might be inclined to help, and they withdraw from contact with the police. Several studies have shown shocking findings about refusals to call 911 or to cooperate with the police even in active crime investigations happening right in the neighborhood where witnesses live.

Eroding Trust

Jonathan Simon (2007) reviews a range of changes in American politics and society stemming from the dramatic politicization of crime that he documents from the 1970s to present. Noting that President Nixon had declared both a war on crime and a war on cancer, he remarks not only that the war on crime seems to have had much greater effects in many areas of politics, education, and criminal justice than the war on cancer, but he notes in his conclusion: "To mix metaphors, governing through crime produces cancer, or more accurately, cancers" (278). His example: 2 million prisoners, with large numbers returning to devastated communities each year, often with little prospect for further education, employment, or productive lives. The danger to the body politic is not only the collective cost of tens of thousands of young men coming out of prison to stressed communities with little hope of economic advancement, but also living in a "stalemate" where we "regard the current state of mass incarceration coexisting with violence-producing criminal markets for narcotics as an acceptable price to be paid for a sense of security in the suburbs" (280).

Many scholars have reviewed the costs and consequences of our nation's experiment with mass incarceration, as we reviewed in Chapter 1. Our focus has been quite narrow, looking only at one state, and at only one aspect of the interactions between the police and the public. Traffic stops are, however, the single most common way in which such interactions occur. For most of us, they are polite, inconvenient and frustrating perhaps, but rare and of no long-term consequence. For a smaller but significant portion of the public, largely Hispanic and black men, these interactions can be quite different. First, they may not be rare, but repeated many times. (Recall our simple bar graphs from Chapter 4 documenting the rate at which different demographic groups experience a search. For middle-age white men, the likelihood of being searched after a stop was around 3 percent; for young black men the likelihood was about 10 percent.) Second, they may not be polite; rather, they clearly convey the suspicion with which the officer views the individual. (Recent evidence from recordings of traffic-stop interactions in Oakland, California suggests that even the language officers use with white and minority drivers is starkly different: respectful with white drivers, less so with minorities; see Voigt et al. 2017). Third, the justification for the stop may be unclear, more a pretext for an officer to look inside the car than a simple moving violation. This is particularly notable when we think of our vision of a speeding ticket from a Highway Patrol trooper on an interstate highway as compared to a more pretextual stop in an urban environment such as the one we looked at in the first pages of this book. Individuals know when they were stopped for good reason as compared to a pretext (see Epp et al. 2014).

Alienating large numbers of drivers may well be an acceptable consequence of good policing if it generates dramatic reductions in crime and is accurately targeted at those who are breaking the law. But when the targets of these aggressive techniques of policing are often falsely accused,

their alienation may be even greater than if they had been guilty of something. Indeed, we noted considerable work in Chapter 1 that showed that
guilty people do not contest the outcomes of their experiences with the
judicial system if they feel the process has been fair. But innocent people
who feel they were not treated fairly can naturally be quite upset. Our
concern has never been with guilty criminals. Rather, we have documented
that many innocent people, who may live in a "high crime area" or have
certain visible characteristics (such as being young, poor, male, and with
brown skin) are much more likely to have adverse encounters with the
police. When this happens often enough, alienation, frustration, and
anger are certainly predictable consequences. Over the past generation,
with the war on crime, police officers have been encouraged to engage in
practices that encourage the use of demographic profiles. In this book we
have documented that they may have higher costs than previously understood. Reducing trust, generating anger, and producing alienation in a
large segment of the community are high costs indeed. Because the costs
have been borne by the members of the community with the least ability
to seek redress, and those with greatest access to power and influence
may be completely unaware of them, these costs have never been part of
the political discussion. They should be. They tear at the very fabric of
democracy.

What Can be Done?

Our analysis presents a bleak picture of policing in one state, but we are
actually very hopeful that the situation can improve. A number of reforms
could be implemented at minimal cost (in fact, many of them might actually save money and time) and would not require any major updates to
existing laws. The preceding chapters have outlined all of these possibilities. Here we briefly summarize them in two categories.

1) *Improve Efficiency*
In US politics, a common criticism of government is that it lacks efficiency.
Often these claims are of dubious (or at least undocumented) quality, but
when it comes to traffic stops, a greater emphasis on efficiency is sorely
needed. It is hard to summarize the logic behind using traffic stops to
fight crime any better than the CA highway patrol officer, who famously
quipped to a reporter that the enterprise was a "sheer numbers game." If
a large proportion of the population was regularly committing felonies,
then the police could stop cars at random and still catch many criminals,

but that is simply not the case, even in the country's most dangerous communities. If failed searches were costless, then low contraband-hit rates would not signify, but this also is not the case. Besides the momentary inconvenience to the motorist (and also the officer who could be using their time in more productive ways), searches are humiliating; repeated searches are ominous, scary, and alienating.

The math is simple, and laid out in Table 5.6. From 20 million traffic stops, 2.4 percent lead to a search. Of those, just 33 percent led to contraband (0.8 percent of stops), and just 12 percent of the searches led to a contraband-arrest combination (0.29 percent of stops). That is, 99.7 percent of traffic stops fail to generate a drug or contraband arrest. The "sheer numbers game" the California trooper describes is a bad gamble.

Furthermore, it is unclear that there is any relationship between aggressive use of traffic stops as an opportunity to conduct criminal investigations and the crime rate. That is, given the meager pay-offs in terms of contraband and arrest following from traffic stops, moving away from their aggressive use may have little down-side in terms of fighting crime. And, as we showed in Chapter 9, it can be very beneficial in promoting public trust, which in turn can be helpful for stopping crime. It might be that when we look at trends in crime rates and correlate those with shifts in policy, that we have the causal arrows backwards. Declining crime rates may provide the window of political opportunity to promote policies consistent with better community engagement. Rising crime rates may make it politically difficult to enact such reforms, especially if the police feel that they are under pressure to use all means possible to bring the crime rate back down. Our hunch is that crime rates are driven by many factors, but not much by how many cars are searched after traffic stops. Perhaps, then, we should think of the political dynamics of rising and falling crime rates as the reason why police departments choose to ratchet up or ratchet down various crime fighting policies. Our analysis suggests that ratcheting up the use of traffic stops as a crime fighting strategy has little positive effect on crime but dramatically negative effects on racial disparities, on alienation and trust in the minority community, and on community cooperation with the police.

One simple reform would be for police chiefs and administrators to assign a value to a fruitless search, those that lead to nothing. Currently, as we have discussed, and with full legal justification, searches that lead to nothing are considered to be "momentary inconveniences" for those individuals so bothered. A look at the numbers can reveal, however, just how many such inconveniences are created, and for so little value to society. Table 5.2, for example, showed that just 29 percent of all searches led to the discovery of any contraband. While this number was higher (55 percent) for probable cause searches, recall as well that contraband, when found, is typically in very small amounts. When we look at searches leading to arrest, as we did in Table 5.4, we find that just 12 percent of searches lead to arrest, and only 23 percent of probable cause searches. We have the opportunity to revise police training, and we believe we should. Given the numbers we have laid out here, it seems reasonable to teach our officers that each interaction with a citizen is a chance to teach trust or alienation. Trust has important social values, and fruitless searches may lead to alienation, especially when the same individual (or those in their social network) are subjected to them repeatedly. Empirically, police officers are very poor predictors of contraband. The vast majority of searches come up dry. High numbers of searches lead to no findings at all or to minimal findings of contraband, so minimal that the officer initiating the search decides not to arrest the individual. While it may be true that "you have to kiss a lot of frogs before you find your prince" it is certainly worth recognizing that those frogs may not like being kissed, and that repeatedly doing so may generate predictable alienation. The simple solution: recognize the inefficiency of searches following routine traffic stops and assign a cost or a value to a citizen's right to privacy and trust.

Focusing on efficiency as an area for improvement has the benefit that everyone (liberal or conservative) can agree that efficiency is a laudable goal. One immediate step that police agencies can take to improve efficiency is to take a long and hard look at the use of consent searches. Our analysis suggests that in almost every jurisdiction consent searches are worse than probable cause searches (the other discretionary search type) at uncovering contraband. Consent searches also tend to be more racially disparate than other searches. This is not surprising. If an officer has a good reason to search a motorist or vehicle, then they can do so with probable cause. Consent searches are essentially fishing expeditions; the perfect embodiment of inefficiency in traffic stops. If police agencies worry about eliminating consent searches altogether, then steps can at least be taken to ensure that drivers are very clear on their right to refuse a search under these circumstances. Fayetteville and Durham have already moved in this direction by introducing written consent forms that a driver must sign before an officer is allowed to conduct such a search. We applaud the use of written consent forms as have been mandated in several jurisdictions. We are concerned that the advent of police-worn body cameras has been used as a reason why written consent forms need not be adopted. A written consent form such as the one reproduced in Appendix D ensures that individuals be aware of their rights to maintain privacy. Clear empirical evidence suggests that use of the reform reduces compliance with the officer's request (or reduces those requests) by over 90 percent. This, if nothing else, suggests that citizens feel compelled to agree to an officer's verbal request for consent. That by itself should suggest a constitutional argument for reducing the use of such searches, as the "consent" may be more theoretical than practical. But our argument goes beyond that, or is weaker than that. Our argument is that if we assign a value to citizen trust and cooperation with the police, the alienation that follows from repeated requests for search is just not worth it. It has little crime-fighting value; we saw in Table 5.4 that over 90 percent of consent searches come up dry or do not lead to arrest. Given the slight value in crime fighting, the cost in alienation seems high.

Beyond reducing searches, agencies should ask about the public safety value of traffic stops in general, in particular those for "investigatory" reasons. Certainly, when an officer is in pursuit of a criminal and the officer finds them in a car they should be stopped. But the routine use of the traffic code as a pretext to stop and investigate a driver, often on a hunch rather than on any kind of firm evidence of criminal activity, should be questioned. There is no doubt that the police have the right to pull over a car and engage in a conversation with a driver if the car has, for example, a cracked tail light or an obscured license plate. But court rulings allowing these activities do not make them effective crime-fighting strategies, particularly if we assign any value at all to the freedom of individuals to be free from unwanted police scrutiny. The numbers we have laid out in this book make clear that routine traffic stops are not good ways to find "bad guys" and also that when the police focus on investigations rather than on traffic safety, the racial disparities in their searches increase. Focusing on traffic safety, speeders, and stop-sign runners rather than those with expired tags, cracked tail lights, or who appear to be Hispanic and may not have immigration papers has the benefit of directly affecting community safety while not alienating those pulled over, who know that the stated reason for the traffic stop was in fact a pretext. It would be one thing if these investigatory stops routinely generated evidence of criminal behavior. But they do not. And they are more costly in terms of public trust than most have previously realized. Police agencies throughout the nation should take a hard look at the costs and benefits of these routine practices.

Another important avenue for improvement is to engage with the data. Throughout the book, we have lamented that although police officers meticulously file forms after every stop, the data is not aggregated and redistributed to police agencies in a way amenable to executive oversight. While the data collection was originally conceived of as a mean of assessing racial disparities (and is of great value in that regard) it has other potentials as well. It is a valuable record of what officers have been doing on the motorways and may therefore be useful in fine-tuning police strategies. This is especially true because while we have a limited capacity to link stops to particular patrol routes, police chiefs could presumably connect the dots for their own agencies with little difficulty. It would then be possible to determine what patrols (and which officers) have relatively low hit rates, and adjust resources accordingly. Of course, we can also hope that police chiefs would use the data to facilitate what may be difficult conversations with officers who show a proclivity for searching minority drivers. One can imagine that with minimal investment the NC DOJ could routinely issue data-driven reports to police agencies, highlighting statistics of interest such as arrest, search, and contraband hit rates, all broken down by race, gender, and age group.

It is also important that the local community remain involved and aware of data collection processes. In fact, while it is unfortunate that no Attorney General since 2000 has seen fit to follow the legislative mandate to report on the data, a recent example from Texas suggests that officially sponsored analyses may not be the best solution. In Texas, under pressure to respond to racial disparities in stops, chief law enforcement officers assembled a hand-picked research team, which, unsurprisingly, led to media accusations of bias (see Walsh 2017). A better approach may be if state DOJs follow the North Carolina example of making the data easily and openly available on-line; they may then benefit from the equivalent of crowd-sourcing the analysis of police data. This may be unwelcome to various police agencies because they will not hand-pick the analyst. But it may lead to more sophisticated and, most importantly, unbiased analyses. The analyst, being unpaid and disconnected from any particular stake-holder, will be exploring the data for the patterns embedded in it, not seeking to curry favor with this or that funding agency, particularly the one being scrutinized. Historically, efforts of police departments to police themselves compare relatively badly to the research enabled by open source projects, such as the Stanford Open Data project (https://openpolicing.stanford.edu/) or https://opendatapolicing.com/, because when independent scholars and researchers analyze the data, they are not under contract to the agency they are seeking to understand.

2) *Strengthen Democracy on the Ground*

A second piece of the puzzle is to make sure that minority voices are a prominent part of the political landscape, especially in regions of the country where minorities make up a sizeable part of the population. The intensive scrutiny directed toward members of poor or minority communities by the police does not occur in more affluent, white parts of town in large part because it is politically unfeasible. If middle-class whites were searched at the same rate as young black men (with as little to show for it), state capitols would soon be ringing with calls to reform the police. It is the extremely targeted nature of aggressive police tactics that makes them possible. Those who might complain often lack political voice and connections in government.

Chapter 8 showed just how important minority representation can be when it comes to policing. In municipalities where African-Americans have more political leverage, we found that racial disparities in stops were less severe on average. And, of course, the law mandating the collection of the data that made this book possible was introduced by African-American legislators. The question of how to get more minorities elected is a book-length topic in its own right (see Segura and Bowler 2005). Here we simply note that there is strong evidence of a vicious cycle of aggressive policing leading to less community involvement, thereby enabling the aggressive policing tactics. This takes place at the individual level as it affects citizens' orientation toward government, as intense police scrutiny may alienate people, making them less inclined to participate in politics, as we have reviewed. It also can occur through legal and institutional means. For example, many states prevent citizens with felony convictions from voting. In a number of US states that means as many as 25 percent of black men are barred from the voting booth; a practice Alexander (2010) refers to as "the new Jim Crow." Voter suppression takes many forms. In this book we have explicitly linked political power with disparities in policing. Where black political power can be reduced – through gerrymandering, voter suppression, felon disenfranchisement, purging voter rolls, or other means – racially disparate patterns of policing are easier to maintain.

We would also be remiss if we did not mention recent efforts in North Carolina at restricting the minority vote. In 2013, NC Governor Pat McCrory signed what was then one of the nation's strictest voter ID laws, which required that citizens show a government-issued ID to vote, cut down on the number of early voting days, eliminated same-day voter registration, and eliminated pre-voter registration for teenagers. The law sparked immediate controversy and was quickly challenged in the courts, culminating in 2016 when a federal court ruled that the law was unconstitutional. The justices were swayed in large part by evidence that NC lawmakers had, while drafting the legislation, requested information on racial differences in voting behavior and then outlawed the types of IDs more commonly used by black citizens. Similarly, after learning that African-Americans were more likely to vote during the first seven days of early voting, lawmakers eliminated those days. "The federal court in Richmond found that the primary purpose of North Carolina's wasn't to stop voter fraud, but rather to disenfranchise minority voters. The judges found that the provisions 'target African Americans with almost surgical precision'" (Ingraham 2016). The court's decision noted: "Thus, in what comes as close to a smoking gun as we are likely to see in modern times, the State's very justification for a challenged statute hinges explicitly on race – specifically its concern that African Americans, who had overwhelmingly voted for Democrats, had too much access to the franchise" (*North Carolina State Conference of the NAACP v. McCrory* 2016, 13).

African-Americans tend overwhelmingly to vote for Democrats, so naturally Republican elected officials are inclined to be unfriendly. But the impact of the type of voter suppression the courts found in our state go well beyond elections themselves. The degree of voice offered to minority voters has a powerful impact on many elements of citizenship, from how much we value government to what we expect from it, to whether we feel a part of it, and, as we have documented here, to how government agencies such as police departments treat members of different racial groups.

Disenfranchisement of minority voters has a long and ugly history in the USA, particularly in the Southern states. In this book, we have seen some of its consequences: when minorities lack a political voice, they are subjected to a more intensive police scrutiny. We are encouraged that the NC legislature's attempt at disenfranchisement was struck down. Making it easier for minorities (and everyone else) to vote may go a long way toward resolving the issues we have documented.

A Hopeful Story of Change

We started this book with a surprising story about a police encounter with a driver in Durham, leading to an officer being shot but the driver acquitted of charges of assault; the trial demonstrated the low level of confidence and trust in the police, as the jury apparently rejected the testimony of the officer who was shot. We also noted in Chapter 9 how a new Chief in Durham may be making progress in reforming local practices to improve community trust. The Department could not have gotten a bigger PR boost than an article which appeared in the *Raleigh News and Observer* in late June 2017. Courtney Bailey, a black woman, was pulled over after speeding, not wearing a seat belt, and with an expired registration. Explaining to officer Dan Strandh that she had exactly six cents in the bank and one dollar in the glove compartment, she did not expect what came next: he accompanied her to an auto repair shop and paid $200 to replace the bald tire that was preventing her from passing inspection and to get her registration renewed; he also forgave the three tickets. According to the article:

"I didn't know what to do with it, other than cry. I boohooed my face off."
Bailey's original [Facebook] post had nearly 280,000 views as of Friday. The Durham Police Department was among thousands to share it.
Bailey used the opportunity to encourage people to be open-minded about others.
"All black people ain't criminals, all police ain't looking to kill us," she said. "Something has to give, and especially after today I'm willing to give it a chance." (Moody 2017)

While no one expects officers to pay for poor people's registration tags, or to fix their cars, in fact many officers, like school teachers, work hard to help those in need, often at considerable personal financial sacrifice. A sandwich here, a meal there, a helping hand goes a long way. With the news media focusing on officers helping citizens rather than on a court ruling that an officer was so wrong that the person accused of shooting him was not convicted in a trial, it is clear that the story in Durham may be changing.

Ms. Bailey may be particularly prescient in arguing that "something has to give" and indicating that she is willing to "give it a chance." Our book has documented many trends and patterns that could be unfamiliar to many readers, but so familiar to others they wonder why we even had to go to the trouble to document it, so well is it known in their communities. We do believe these trends are deeply troubling and that Ms. Bailey is right in saying things have to change. We believe there are many simple reforms that police throughout the state and nation can adopt at no or very low cost in terms of fighting crime which will reduce racial disparities in policing, enhance trust, improve feelings of inclusion and citizenship, and lead to greater cooperation and working together with the police in particular. We hope that we collectively will give it a chance.

Appendix A: Text of SB 76 as Enacted in 1999*

GENERAL ASSEMBLY OF NORTH CAROLINA
SESSION 1999
SESSION LAW 1999-26
SENATE BILL 76
AN ACT TO REQUIRE THE DIVISION OF CRIMINAL STATISTICS
TO COLLECT AND MAINTAIN STATISTICS ON TRAFFIC LAW
ENFORCEMENT.

The General Assembly of North Carolina enacts:

Section 1. G.S. 114-10 reads as rewritten:
"§ 114-10. Division of Criminal Statistics.

The Attorney General shall set up in the Department of Justice a division to be designated as the Division of Criminal Statistics. There shall be assigned to this Division by the Attorney General duties as follows:

(1) To collect and correlate information in criminal law administration, including crimes committed, arrests made, dispositions on preliminary hearings, prosecutions, convictions, acquittals, punishment, appeals, together with the age, race, and sex of the offender, and such other information concerning crime and criminals as may appear significant or helpful. To correlate such information with the operations of agencies and institutions charged with the supervision of offenders on probation, in penal and correctional institutions, on parole and pardon, so as to show the volume, variety and tendencies of crime and criminals and the workings of successive links in the machinery set up for

the administration of the criminal law in connection with the arrests, trial, punishment, probation, prison parole and pardon of all criminals in North Carolina.

(2)   To collect, correlate, and maintain access to information that will assist in the performance of duties required in the administration of criminal justice throughout the State. This information may include, but is not limited to, motor vehicle registration, drivers' licenses, wanted and missing persons, stolen property, warrants, stolen vehicles, firearms registration, sexual offender registration as provided under Article 27A of Chapter 14 of the General Statutes, drugs, drug users and parole and probation histories. In performing this function, the Division may arrange to use information available in other agencies and units of State, local and federal government, but shall provide security measures to insure that such information shall be made available only to those whose duties, relating to the administration of justice, require such information.

(2a) To collect, correlate, and maintain the following information regarding traffic law enforcement by State law enforcement officers:

a. The number of drivers stopped for routine traffic enforcement by State law enforcement officers and whether or not a citation or warning was issued;

b. Identifying characteristics of the drivers stopped, including the race or ethnicity, approximate age, and gender;

c. The alleged traffic violation that led to the stop;

d. Whether a search was instituted as a result of the stop;

e. Whether the vehicle, personal effects, driver, or passenger or passengers were searched, and the race or ethnicity, approximate age, and gender of each person searched;

f. Whether the search was conducted pursuant to consent, probable cause, or reasonable suspicion to suspect a crime, including the basis for the request for consent, or the circumstances establishing probable cause or reasonable suspicion;

g. Whether any contraband was found and the type and amount of any such contraband;

h. Whether any written citation or any oral or written warning was issued as a result of the stop;

i. Whether an arrest was made as a result of either the stop or the search;

j. Whether any property was seized, with a description of that property;

k. Whether the officers making the stop encountered any physical resistance from the driver or passenger or passengers;

l. Whether the officers making the stop engaged in the use of force against the driver, passenger, or passengers for any reason;

m. Whether any injuries resulted from the stop; and

n. Whether the circumstances surrounding the stop were the subject of any investigation, and the results of that investigation.

The information required by this subdivision need not be collected in connection with impaired driving checks under G.S. 20-16.3A or other types of roadblocks, vehicle checks, or checkpoints that are consistent with the laws of this State and with the State and federal constitutions, except when those stops result in a warning, search, seizure, arrest, or any of the other activity described in sub-subdivisions d. through n. of this subdivision.

(3) To make scientific study, analysis and comparison from the information so collected and correlated with similar information gathered by federal agencies, and to provide the Governor and the General Assembly with the information so collected biennially, or more often if required by the Governor.

(4) To perform all the duties heretofore imposed by law upon the Attorney General with respect to criminal statistics.

(5) To perform such other duties as may be from time to time prescribed by the Attorney General.

(6) To promulgate rules and regulations for the administration of this Article."

Section 2. This act shall not be construed to obligate the General Assembly to make any appropriation to implement the provisions of this act. Each department and agency to which this act applies shall implement the provisions of this act from funds otherwise appropriated to that department or agency.

Section 3. This act becomes effective January 1, 2000, and applies to law enforcement actions occurring on or after that date.

In the General Assembly read three times and ratified this the 14th day of April, 1999.

s/   Dennis A. Wicker
President of the Senate
s/   James B. Black
Speaker of the House of Representatives
s/   James B. Hunt, Jr.
Governor
Approved 9:35 a.m. this 22nd day of April, 1999

Appendix B: Status of the Law as of 2017

A number of revisions to the 1999 law have been made in the years since 1999.[1] Whereas the original law applied only to "state law enforcement officers," it was expanded as of January 1, 2002, to apply to the vast bulk of law enforcement officers throughout the state, and to specify that each agency should assign an anonymous ID number to each officer, and that this ID number (but not the personal information associated with it) would be a public record. Small changes were made in 2009 to specify how officers should handle a situation where they arrest a driver who has custody of minor children during the time of the arrest. As of July 2017, the relevant section of the state code reads as follows (taken from the link at: http://trafficstops.ncsbi.gov/):

§ 143B-903. Collection of traffic law enforcement statistics.

(a) In addition to its other duties, the Department of Public Safety shall collect, correlate, and maintain the following information regarding traffic law enforcement by law enforcement officers:

(1) The number of drivers stopped for routine traffic enforcement by law enforcement officers, the officer making each stop, the date each stop was made, the agency of the officer making each stop, and whether or not a citation or warning was issued.

(2) Identifying characteristics of the drivers stopped, including the race or ethnicity, approximate age, and sex.

(3) The alleged traffic violation that led to the stop.

(4) Whether a search was instituted as a result of the stop.

(5)　Whether the vehicle, personal effects, driver, or passenger or passengers were searched, and the race or ethnicity, approximate age, and sex of each person searched.

(6)　Whether the search was conducted pursuant to consent, probable cause, or reasonable suspicion to suspect a crime, including the basis for the request for consent, or the circumstances establishing probable cause or reasonable suspicion.

(7)　Whether any contraband was found and the type and amount of any such contraband.

(8)　Whether any written citation or any oral or written warning was issued as a result of the stop.

(9)　Whether an arrest was made as a result of either the stop or the search.

(10)　Whether any property was seized, with a description of that property.

(11)　Whether the officers making the stop encountered any physical resistance from the driver or passenger or passengers.

(12)　Whether the officers making the stop engaged in the use of force against the driver, passenger, or passengers for any reason.

(13)　Whether any injuries resulted from the stop.

(14)　Whether the circumstances surrounding the stop were the subject of any investigation, and the results of that investigation.

(15)　The geographic location of the stop; if the officer making the stop is a member of the State Highway Patrol, the location shall be the Highway Patrol District in which the stop was made; for all other law enforcement officers, the location shall be the city or county in which the stop was made.

(b) For purposes of this section, "law enforcement officer" means any of the following:

(1)　All State law enforcement officers.

(2)　Law enforcement officers employed by county sheriffs or county police departments.

(3)　Law enforcement officers employed by police departments in municipalities with a population of 10,000 or more persons.

(4)　Law enforcement officers employed by police departments in municipalities employing five or more full-time sworn officers for every 1,000 in population, as calculated by the Department for the calendar year in which the stop was made.

(c) The information required by this section need not be collected in connection with impaired driving checks under G.S. 20-16.3A or other types of roadblocks, vehicle checks, or checkpoints that are consistent with the laws of this State and with the State and federal constitutions, except when those stops result in a warning, search, seizure, arrest, or any of the other activity described in subdivisions (4) through (14) of subsection (a) of this section.

(d) Each law enforcement officer making a stop covered by subdivision (1) of subsection (a) of this section shall be assigned an anonymous identification number by the officer's employing agency. The anonymous identifying number shall be public record and shall be reported to the Department to be correlated along with the data collected under subsection (a) of this section. The correlation between the identification numbers and the names of the officers shall not be a public record, and shall not be disclosed by the agency except when required by order of a court of competent jurisdiction to resolve a claim or defense properly before the court.

(e) Any agency subject to the requirements of this section shall submit information collected under subsection (a) of this section to the Department within 60 days of the close of each month. Any agency that does not submit the information as required by this subsection shall be ineligible to receive any law enforcement grants available by or through the State until the information which is reasonably available is submitted.

(f) The Department shall publish and distribute by December 1 of each year a list indicating the law enforcement officers that will be subject to the provisions of this section during the calendar year commencing on the following January 1. (1939, c. 315, s. 2; 1955, c. 1257, ss. 1, 2; 1969, c. 1267, s. 1; 1995, c. 545, s. 2; 1999-26, s. 1; 1999-225, s. 1; 2000–67, s. 17.2(a); 2001–424, s. 23.7(a); 2002–159, s. 18(a), (b); 2009–544, s. 1; 2012–182, s. 1; 2014–100, ss. 17.1(h), (tt).)

§ 143B-902. Powers and duties of the Department of Public Safety with respect to criminal information.

...

(3)   To make scientific study, analysis and comparison from the information so collected and correlated with similar information gathered by federal agencies, and to provide the Governor and the General Assembly with the information so collected biennially, or more often if required by the Governor.

Appendix C: SBI-122 Form

 TRAFFIC STOP REPORT

Agency Name   Date (Month/Day/Year) Time

County of Stop   Officer ID Number

City of Stop

Part I

Initial Purpose of Traffic Stop *(check only one)*

☐ Checkpoint ☐ Other Motor Vehicle Violation ☐ Stop Light / Sign Violation
☐ Driving While Impaired ☐ Safe Movement Violation ☐ Vehicle Equipment Violation
☐ Investigation ☐ Seat Belt Violation   ☐ Vehicle Regulatory Violation
       ☐ Speed Limit Violation

Vehicle Driver Information

Driver's Age _____ Driver's Race ☐ White ☐ Black ☐ Native American ☐ Asian ☐ Othe

Driver's Sex ☐ Male ☐ Female

Driver's Ethnicity ☐ Non-Hispanic ☐ Hispanic *(Person of Mexican, Puerto Rican, Cuban, Central or South American, or other Spanish Culture)*

Enforcement Action Taken as a Result of the Traffic Stop *(check only one)*

☐ Citation Issued ☐ On-View Arrest ——→ If arrest made, who was arrested?
☐ No Action Taken ☐ Verbal Warning ☐ Driver
       ☐ Written Warning ☐ Passenger(s)

Physical Resistance Encountered

Did Officer(s) encounter any physical resistance from Driver and/or Passenger(s)? ☐ Yes ☐ No
Did Officer(s) engage in the use of force against the Driver and/or Passenger(s)? ☐ Yes ☐ No
Did injuries occur to the Officer(s) as a result of the stop? ☐ Yes ☐ No
Did injuries occur to the Driver as a result of the stop? ☐ Yes ☐ No
Did injuries occur to the Passenger(s) as a result of the stop? ☐ Yes ☐ No

Vehicle/Driver/Passenger(s) Search

Was a search initiated subsequent to the traffic stop? ☐ Yes* ☐ No
    *If search was initiated, complete Part II

SBI-122 (Rev. 12/09)

Traffic Stop Report

Part II

Type of Search *(check only one)*

☐ Consent   ☐ Search Warrant   ☐ Probable Cause   ☐ Search Incident to Arrest   ☐ Protective Frisk

Basis for Search

☐ Erratic/Suspicious Behavior   ☐ Observation of Suspected Contraband   ☐ Suspicious Movement

☐ Informant's Tip   ☐ Other Official Information   ☐ Witness Observation

Person(s)/Vehicle Searched

Was the Vehicle Searched?	☐ Yes ☐ No
Was the Driver Searched?	☐ Yes ☐ No
Was a Passenger(s) Searched?	☐ Yes ☐ No
Were the Personal Effects of the Driver and/or Passenger(s) Searched?	☐ Yes ☐ No

Identify the sex, race, and ethnicity of each passenger searched

	Age	Sex		Race					Ethnicity	
		Male	Female	White	Black	Native American	Asian	Other	Hispanic	Non-Hispanic
Passenger 1										
Passenger 2										
Passenger 3										
Passenger 4										

Contraband Found

Contraband found as a result of the search: ☐ None   **OR** complete the following:

☐ Drugs _____ Ounces _____ Pounds _____ Dosages _____ Grams _____ Kilos

☐ Alcohol _____ Pints _____ Gallons

☐ Money _____ Dollar Amount

☐ Weapons _____ Number of Weapons

☐ Other _____ Dollar Amount

Property Seized

Property seized as a result of the search: ☐ None   **OR** complete the following:

☐ Motor Vehicle   ☐ Personal Property   ☐ Other Property

Office Use Only	Date	Initials
Reviewed		
Entered		

SBI-122 (Rev. 12/09)

Appendix D: Durham Police Department Written Consent to Search Form

Durham Police Department
505 W. Chapel Hill St. Durham, NC 27701
919-560-4427

Consent to Search Form

Person to be Searched   IR#:

☐ Person

I, _____, agree to allow law enforcement to perform a complete search of my
person, including all property on my person.

Property to be Searched

☐ Vehicle   Plate: _____   VIN: _____
             Make: _____   Model: _____

☐ Premises   Address: _____
             Description: _____

☐ Electronic Device   Type of Device: _____
             Make: _____   Model: _____
             Serial Number: _____

Passwords/log-ins/specific directions for entry: _____

☐ Other (Describe property): _____

I, _____, own, possess, or have authority over the property described
above and do hereby agree to allow law enforcement to perform a complete search of the property
listed above, to include all property located on or within the vehicle, premise, electronic device,
or other property listed above.

I have been advised of my right to refuse to consent to this search. I give this consent voluntarily,
without any promises made to me, or threats of any kind made against me. I understand any evidence
of a crime may be seized as a result of this search.

Signature: _____   Date/Time: _____

☐ Check if consent denied

Person Authorizing

Name: _____

Date of Birth: _____   Age: _____   Phone Number: _____

Address: _____

Officer Name: _____   Employee ID#: _____

Division/District/Unit: _____   Contact #: _____

Officer Signature: _____   Date/Time: _____

General Order 4004 A-1 R-1   Submit original to records.
REV 8/14   Copies may be kept with case file.

Durham Police Department
505 W. Chapel Hill St. Durham, NC 27701
919-560-4427

Formulario De Consentimiento Para Effectuar Un Registro

Persona Que Va Ser Sometido A Un Registro   IR#:

☐ Persona

Yo, _____, accedo a un registro completa de mi persona, incluyendo toda la propiedad que llevo en mi persona a los Oficiales de Policía.

Propiedad Que Va Ser Registrada

☐ Vehículo: Placa : _____   VIN: _____
              Marca : _____   Modelo: _____

☐ Local   Dirección : _____
             Descripción : _____

☐ Aparato Electrónico   Tipo de Aparato: _____
              Marca : _____   Modelo : _____
              Número de Serie : _____

Clave/iniciar sesión/instrucciones
específicas para entrar:

☐ Otra (Describe propiedad):

Yo, _____, dueño, poseo, o tengo autoridad sobre la propiedad descrita arriba y accedo a un registro completa de la propiedad escrita arriba, incluyendo toda la propiedad situada en o adentro de mi vehículo, local, aparato electrónico, u otra propiedad escrita arriba.

Yo he sido informado de mi derecho a negar a dar mi consentimiento. Yo doy este consentimiento voluntariamente, sin promesas dirigidas hacia mí, o amenazas de cualquier tipo hechas en contra de mí. Yo entiendo que toda evidencia de un crimen, objeto(s) o sustancia(s) ilegal(es) puede(n) ser confiscado(s) como el resultado de este registro.

Firma: _____   Fecha/Hora: _____

☐ Marque si autorización es negada

Persona Que Autoriza

Nombre : _____
Fecha de nacimiento: _____   Edad: _____   Número de teléfono: _____
Dirección: _____

Officer Name: _____   Employee ID#: _____
Division/District/Unit: _____   Contact #: _____
Officer Signature: _____   Date/Time: _____

General Order 4004 A-1 R-1
REV 8/14   Submit original to records.
                                            Copies may be kept with case file.

Appendix E: Shortcomings in the Official Data

Our study can only be as good as the data on which it is based, so we take seriously questions of data quality and here list some of the flaws and limitations that we know permeate the official records that we use. In our online appendix, we go into much greater detail on each of these issues, documenting their existence, discussing why they are important, explaining our efforts to make sure that they do not bias our analysis, and what revisions could be made to the data collection process to mitigate them or eliminate them altogether. In all, while we believe that analysts should be aware of these flaws and that state agencies should work to correct them, we do not believe that they pose a fundamental problem to the integrity of the data already collected. This is because the problems affect a relatively small percentage of the total data and with 20 million stops on record, the trends and patterns we document in the book are highly robust. The flaws and limitations are as follows:

1. The officer ID numbers are meant to be unique but different agencies sometimes assign different officers the same ID. More widespread are typographical errors; 58,997 officer ID numbers occur fewer than five times in the database.
2. The SBI-122 form asks officers to record contraband as either drugs, alcohol, money, weapons, or "other," but these broad categories may mask important differences between, say, marijuana and heroin.
3. A more serious problem with the contraband data is that very low contraband amounts appear to be rounded down to zero either

by local agency computers or by the NC DOJ computers when the data is compiled.

4. Yet another issue with the recording of contraband is that the NC DOJ data files link contraband hits with stops, rather than with the individual motorists who were involved with a stop. This is problematic when there is a passenger involved in the stop as it is impossible to tell if the contraband was found on the driver or the passenger.

5. Only a single search type is recorded, though officers may record more than one. From discussions with officers and chiefs, it appears that some widely used software programs simply record the first search type in the numeric list of search types used.

6. Perusing the data, it is clear that an inordinate number of stops occur at exactly midnight. Of all 20 million traffic stops from 2002 through 2016, 51 percent were recorded as having occurred at midnight (hour 00). Time should be properly recorded. The State Highway Patrol in particular should review its procedures to ensure that time is recorded as required by law.

7. While the law requires every agency covered by the law to report each traffic stop, it is clear that many stops are missing. We have compiled monthly totals of traffic stops for every agency in the state database, and the patterns there clearly suggest massive failure to report, or reports lost through computer or other types of error.

8. Passengers and checkpoint stops are recorded only when there is an adverse outcome. Thus, it is impossible to calculate any rates for such things as search or arrest, since we do not know the baseline of how many passengers or checkpoint stops were present.

9. The data on the city where the stop took place is evidently typed into the SBI software by hand and thus typographical errors and inconsistencies abound. The city of Winston-Salem appears with more than thirty different spellings. Kings Mountain appears with bewildering combinations of close and distant spellings and capitalization patterns.

10. There are also a number of small, miscellaneous errors. For example, 5,636 drivers are listed as younger than fifteen, while 544 are listed as 110 years old.

11. In some cases, an officer may continue to engage in a "voluntary encounter" with the driver or passengers after the driver is technically free to go on his or her way. These data should be recorded

if they follow from the same encounter that was initiated by the traffic stop, and a revised law should specify this.

12. In the online appendix, we also discuss a number of shortcomings with the data collection that are documented by Deborah Weisel in her report published by the NC Association of Chiefs of Police and NC Sheriffs' Association. We review and summarize the recommendations made there as well.

13. We include recommendations for information on contextual factors that a revised SBI-122 form could take into account. These include: GIS coordinates of where the traffic stop occurred, the make and model of the driver's car, the posted speed limit and the observed speed, if the vehicle was a rental car, and the race, gender, and years of service of the officer who made the stop.

14. Finally, we recommend that, wherever possible, the NC DOJ should facilitate collaborative efforts with other states, pooling traffic stops data in a central location. We also believe police agencies themselves would benefit from receiving the compiled data back from the NC DOJ in a user-friendly format to facilitate periodic review of officer-level patterns.

Notes

1 Suspect Citizens

1 Of course, even when disparities are indicative of actual rates of criminal behavior in underlying populations that does not mean that such disparities are harmless or legitimate. As Tonry points out, the roots of criminal behavior are closely tied to larger social inequalities in health care, education, and employment.

2 A Legislative Mandate to Address Concerns about Racial Profiling

1 Rep. Ramero told a poignant story in the presence of the Director of Public Safety (e.g., the Texas Highway Patrol) about being stopped repeatedly while a young driver and in particular of being searched on the grounds of his own high school while friends and teachers watched. This humiliation and trauma clearly remained fresh in his mind as he considered efforts to limit police discretion to engage in such actions. As a lawmaker, he had the opportunity to address the question directly, though the proposed legislation to prohibit "pretextual" traffic stops was voted down after significant law enforcement opposition (see Silver 2017).

3 Who Gets Stopped?

1 As we note in Appendix E, much of the surge in 2007 may come from a large increase in stops reported by the SHP. We do not know if this reflects a real increase or a change in reporting practice. The website for this book (www.unc.edu/~fbaum/books/SuspectCitizens/index.html) provides many supplementary materials, including Figure E-1 that documents trends in reported stops.

2   Note that demographic trends slowly evolve over time, so our stop rates are estimates and may get more inaccurate as we move away from 2010, when the population data are most accurate.

3   While Figure 3.3c excluded thirty-one outliers, these correlation statistics include all values.

4 What Happens After a Stop?

1   Note that large numbers of stops, in particular those associated with the SHP, are missing the time variable so are not included in this analysis.

5 Finding Contraband

1   We found some support for this possibility in the last chapter. Recall that black drivers were more likely than whites to have their traffic stops result in "no action" being taken by the police. Verbal and written warnings are also possible stop outcomes, so no action literally means that the police took no action, not even verbally admonishing the driver. A no-action stop raises questions about why the stop was initiated in the first place, perhaps simply as a means of maximizing police–citizen interactions. If police are more suspicious of black drivers, as we have argued, then it is unsurprising that blacks are more likely to experience no-action stops. And, while North Carolina does not record the alleged speed of a violator, Texas does. In Texas, generally speaking, faster speeders are less likely to be searched: they get a ticket. But among those pulled over for speeding less than 10 mph over the limit, chances of search are higher (see Baumgartner, Christiani, and Roach 2016). The marginal violation speeding stops may be pretexts for something else, a desire to conduct an investigation.

2   Operation Pipeline was a highway interdiction program initiated by the DEA in 1984. It focused police patrols on "drug corridors" – interstate highways running up the East and West Coasts from Mexico.

3   In the online appendix to this chapter, we look at how arrest rates vary by the amounts of contraband found. We discover that even relatively large amounts of contraband only sometimes lead to an arrest.

4   The online appendix to this chapter replicates Figure 5.2 for NC police agencies by aggregating across all the officers associated with each agency. (See Figure 5A-1.) The pattern is the same, however. There is great variability in contraband hit rates; some agencies find contraband in more than 50 percent of searches, while others have hit rates of less than 10 percent.

5   Gender differences in hit rates are minor, though the search rates differ dramatically. For white, black, and Hispanics, the search rates for males are 1.96, 5.54, and 3.44; among females, 1.01, 1.29, and 0.80. Hit rates are 35.78, 33.22, and 21.53 among males, and 35.5, 33.67, and 27.37 among females. Hits followed by arrest are 11.84, 13.25, and 8.28 among males; 11.6, 11.36, and 7.19 among females.

6   Ideally we would also control for the neighborhood where the stop was conducted, but the SBI-122 does not record this. However, the analysis gains from the officer-level fixed effect controls, as officers will often work the same "beat" for extended periods of time. By controlling for individual officers, we therefore gain some leverage on the degree to which different patrols affect searching behavior.

6 Search and Arrest Patterns by Officer and Agency

1   A large number of officer ID numbers appear just once in the database, as described in Appendix E. Most likely, these are data entry errors.
2   Of course, as we discussed in Chapter 3, whites and blacks may not drive or be on the roadways in the same proportion that they are in the population. In fact, whites tend to drive more, so if anything we might expect whites to be an even higher proportion of traffic stops if those stops were proportionate to each group's share of drivers. Note that just being on the roadway does not necessarily make one equally likely to be pulled over since that should focus on speeders or others who violate the law. We do not know which drivers are violating the law, however. But, as we reviewed in earlier chapters, virtually all drivers violate some law.
3   Recall that we classify stops for speeding, stoplight violations, impaired driving, and safe movement violations as "safety" related and stops for vehicular equipment or registration issues, seatbelt violations, investigations, and other types of stops as "investigatory."

8 Black Political Power and Disparities in Policing

1   We have run models with different versions of a racial threat variable (reaching its peak value when the minority presence is at different levels from 20 to 50 percent) for municipalities in North Carolina. None of those models out-perform the ones we present below, and on average the models reinforce the findings presented here. The models themselves can be seen in the online appendix to this chapter.
2   Two additional factors that may influence disparities in treatment are the level of segregation in an area and the racial composition of the police force. Information for both factors is publicly available. However, its inclusion biases the results, by generating non-random missingness in the data set. Essentially, those departments likely to respond to surveys asking about policing practices have higher levels of black political power, and those cities that a segregation score has been calculated for are much larger than average. See the online appendix to this chapter for further discussion of these issues.
3   Black-white disparities are robust to the more enhanced specification (i.e. regression). For a discussion of this, see the online appendix to this chapter.
4   There are thirty-six agency-year instances of a search ratio lower than 1, and twenty-two agencies account for this. They are the police departments

for: Boone, Butner, Claremont, Conover, Eden, Greenville, Holly Ridge, Kings Mountain, Kinston, Mebane, Mint Hill, Monroe, New Bern, Pineville, Rolesville, Sanford, Spring Lake, Tarboro, Troutman, Waxhaw, Weldon, and Youngsville. There are eight agency-year instances of a search ratio greater than 4.00, and eleven agencies account for this. They are the police departments for: Archdale, Asheboro, Carrboro, Durham, Fletcher, Fuquay-Varina, Havelock, Morrisville, New Bern, Troutman, and Wilkesboro. There are 204 agency-years that have a light outcome ratio of less than 1; and 203 agency-years that have a citation outcome ratio of less than 1.

5 To calculate voter turnout, we started with the voting history and voting registration information for each county in North Carolina from the Board of Election's website: www.ncsbe.gov/other-election-related-data. Each file was then merged together to identify in which elections each individual voted. This file was then collapsed by race of voter, election, and municipal description. The totals resulting from this are taken as the number of voters that turned out to vote in each election by race. We then compared voting turnout rates to the 2010 Census population estimates to calculate voter turnout by race. This process was automated and conducted in R.

6 While many studies that look at the relationship between police behavior and race use the race of the mayor as the key explanatory variable (for examples see: Stucky 2011, Saltzstein 1989), we do not. Rather we adopt a more holistic definition of city government to include both the city council and mayor. While this was done because we believe this is theoretically justified, it was also because there were almost no black mayors in North Carolina during the time period of our study.

7 The factor analysis was completed in R using the fa command within the psych package. The factor analysis used an oblique minimizing rotation (oblimin) and minimum residual OLS to estimate the factor. The standardized factor loadings are: 0.70 for the percent of local government that is black, 0.92 for the percent of the voting population that is black, and 0.92 for the percent of the population that is black. The correlation of scores with factors is 0.96. The multiple R square of score with factors is 0.92. The minimum correlation of possible factor scores is 0.85.

8 For an example report see: https://ucr.fbi.gov/. The specific information comes from Table 8 in the annual Crime Report in the United States.

9 An HLM regression rather than an OLS regression is fit, because observations are clustered by city as shown by the ANOVA presented in the online appendix. However, each observation contains some information static at the agency level. As a result, an HLM rather than FE in an OLS are used.

10 Two variables that might also influence outcomes, but are excluded in the analysis presented here, are the percent of cops who are black working in a given city and the level of segregation in a given city. Inclusion of both variables excludes approximately half of the observations. This missingness appears to be directly related to the level of political power in a given city. As a result, neither variable is used in the analysis presented here. See the online appendix, for further discussion of this matter and how it affects our results.

11 The factor analysis was completed in R using the fa command within the psych package. The factor analysis used an oblique minimizing rotation (oblimin) and minimum residual OLS to estimate the factor. The standardized factor loadings are: 0.88 for the race of the sheriff, 0.78 for the percent of the voting population that is black, and 0.49 for the percent of the population that is black. The correlation of scores with factors is 0.92. The multiple R square of score with factors is 0.85. The minimum correlation of possible factor scores is 0.69.

9 Reforms that Reduce Alienation and Enhance Community Safety

1 www.ncsl.org/research/health/state-seat-belt-laws.aspx
2 The ARIMA model estimated for Fayetteville followed the form (1,0,1). The AIMA model estimated for Durham followed the form (4,1,0). The ARIMA model estimated for Chapel Hill followed the form (4,0,0).
3 The ARIMA model estimated for Fayetteville followed the form (1,1,1). The ARIMA model estimated for Durham followed the form (3,1,2). The ARIMA model estimated for Chapel Hill followed the form (0,1,1).

Appendix A

* Taken from the North Carolina General Assembly website: www.ncleg.net/Sessions/1999/Bills/Senate/HTML/S76v6.html
1 For various amendments to the 1999 law, see: 2001 revisions: www.ncleg.net/Sessions/2001/Bills/Senate/HTML/S1005v7.html and www.ncleg.net/Sessions/2001/Bills/Senate/HTML/S1217v6.html. For the 2009 amendments, see http://ncleg.net/Sessions/2009/Bills/Senate/HTML/S464v6.html. In 2012, Sen. Goolsby introduced Senate Bill 923, which proposed simply to repeal the data collection law entirely. This bill was filed on May 29, 2012, referred to the Judiciary I Committee on May 30, and died there. For the bill text, see: www.ncleg.net/Sessions/2011/Bills/Senate/HTML/S923v1.html; for the legislative outcome, see: www.ncleg.net/gascripts/BillLookUp/BillLookUp.pl?Session=2011&BillID=SB923&submitButton=Go.

References

Alexander, Michelle. 2010. *The New Jim Crow: Mass Incarceration in the Age of Colorblindness*. New York: The New Press.

Alpert, Geoffrey P., Michael R. Smith, and Roger G. Dunham. 2004. Toward a Better Benchmark: Assessing the Utility of Not-at-fault Traffic Crash Data in Racial Profiling Research. *Justice Research and Policy* 6, 1: 43–69.

Anderson, Elijah. 1978. *A Place on the Corner*. Chicago, IL: University of Chicago Press.

    1990. *Streetwise: Race, Class, and Change in an Urban Community*. Chicago, IL: University of Chicago Press.

    1999. *Code of the Street*. New York: W. W. Norton.

Anderson, Kristin J. 2010. *Benign Bigotry: The Psychology of Subtle Prejudice*. New York: Cambridge University Press.

Banks, R. Richard. 2003. Beyond Profiling: Race, Policing, and the Drug War. *Stanford Law Review* 56, 3: 571–603.

Barksdale, Andrew. 2010. NAACP concerned police are searching more blacks. *Fayetteville Observer*. December 4.

    2011. Data raise concerns of racial profiling. *Fayetteville Observer*. May 1.

    2012a. Ousted Iman criticizes council. *Fayetteville Observer*. April 2.

    2012b. Report: Blacks, Hispanics in North Carolina get searched by police more than whites. *Fayetteville Observer*. June 22.

    2014. Fayetteville police making fewer traffic stops. *Fayetteville Observer*. August 17.

Bates, Timothy. 2010. Driving While Black in Suburban Detroit. *Du Bois Review: Social Science Research on Race* 7, 1: 133–150.

Baumgartner, Frank R. and Derek A. Epp. 2012. North Carolina Traffic Stop Statistics Analysis. Report to the North Carolina Advocates for Justice. February 1. Available at: www.unc.edu/~fbaum/papers/Baumgartner-Traffic-Stops-Statistics-1-Feb-2012.pdf

Baumgartner, Frank R. and Bryan D. Jones. 1993. *Agendas and Instability in American Politics*. Chicago, IL: University of Chicago Press.

Baumgartner, Frank R., Leah Christiani, and Kevin Roach. 2016. Analyzing Racial Disparities in Traffic Stops Statistics from the Texas Department of Public Safety. Report to the Texas House of Representatives, Committee on County Affairs, September 20. Available at: www.unc.edu/~fbaum/TrafficStops/Baumgartner-Testimony-20Sept2016.pdf

Baumgartner, Frank R., Leah Christiani, Derek A. Epp, Kevin Roach, and Kelsey Shoub. 2017. Racial Disparities in Traffic Stop Outcomes. *Duke Forum for Law and Social Change* 9: 21–53.

Baumgartner, Frank R., Derek A. Epp, Kelsey Shoub, and Bayard Love. 2017. Targeting Young Men of Color for Search and Arrest during Traffic Stops: Evidence from North Carolina, 2002–2013. *Politics, Groups, and Identities* 5, 1: 107–131.

Bender, Steven W. 2003. *Greasers and Gringos: Latinos, Law, and the American Imagination*. New York: New York University Press.

Blalock, Hubert. 1967. *Toward a Theory of Minority-group Relations*. New York: John Wiley.

Blauner, Robert. 1972. *Racial Oppression in America*. New York: Harper and Row.

Blinder, Alan. 2017. Ex-officer who shot Walter Scott pleads guilty in Charleston. *New York Times*. May 2.

Blythe, Anne. 2016. Johnston County traffic stop led to illegal search, appellate judges say. *Raleigh News and Observer*. September 21.

Boeckmann, Robert J., and Tom R. Tyler. 2002. Trust, Respect, and the Psychology of Political Engagement. *Journal of Applied Social Psychology* 32, 10: 2067–2088.

Bonilla-Silva, Eduardo, Amanda Lewis, and David G. Embrick. 2004. I Did Not Get That Job Because of a Black Man ... : The Story Lines and Testimonies of Color-Blind Racism. *Sociological Forum* 19, 4: 555–581.

Bonner, Lynn. 1999a. Bill probes traffic stops for "driving while black." *Raleigh News and Observer*. February 18. A1.

 1999b. House OKs bill to track "driving while black." *Raleigh News and Observer*. April 2. A1.

Boushey, Graeme and Adam Luedtke. 2011. Immigrants across the U.S. Federal Laboratory: Explaining State-Level Innovation in Immigration Policy. *State Politics and Policy Quarterly* 11, 4: 390–414.

Bratton, Kathleen A. 2005. Critical Mass Theory Revisited: The Behavior and Success of Token Women in State Legislatures. *Politics and Gender* 1, 1: 97–105.

Bratton, Kathleen A., and Leonard P. Ray. 2002. Descriptive Representation, Policy Outcomes, and Municipal Day-Care Coverage in Norway. *American Journal of Political Science* 46, 2: 28–39.

Bridges, Virginia. 2015a. Durham police officer describes 2012 shooting, struggle. *Raleigh News and Observer*. August 4.

 2015b. Riley found guilty of robbery, not guilty of shooting Durham officer. *Raleigh News and Observer*. August 14.

 2015c. Ousted Durham Police Chief Lopez rebuts critics. *Raleigh News and Observer*. September 16.

2015d. Durham's probable-cause searches rise after consent policy is implemented. *Raleigh News and Observer.* July 21.

2015e. Durham discusses community and police divide. *Raleigh News and Observer.* July 21.

2017. Durham traffic stops, searches down; concerns about disparities continue. *Raleigh News and Observer.* May 10.

Burch, Traci. 2013. *Trading Democracy for Justice.* Chicago, IL: University of Chicago Press.

Burstein, Paul. 1979. Public Opinion, Demonstrations, and the Passage of Antidiscrimination Legislation. *Public Opinion Quarterly* 43, 2: 157–172.

Burstein, Paul, and April Linton. 2002. The Impact of Political Parties, Interest Groups, and Social Movement Organizations on Public Policy: Some Recent Evidence and Theoretical Concerns. *Social Forces* 82, 2 (December): 381–408.

Cammisa, Anne Marie, and Beth Reingold. 2004. Women in State Legislatures and State Legislative Research: Beyond Sameness and Difference. *State Politics and Policy Quarterly* 4, 2: 181–210.

Canon, David T. 1999. *Race, Redistricting, and Representation: The Unintended Consequences of Black Majority Districts.* Chicago, IL: University of Chicago Press.

Capps, Randy, Marc R. Rosenblum, Muzaffar Chishit, and Cristina Rodriguez. 2011. Delegation and Divergence: 287(g) State and Local Immigration Enforcement. Migration Policy Institute. Available at: www.migrationpolicy. org/research/delegation-and-divergence-287g-state-and-local-immigration-enforcement

Carnes, Nicholas. 2012. Does the Numerical Underrepresentation of the Working Class in Congress Matter? *Legislative Studies Quarterly* 37, 1: 5–34.

2013. *White-Collar Government: The Hidden Role of Class in Economic Policy Making.* Chicago, IL: University of Chicago Press.

Chaney, Carole Kennedy, and Grace Hall Saltzstein. 1998. Democratic Control and Bureaucratic Responsiveness: The Police and Domestic Violence. *American Journal of Political Science* 42, 3: 745–768.

Chavez, Jorge M. and Doris Marie Provine. 2009. Race and the Response of State Legislatures to Unauthorized Immigrants. *The Annals of the American Academy of Political and Social Science* 623, 1: 78–92.

Chavez, Leo Ralph. 2008. *The Latino Threat: Constructing Immigrants, Citizens, and the Nation.* Stanford, CA: Stanford University Press.

Clark, Christopher J. 2017a. Personal Communication. Email, June 30.

2017b. *A Seat at the Table: Causes and Consequences of Black Descriptive Representation in the American States.* Manuscript. Chapel Hill: University of North Carolina Department of Political Science.

Clark, Rebecca. 2013. Judge rules police targeted Hispanics in I-85 stops. *GastonGazette.com.* May 16.

Clear, Todd R., and Natasha A. Frost. 2014. *The Punishment Imperative: The Rise and Failure of Mass Incarceration in America.* New York: New York University Press.

Correll, J. 2009. Racial Bias in the Decision to Shoot? *The Police Chief* 76, 5: 54–58.

Correll, J., B. Park, C. M. Judd, and B. Wittenbrink. 2002. The Police Officer's Dilemma: Using Ethnicity to Disambiguate Potentially Threatening Individuals. *Journal of Personality and Social Psychology* 83, 6: 1314–1329.

Correll, J., B. Park, C. M. Judd, B. Wittenbrink, and M. S. Sadler. 2007. Across the Thin Blue Line: Police Officers and Racial Bias in the Decision to Shoot. *Journal of Personality and Social Psychology* 92, 6: 1006–1023.

D'Alessio, Stewart J. and Lisa Stolzenberg. 2003. Race and the Probability of Arrest. *Social Forces* 81: 1381–1397.

Desmond, Matthew, Andrew V. Papachristos, and David S. Kirk. 2016. Police Violence and Citizen Crime Reporting in the Black Community. *American Sociological Review* 81, 5: 856–876.

Dingeman, M. Kathleen and Ruben G. Rumbaut. 2010. The Immigrant–Crime Nexus and Post Deportation Experiences. *University of La Verne Law Review* 31, 2: 363–383.

Drake, Bruce. 2015. *Divide between Blacks and Whites on Police Runs Deep*. Washington, DC: Pew Research Center. April 28. Available at: www.pewresearch.org/fact-tank/2015/04/28/blacks-whites-police/

Durham, North Carolina, City of, Executive Command Staff of the Durham Police Department. 2014. Durham Response to the FADE Coalition Policy Recommendations: Final Report to the Durham City Manager. Retrieved September 1 2014 from: http://durhamnc.gov/ich/op/DPD/Documents/FADE%20Coalition%20Response.pdf

Dwyer, Timothy. 2003. Near misses of sniper manhunt detailed. *Washington Post*. September 30.

Easton, David. 1965. *A Framework for Political Analysis*. Englewood Cliffs, NJ: Prentice-Hall.

Eberhardt, Jennifer L., Nilanjana Dasgupta, and Tracy L. Banaszynski. 2003. Believing is Seeing: The Effects of Racial Labels and Implicit Beliefs on Face Perception. *Personality and Social Psychology Bulletin* 29, 3: 360–370.

Eberhardt, Jennifer L., Paul G. Davies, Valerie J. Purdie-Vaughns, and Sheri Lynn Johnson. 2006. Looking Deathworthy: Perceived Stereotypicality of Black Defendants Predicts Capital-Sentencing Outcomes. *Psychological Science* 17, 5: 383–386.

Eberhardt, Jennifer L., Phillip Atiba Goff, Valerie J. Purdie, and Paul G. Davies. 2004. Seeing Black: Race, Crime, and Visual Processing. *Journal of Personality and Social Psychology* 87, 6: 876–893.

Editorial Board. 1999a. Who's being stopped? *Raleigh News and Observer*. February 19.

1999b. Patrol bias: Numbers won't tell the real story – let's get to the bottom of the "driving while black" complaint. *Greensboro News and Record*. February 27.

1999c. Getting the facts. *Winston-Salem Journal*. March 2.

Eith, Christine, and Matthew R. Durose. 2011. *Contacts between Police and the Public, 2008*. Washington, DC: US Department of Justice, Bureau of Justice Statistics, NCJ 234599 (October).

Epp, Charles R., Steven Maynard-Moody, and Donald Haider-Markel. 2014. *Pulled Over: How Police Stops Define Race and Citizenship*. Chicago, IL: University of Chicago Press.

Ewing, Walter A., Daniel E. Martinez, and Ruben G. Rumbaut. 2015. *The Criminalization of Immigration in the United States*. Washington DC: American Immigration Council. Available at: www.americanimmigrationcouncil.org/research/criminalization-immigration-united-states

Fishman, Charles. 1991. Sheriff Bob Vogel: He's the mayor of I-95, and a terror to drug smugglers. *Orlando Sentinel*, August 11.

Fridell, Lorie, Robert Lunney, Drew Diamond, and Bruce Kubu. 2001. *Racially Biased Policing: A Principled Response*. Washington, DC: Police Executive Research Forum.

Frontline. n.d. The Legacy of Rodney King. Available at: www.pbs.org/wgbh/pages/frontline/shows/lapd/race/king.html

GAO. 2000. *Racial Profiling*. Washington, DC: General Accounting Office report GAO/GGD-00-41. March.

Gilliam, Franklin D., Jr., and Shanto Iyengar. 2000. Prime Suspects: The Influence of Local Television News on the Viewing Public. *American Journal of Political Science* 44, 3: 560–573.

Glaser, Jack. 2006. The Efficacy and Effect of Racial Profiling: A Mathematical Simulation Approach. *Journal of Policy Analysis and Management* 25, 2: 395–416.

2015. *Suspect Race: Causes and Consequences of Racial Profiling*. New York: Oxford University Press.

Glaser, Jack, Katherine Spencer, and Amanda Charbonneau. 2014. Racial Bias and Public Policy. *Policy Insights from the Behavioral and Brain Sciences* 1, 1: 88–94.

Goffman, Alice. 2014. *On the Run: Fugitive Life in an American City*. Chicago, IL: University of Chicago Press.

Gordon, Michael. 2015a. Racial disparity in Charlotte traffic stops grows, study finds. *Charlotte Observer*. April 11.

2015b. The personal side of traffic stops. *Charlotte Observer*. April 11.

Griffin, Anna. 1999. Traffic stops and race are debated – bill would require state to keep tabs. *Charlotte Observer*. April 2. A1.

Grine, Alyson A. and Emily Coward. 2014. *Raising Issues of Race in NC Criminal Cases*. Chapel Hill, NC: UNC School of Government.

Gronberg, Ray. 2014. *Durham Adopts Written-Consent Policy for Searches*. Durham, NC: Southern Coalition for Social Justice. September 16. Available at: www.southerncoalition.org/durham-adopts-written-consent-policy-for-searches/

Grose, Christian R. 2011. *Congress in Black and White: Race and Representation in Washington and at Home*. New York: Cambridge University Press.

Grubb, Tammy. 2016a. Chapel Hill police take aim at more openness, less racial bias. *Raleigh News and Observer*. October 11.

2016b. Crowd fills Chapel Hill Town Hall for dialogue about race, police. *Raleigh News and Observer*. October 25.

Hackney, Amy A., and Jack Glaser. 2013. Reverse Deterrence in Racial Profiling: Increased Transgressions by Nonprofiled Whites. *Law and Human Behavior* 37, 5: 348–353.

Hansen, Eric R., and Sarah A. Treul. 2015. The Symbolic and Substantive Representation of LGB Americans in the US House. *Journal of Politics* 77, 4: 955–967.

Harris, David A. 1997. Driving While Black and all other Traffic Offenses: The Supreme Court and Pretextual Traffic Stops. *Journal of Criminal Law and Criminology* 87, 2: 544–582.

1999a. *Driving While Black: Racial Profiling on our Nation's Highways. ACLU Special Report.* New York: American Civil Liberties Union. Available at: www.aclu.org/racial-justice/driving-while-black-racial-profiling-our-nations-highways

1999b. The Stories, the Statistics, and the Law: Why "Driving While Black" Matters. *Minnesota Law Review* 84: 265–326.

2002a. *Profiles in Injustice: Why Racial Profiling Cannot Work.* New York: New Press.

2002b. Racial Profiling Revisited: "Just Common Sense" in the Fight against Terror? *Criminal Justice* 17: 36–41, 59.

Hecker, Sean. 1996. Race and Pretextual Traffic Stops: An Expanded Role for Civilian Review Boards. *Columbia Human Rights Law Review*: 551.

Hetey, Rebecca C., and Jennifer L. Eberhardt. 2014. Racial Disparities in Incarceration Increase Acceptance of Punitive Policies. *Psychological Science* 25, 10: 1949–1954.

Hickman, Matthew J. 2005. *Traffic Stop Data Collection Policies for State Police, 2004.* Washington, DC: Bureau of Justice Statistics. NCJ 209156. June.

Horowitz, Donald L. 1985. *Ethnic Groups in Conflict.* Berkeley: University of California Berkeley Press.

Huerta-Bapat, Carmen. 2017. *The Racial Profiling of Latinos in North Carolina.* PhD dissertation. Department of Sociology, UNC-Chapel Hill.

Humes, Karen R., Nicholas A. Jones, and Roberto R. Ramirez. 2011. *Overview of Race and Hispanic Origin: 2010. 2010 Census Briefs.* Washington DC: US Bureau of the Census C2010BR-02 (March).

Ingraham, Christopher. 2016. The "smoking gun" proving North Carolina Republicans tried to disenfranchise black voters. *Washington Post.* July 29.

Intravia, Jonathan, et al. 2016. Neighborhood Disorder and Generalized Trust: A Multilevel Mediation Examination of Social Mechanisms. *Journal of Criminal Justice* 46: 148–158.

Jaret, Charles. 1999. Troubled by Newcomers: Anti-immigrant Attitudes and Action during Two Eras of Mass Immigration to the United States. *Journal of American Ethnic History* 18, 3: 9–39.

Johnson, Kevin R. 2004. *The "Huddled Masses" Myth: Immigration and Civil Rights.* Philadelphia: Temple University Press.

Keiser, Lael R., Vicky M. Wilkins, Kenneth J. Meier, and Catherine A. Holland. 2002. Lipstick and Logarithms: Gender, Institutional Context, and Representative Bureaucracy. *American Political Science Review* 96, 3: 553–564.

Kelley, Angela Maria, Marshall Fitz, and Philip E. Wolgin. 2012. Latinos voice continued concerns about S.B. 1070. *Center for American Progress Action Fund.* August 3.

Killian, Joe. 2015. *New York Times* story spotlights racial disparities in Greensboro policing. *Greensboro News and Record.* October 27.

King, B. G., Bentele, K. G., and Soule, S. A. 2007. Protest and Policy Making: Explaining Fluctuation in Congressional Attention to Rights Issues: 1960–1986. *Social Forces* 86: 137–163.

Kirkpatrick, Christopher. 1999. Official: Insurers might deny policies if N.C. tracks traffic-stop drivers' race. *Durham Herald Sun.* March 3. C5.

Knowles, John, Nicola Persico, and Petra Todd. 2001. Racial Bias in Motor Vehicle Searches: Theory and Evidence. *Journal of Political Economy* 109, 1: 203–229.

Lach, Alex. 2012. The top 5 reasons why S.B. 1070 damages America. *Center for American Progress.* June 5.

LaFraniere, Sharon and Andrew W. Lehren. 2015. The disproportionate risks of driving while black. *New York Times.* October 24.

Lamberth, John. 1994. Revised Statistical Analysis of the Incidence of Police Stops and Arrests of Black Drivers/Travelers on the New Jersey Turnpike between Exits or Interchanges 1 and 3 from years 1988 through 1991. Available at: www.mass.gov/eopss/docs/eops/faip/new-jersey-study-report.pdf

   1996. *A Report to the ACLU.* New York: American Civil Liberates Union. Available at: http://archive.aclu.org/court/lamberth.html

Lange, James E., Mark B. Johnson, and Robert B. Voas. 2005. Testing the Racial Profiling Hypothesis for Seemingly Disparate Traffic Stops on the New Jersey Turnpike. *Justice Quarterly* 22: 193–223.

Lerman, Amy E., and Vesla M. Weaver. 2014. *Arresting Citizenship.* Chicago, IL: University of Chicago Press.

Leskanic, Todd. 2012. Group's leader charges conspiracy. *Fayetteville Observer.* June 8.

Lipsky, Michael. 1968. Protest as a Political Resource. *American Political Science Review* 62: 1144–1158.

   1980. *Street-Level Bureaucracy: Dilemmas of the Individual in Public Services.* New York: Russell Sage Foundation.

Mance, Ian A. 2012. Racial Profiling in North Carolina: Racial Disparities in Traffic Stops 2000 to 2011. *Trial Briefs* (June): 23–27.

Martinez, Ramiro, Jr. 2002. *Latino Homicide: Immigration, Violence, and Community.* New York: Routledge.

Maxwell, Tonya. 2016. In traffic stops, disparity in black and white, *Asheville (NC) Citizen Times.* August 27.

McAdam, Doug. 1988. *Freedom Summer.* New York: Oxford University Press.

   2002. The War at Home: Antiwar Protests and Congressional Voting, 1965 to 1973. *American Sociological Review* 67, 5 (October): 696–721.

Meares, Tracey. 2009. The Legitimacy of Police among Young African-American Men. *Marquette Law Review* 92, 4: 651–666.

Meares, Tracey L., Tom R. Tyler, and Jacob Gardener. 2016. Lawful or Fair? How Cops and Laypeople perceive Good Policing. *Journal of Criminal Law and Criminology* 105, 2: 297–344.

Meehan, Albert J. and Michael C. Ponder. 2006. Race and Place: The Ecology of Racial Profiling African American Motorists. *Justice Quarterly* 19: 399–430.

Miller, Cheryl M. 1990. Agenda-Setting by State Legislative Black Caucuses: Policy Priorities and Factors of Success. *Policy Studies Review* 9, 2: 339–354.

Moody, Aaron. 2017. She expected traffic tickets. Instead, a cop bought her a new tire. *Raleigh News and Observer*. June 30.

Mooneyham, Scott. 1999. Lawmaker: Patrol stops and searches too often. *Charlotte Observer*. March 26. C4.

Morin, Rich, et al. 2017 *Behind the Badge: Amid Protests and Calls for Reform, how Police View their Jobs, Key Issues and Recent Fatal Encounters between Blacks and Police*. Washington, DC: Pew Research Center.

Mucchetti, Anthony E. 2005. Driving While Brown: A Proposal for Ending Racial Profiling in Emerging Latino Communities. *Harvard Latino Law Review* 8: 1.

Mueller, Benjamin, and Al Baker. 2016. A mother is shot dead on a playground, and a sea of witnesses goes silent. *New York Times Magazine*. October 7.

Nash, Parker Lee. 1999. GOP paying court to area black leaders. *Greensboro News and Record*. February 25.

Nguyen, Mai Thi and Hannah Gill. 2015. Interior Immigration Enforcement: The Impacts of Expanding Local Law Enforcement Authority. *Urban Studies* 53, 2: 1–22.

North Carolina General Assembly. 2015. North Carolina Controlled Substances Act (G.S. 90–95(h)). Available at: www.ncleg.net/EnactedLegislation/Statutes/HTML/BySection/Chapter_90/GS_90-95.html

North Carolina State Conference of the NAACP v. *McCrory*. 831 F.3d 204 (4th Circuit 2016).

O'Connor, Paul. 2001. Law by special provision. *Chapel Hill News*. June 3.

Oppel, Richard A. 2014. Activists wield search data to challenge and change police policy. *New York Times*. November 20.

Pager, Devah. 2007. *Marked: Race, Crime, and Finding Work in an Era of Mass Incarceration*. Chicago, IL: University of Chicago Press.

Parascandola, Rocco, Tina Moore, and Corky Siemaszko. 2014. Police Commissioner Bill Bratton declares war on dirty cops, says he will rid NYPD of those who are "poisoning the well." *New York Daily News*. October 3.

Patterson, Dennis. 1999a. Do troopers target black drivers? State officials to launch study with help of N.C. State. *Durham Herald Sun*. February 28. B8.
  1999b. Senate endorses driving-while-black analysis. *Charlotte Observer*. March 10. C5.

Peralta, Eyder and Cheryl Corley. 2016. The driving life and death of Philando Castile. *NPR Morning Edition*. July 15. Available at: www.npr.org/sections/thetwo-way/2016/07/15/485835272/the-driving-life-and-death-of-philando-castile

Persico, Nicola and Petra Todd. 2008. The Hit Rates Test for Racial Bias in Motor-Vehicle Searches. *Justice Quarterly* 25, 1: 52.

Pitts, Leonard, Jr. 2017. *Something's wrong when the law-abiding are afraid of police*. MiamiHerald.com. June 13.

Plant, E. A., and Peruche, B. M. 2005. The Consequences of Race for Police Officer's Responses to Criminal Suspects. *Psychological Science* 16, 3: 180–183.

Ramsey, Mike. 1999. Getting to know you: Reggie Shuford; city native fights bias against black drivers. *Wilmington Star-News*. May 30.

Rankin, Bill. 2017. Judge: Racial profiling led to illegal arrest of ex-Hawk Mike Scott. *The Atlanta Journal-Constitution*. May 4.

Rattan A., C. S. Levine, C. S. Dweck, and J. L. Eberhardt. 2012. Race and the Fragility of the Legal Distinction between Juveniles and Adults. *PLoS ONE* 7, 5: e36680.

Reaves, Brian A. 2011. *Census of State and Local Law Enforcement Agencies, 2008.* Washington, DC: US Department of Justice, Bureau of Justice Statistics, NCJ 233982 (July).

Remsberg, Charles. 1995. *Tactics for Criminal Patrol: Vehicle Stops, Drug Discovery and Officer Survival.* Glen Ellyn, IL: Calibre Press.

Rhee, Foon. 1999. Minorities not targeted, patrol plans to show. *Charlotte Observer*. February 26.

Robles, Frances, and Shaila Dewan. 2015. Skip child support. Go to jail. Lose job. Repeat. *New York Times*. 19 April.

Rothstein, Bo, and Dietlind Stolle. 2008. The State and Social Capital: An Institutional Theory of Generalized Trust. *Comparative Politics* 40, 4: 441–459.

Sagar, H. A., and J. W. Schofield. 1980. Racial and Behavioral Cues in Black and White Children's Perceptions of Ambiguously Aggressive Acts. *Journal of Personality and Social Psychology* 39, 4: 590–598.

Saltzstein, Grace Hall. 1989. Black Mayors and Police Policies. *Journal of Politics* 51: 525–44.

Santiago, Leyla and Matthew Burns. 2015. McCrory signs bill outlawing sanctuary cities in NC. *WRAL*. October 28.

Schuck, Peter H. 2006. *Meditations of a Militant Moderate: Cool Views on Hot Topics.* Lanham, MD: Rowman and Littlefield.

Schwartz, Jeremy, and Eric Dexheimer. 2017. Texas lawmakers call for stronger prohibitions on racial profiling. *Austin American-Statesman*. February 3.

Segura, Gary M. and Shaun Bowler (eds.) 2005. *Diversity in Democracy: Minority Representation in the United States.* Charlottesville: University of Virginia Press.

Sharkey, Patrick. 2013. *Stuck in Place: Urban Neighborhoods and the End of Progress Toward Racial Equality.* Chicago, IL: University of Chicago Press.

Silver, Johnathan. 2017. Texas Gov. Abbot signs "Sandra Bland Act" into law. *The Texas Tribune*. June 15.

Simes, Jessica T. and Mary C. Waters. 2014. The Politics of Immigration and Crime. *The Oxford Handbook of Ethnicity, Crime, and Immigration*, eds. Sandra M. Bucerius and Michael Tonry. New York: Oxford University Press, pp. 457–483.

Simoiu, Camelia, Sam Corbett-Davies, and Sharad Goel. 2017. The Problem of Infra-marginality in Outcome Tests for Discrimination. *Annals of Applied Statistics* 11, 3: 1193–1216.

Simon, Jonathan. 2007. *Governing through Crime.* New York: Oxford University Press.

Skogan, Wesley G. 2008. Assymetry in the Impact of Encounters with Police. *Policing and Society* 16, 2: 99–126.

Smith, Douglas A., Christy A. Visher and Laura A. Davidson. 1984. Equity and Discretionary Justice: The Influence of Race on Police Arrest Decisions. *The Journal of Criminal Law and Criminology* 75: 234–249.

Smith, Michael R. and Matthew Petrocelli. 2001. Racial Profiling? A Multivariate Analysis of Police Traffic Stop Data. *Police Quarterly* 4: 4–27.

Smith, Michael R., Matthew Makarios, and Geoffrey Alpert. 2006. Differential Suspicion: Theory Specification and Gender Effects in the Traffic Stop Context. *Justice Quarterly* 23: 271–295.

Smith, William R., Donald Tomaskovic-Devey, Matthew T. Zingraff, H. Marcinda Mason, Patricia Y. Warren, and Cynthia Pfaff Wright. 2004. *The North Carolina Highway Traffic Study*. US Department of Justice, Office of Justice Programs, Final Report Document No.: 204021. Available at: www.ncjrs.gov/pdffiles1/nij/grants/204021.pdf

Stucky, Thomas D. 2005. Local Politics and Police Strength. *Justice Quarterly* 22: 139–169.

2011. The Conditional Effects of Race and Politics on Social Control: Black Violent Crime Arrests in Large Cities, 1970 to 1990. *Journal of Research in Crime and Delinquency* 49, 1: 3–30. DOI: 10.1177/0022427810393020.

Sullivan, Brenda. 2000. Even at the Turning Tide: An Analysis of the North Carolina Legislative Black Caucus. *Journal of Black Studies* 30, 6: 815–838.

Tal, Gil, and Susan Handy. 2005. *The Travel Behavior of Immigrants and Race/Ethnicity Groups: An Analysis of the 2001 National Household Transportation Survey*. Davis: University of California at Davis Institute of Transportation Studies. Available at: http://its.ucdavis.edu/research/publications/publication-detail/?pub_id=67

Thibaut, John, and Laurens Walker. 1975. *Procedural Justice: A Psychological Analysis*. Hillsdale, NJ: Lawrence Erlbaum Associates.

Tomaskovic-Devey, Donald, and Patricia Warren. 2009. Explaining and Eliminating Racial Profiling. *Contexts* 8: 34–39.

Tomaskovic-Devey, Donald, Marcinda Mason, and Matthew Zingraff. 2004. Looking for the Driving While Black Phenomena: Conceptualizing Racial Bias Processes and their Associated Distributions. *Police Quarterly* 7: 3–29.

Tomaskovic-Devey, Donald, Cynthia Wright, Ron Czaja, and Kirk Miller. 2006. Self-Reported Speeding Behaviors: Results from a North Carolina Reverse Record Check. *Journal of Quantitative Criminology* 22: 279–297.

Tonry, Michael. 1995. *Malign Neglect: Race, Crime, and Punishment in America*. New York: Oxford University Press.

Triplett, Tim, Robert Santos, Sandra Rosenbloom, and Brian Tefft. 2016. *American Driving Survey: 2014–2015*. Washington, DC: AAA Foundation for Traffic Safety.

Tucker, Susan B., and Eric Cadora. 2003. Justice Reinvestment. *Ideas for an Open Society* 3, 3 (November). New York: Open Society Institute.

Tyler, Tom R., and Robert Folger. 1980. Distributional and Procedural Aspects of Satisfaction with Citizen–Police Encounters. *Basic and Applied Social Psychology* 1, 4: 281–292.

Tyler, Tom R., and Jonathan Jackson. 2014. Popular Legitimacy and the Exercise of Legal Authority: Motivating Compliance, Cooperation and Engagement. *Psychology, Public Policy and Law* 20, 1: 78–95.

Tyler, Tom R., Jonathan D. Casper, and Bonnie Fisher. 1989. Maintaining Allegiance toward Political Authorities: The Role of Prior Attitudes and the Use of Fair Procedures. *American Journal of Political Science* 33, 3: 629–652.

Tyler, Tom R., Jeffrey Fagan, and Amanda Geller. 2014. Street Stops and Police Legitimacy: Teachable Moments in Young Urban Men's Legal Socialization. *Journal of Empirical Legal Studies* 11, 4: 751–785.

Tyler, Tom R., Jonathan Jackson, and Avital Mentovich. 2015. The Consequences of Being an Object of Suspicion: Potential Pitfalls of Proactive Police Contact. *Journal of Empirical Legal Studies* 12, 4: 602–636.

United States Department of Justice (US DOJ), Civil Rights Division. 2015. *Investigation of the Ferguson Police Department.* Washington: US DOJ. March 4.

United States Department of Transportation (US DOT), Federal Highway Administration. n.d. *2009 National Household Travel Survey.* Available at: http://nhts.ornl.gov

United States Immigration and Customs Enforcement. 2017. *Delegation of Immigration Authority Section 287(g) Immigration and Nationality Act.* Washington, DC: Department of Homeland Security. Available at: www.ice. gov/factsheets/287g

USA Today. 2017. Woman after police encounter: "I was so scared". *USAToday. com.* June 6.

Venkatesh, Sudhir. 2006. *Off the Books: The Underground Economy of the Urban Poor.* Cambridge, MA: Harvard University Press.

Voigt, Rob, Nicholas P. Camp, Vinodkumar Prabhakaran, William L. Hamilton, Rebecca C. Hetey, Camilla M. Griffiths, David Jurgens, Dan Jurafsky, and Jennifer L. Eberhardt. 2017. Language from police body camera footage shows racial disparities in officer respect. Proceedings of the National Academy of Science (PNAS). www.pnas.org/cgi/doi/10.1073/pnas.1702413114

Wacquant, Loic. 2009. *Punishing the Poor: The Neoliberal Government of Social Insecurity.* Durham, NC: Duke University Press.

Walker, Samuel. 2003. *Internal Benchmarking for Traffic Stop data: An Early Intervention System Approach.* Omaha, NE: Police Professionalism Initiative, University of Nebraska at Omaha.

Walsh, Sean Collins. 2016. Cameras, complaints, and questions. *Austin American Statesman.* September 9.

Walsh, Sean Collins. 2017. DPS handpicks ex-cop for $194,000 racial profiling analysis. *Austin American Statesman.* June 30.

Warner, Judith Ann. 2005. The Social Construction of the Criminal Alien in Immigration Law, Enforcement Practice and Statistical Enumeration: Consequences for Immigrant Stereotyping. *Journal of Social and Ecological Boundaries* 1, 2: 56–80.

Warren, Patricia Y. 2010. The Continuing Significance of Race: An Analysis Across Two Levels of Policing. *Social Science Quarterly* 91, 4: 1025–1042.

2011. Perceptions of Police Disrespect during Vehicle Stops: A Race-Based Analysis. *Crime and Delinquency* 57, 3: 356–376.

Warren, Patricia Y., and Donald Tomaskovic-Devey. 2009. Racial Profiling and Searches: Did the Politics of Racial Profiling Change Police Behavior? *Criminology and Public Policy* 8, 2: 343–369.

Warren, Patricia, Donald Tomaskovic-Devey, Marcinda Mason, William Smith, and Matthew Zingraff. 2006. Driving While Black: Bias Processes and Racial Disparity in Police Stops. *Criminology* 44: 709–738.

Webb, Gary. 2007. Driving While Black: Tracking Unspoken Law-Enforcement Racism. *Esquire*, January 29. Downloaded from www.esquire.com/news-politics/a1223/driving-while-black-0499 on May 21, 2015. [Originally published as: DWB, *Esquire* 131, 4 (April 1999): 118–127.]

Weisel, Deborah Lamm. n.d. *Racial and Ethnic Disparity in Traffic Stops in North Carolina, 2000–2011: Examining the Evidence.* Fletcher, NC: North Carolina Association of Chiefs of Police. www.ncacp.org/images/stories/documents/racialprofilingstudyreport.pdf

Western, Bruce. 2006. *Punishment and Inequality in America.* New York: Russell Sage Foundation.

Whren v. United States, 517 U.S. 806 (1996).

Williams, Melissa J., and Jennifer L. Eberhardt. 2008. Biological Conceptions of Race and the Motivation to Cross Racial Boundaries. *Journal of Personality and Social Psychology* 94, 6: 1033–1047.

Wise, Jim. 2013. Traffic-stop numbers show racial bias across North Carolina. *Raleigh News and Observer.* September 29.

2014. Written consents are Fayetteville Policy. *Raleigh News and Observer.* September 3.

Withrow, Brian. L. 2003. *Sedgwick County (Kansas) Sheriff's Department: Racial Profiling Study.* Wichita, KS: Wichita State University, Midwest Criminal Justice Institute.

Withrow, Brian L. 2004. Driving while Different: A Potential Theoretical Explanation for Race-Based Policing. *Criminal Justice Policy Review* 15: 344–364.

2006. *Racial Profiling: From Rhetoric to Reason.* Upper Saddle River, NJ: Pearson Prentice Hall.

Withrow, Brian L., and Howard Williams. 2015. Proposing a Benchmark Based on Vehicle Collision Data in Racial Profiling Research. *Criminal Justice Review* 40, 4: 449–469.

WRAL. 2012a. Police group suing Fayetteville over consent search freeze. *WRAL.com.* February 22.

2012b. Judge allows Fayetteville police to continue consent searches. *WRAL.com.* March 1.

2012c. Fayetteville agrees to let court rule on consent search issue. *WRAL.com.* March 12.

2012d. Fayetteville gets new city manager amid consent search controversy. *WRAL.com.* March 27.

2013. Charlotte cop named as Fayetteville police chief. *WRAL.com.* January 9.

2014a. Report: Racial bias exists within Durham Police Department. *WRAL. com*. May 1.

2014b. Durham officials respond to police racial bias recommendations. *WRAL.com*. August 22.

2015a. Lawsuit claiming racial profiling filed against Durham police. *WRAL. com*. April 29.

2015b. "I was terrified": Raleigh man says he became traffic-stop statistic. *WRAL.com*. July 28.

2016. New Durham police chief faces challenges on her first day. *WRAL.com*. June 6.

Index